THE
COMPLETE BOOK
OF
FABRIC PAINTING

THE
COMPLETE BOOK
OF
FABRIC PAINTING

BY LINDA S. KANZINGER

THE ALCOTT PRESS
1986
SPOKANE, WASHINGTON

As well, please share with me your experiences of fabric painting. Let me know
how the ideas and techniques in this book work for you. Send letters to: The
Alcott Press, P.O. Box 857, Spokane, WA. 99210

Library of Congress Cataloging in Publication Data

Kanzinger, Linda S., 1951-
   The complete book of fabric painting.

   Bibliography: p.
   Includes indexes.
   1. Textile painting. I. Title.
TT851.K36   1986   746.6   85-73432
ISBN:0-9616180-0-0

Printed in the United States of America

First Printing 1986

Permission is gratefully acknowledged for reprinting of the following quotes:
p. ix,from THE WELL-BODY BOOK-Mike Samuels, MD and Hal Bennett. Random House,
copyright 1973.
p.xii,from THE POEMS OF W.B.YEATS-edited by Richard J.Finneran, Macmillan
Publishing Company,copyright 1983.
p.22,from THE SNOW GOOSE-Paul Gallico,Alfred A. Knopf,Inc. copyright 1941.
p.64,from KANDINSKY:COMPLETE WRITINGS ON ART-edited by Kenneth C. Lindsay and
Peter Vergo,G.K.Hall and Company,copyright 1982.

Acknowledgement is made for the following:
p.41: Artists' letters to author
p. 142: Artist's letter-Valery Guignon
Copyright © is held by each individual artist for work portrayed

Cover illustrations:(left) Lisa Hensley Rector models cotton huiptl painted
and drawn with Pelican drawing ink, acrylic paint, Design markers, embroidery paints.
(right) "Heart Strings Vest",back view, by Sara Drower. Cotton polyester and
textile paint, quilted, with soft-sculpture hearts.

DEDICATION

To my sisters: Cathy Mottern Butler,
Lisa Hensley Rector, and Jennifer
Hensley Heller

To my mentors: Julia Jay Hensley,
Patricia Clift Tubb, Mary Stuart
Faust, Linda K. Rice

To all the members of the Resort:
for all the good times- Ted Cotrot-
sos, Stephen Garrow, Chuck Johnson,
Beth Brown, Gary Klier, Gary Bochen-
ski, Christie DeMoll, Bruce Hapeman,
Elayne Quirin, Jim Wallace, Carol
Wallace, Sarolta Mackrayni, Carol
Petrelli, Steve Hall, John Gill,
Andy Burger, Jim Janaschek, Gary
Pavek, Gail Streiker, Mike Goerger,
Betsy Jumper, Cathy Martini, Charles
Dorman, John Tuttle

To my husband: Erik C. Jonas

To Dr. Robert M. Hensley: without
whom I would not have gotten started

And to my mother: who bought some
textile paints many years ago and
encouraged me to make things

Research, Writing, Typing, Editing,
Layout, Paste-up, Typesetting, Proof-
ing, Indexing, Publishing, Advertising, Marketing, and Distributing by
the Author

Note: All painted items or drawings
without credit are done by author

ACKNOWLEDGEMENTS

I want to thank my artist, Phyllis Thompson, for providing so many excellent quality drawings for this book.

Thanks to all the artists who corresponded with me,sending slides and photos of their work. Out of the 100 or so artists who contacted me, about 40 are represented in this book.

I appreciate the help of Sue Thompson, Seattle, Washington; Dave Barbara, Cincinnati,Ohio; Jack Straton, Eugene,Oregon; Sarah Chandler, Bellevue, Washington; and Ellen Ross,of Lexington, Kentucky; in photographing a number of items for this book.

Thanks to the people who helped model painted clothing: Beth Brown, Christie DeMoll, Ted Cotrotsos, Stephen Garrow, Ellen Essig Ross, Jennifer Hensley Heller, Lisa Hensley Rector, Douglas Hensley, Judy Hankin, Karen Leeds, Leslie Allen, Patricia Tubb, Laura Dale, Arden Dale, Hope Fox, Carol Petrelli, and Ava Lake.

To Carla Emery, author and self-publisher of THE OLD FASHIONED RECIPE BOOK: thank you for your inspiration.

And to all small press people everywhere.

PHOTO CREDITS

Fig. 11: Chatham Press, Old Greenwich, CT.
Fig. 17: 1964.31.2, The Textile Museum,Washington,D.C.
Fig. 18: Richard A. Pohrt, Flint, MI.
Figs. 27,28,32,34,35,39,40: Dover Publications,New York.
Fig. 41: Charles Uht, Heeramaneck Gallery, New York.
Fig. 103,106: Dover Publications, New York.
Fig. 110: Harvard University Press, Cambridge, MA.
Fig. 116: Rainbird Publishing Group, London.
Figs. 140,141: Verlag Ernst Wasmuth,Tubingen, Germany.
Fig. 147: Rizzoli International Publications, Inc., New York.

Barbara, Dave: Figs. 4,57-C, 90
Bryan, Ray: Fig. 189
Bryan, Steve: Fig. 157
Chandler, Sarah: Figs. 5,82,83,105,108
Galgiani, Phillip: Figs. 52,70
Hartzel, Herman: Figs. A,F,H, 161
Kanzinger, Linda: Figs. 13,14,19,44-46,
64,66,96,115,153,168,170
Larsen, Rob: Figs. C,10,48,73,97

Nickolson, Anne McKenzie: Fig. 175
Richardson, Phyllis: Figs. 7,8
Roizen, Donna: Fig. 74
Ross, Ellen Essig: Figs. 1,3,21,22,91,167
Small,Perry: Figs. 75,166
Straton, Jack: Figs. D, 6,9,57-A,67,88,
89,93-95,98-101,113,120,171
Thompson, Sue: Figs. 20,114,124,130,136

PREFACE:
FABRIC PAINTING IN THE 80's

In the 1980's, fabric painting can stand on its own beside the other forms of surface decoration: batik, silkscreen, fabric printing, plangi(or tie-dye),and shibori. In the past ten years, many of the fiber arts have grown in public awareness and practice. It's no longer relevant or even necessary to compare fabric painting with other painting disciplines. Fabric painting, in the 80's, has come into its own.

However, it is true that certain fabric arts go in and out of style. While it is apparent that the interest in crafts has lessened since its height in the 1970's,any serious artist will find fabric painting to be a sufficiently interesting activity- even a passion- for many years. The problem with the faddishness of fabric painting is that at certain times, it is very difficult to find fabric paints and dyes. Right now,they are in surplus, and it is wonderful to see the interest in fabric painting and therefore the ample supplies.

As the crafts movement has matured, so have the artists working in it. In large cities today, craft fairs are primarily peopled with professional artists doing quality work. In the 1980's, the definition and sense of fabric decoration has expanded to be that of true works of art and creativity. At the same time, fabric painting is flexible enough to include punk-art clothing influenced by the present styles. Other uses of fabric painting today include costumes for the theater, as an art form for the visual arts, as wearable art, and as a home craft.

An Eastern influence affects certain fabric painters of today. Japanese techniques of fabric decoration such as stencil dyeing with paste-resist, nori paste resist techniques, and shibori(which is a method of shaping cloth by pinching,folding,stitching, pleating, wrapping,or twisting, and then binding it in various fashions), are all popular methods being tried in the U.S. today. Painted weaving is also a popular form of fabric painting, both the technique of warp painting as well as the ikat method. It is inspiring that people are continuing to learn these ancient techniques since they are fast dying out among the indiginous population.

Silk is another highly visible material being used today in conjunction with fabric painting. Although much of the work being shown in museums, art shows, and fiber magazines is painted silk, remember that many beautiful items can also be made with cotton and muslin. Quilted jackets, wrap jackets, skirts, summer pants, curtains, purses, and quilts all make up beautifully with painted cotton fabrics. Silk is a beautiful fabric and,when painted on by someone with expertise and experience, a truly unique piece of art is created. The emphasis on silk is a 1980's emphasis, and need not be followed.

Today there are many distributors of fabrics and supplies. You can be adventuresome and experiment with lesser known paints,trying for a new effect;or you can follow the advice and material of the experts. Either way, I'm sure you will end up with an intriguing or unique fabric painted item.

"Clothes can be a way to get yourself into
 a very high and joyful place. Get in touch
 with yourself in the most joyful state you
 can imagine. And then visualize the kind
 of clothes you'd be wearing at that moment.
 Remember how the clothes look and feel, and
 then get yourself real clothes to wear that
 look and feel like that. You might find it
 fun to take castaside clothes and cut,dye,
 and embroider designs on them until they
 express the feelings you would like them
 to express."

THE WELL-BODY BOOK
Mike Samuels, MD and Hal Bennett

TABLE OF CONTENTS

CHAPTER VII

CHAPTER VIII

NOTES TO TEXT

Regarding 'Introduction to Fabric Painting':certain comments about the availability of fabric paints,usage, etc. have changed since fabric painting is now a more well-known craft. Silk, for example, is commonly used whereas in the 1970's, painted T-shirts were more common.

Regarding the discussion on fabric painting versus fabric printing in Chapter I: when this book was first researched, fabric printing was presented in a rather standard way. Since that time, all types of fabric decoration have evolved.

Regarding the usage of the term 'American Indian' rather than 'Native American': I am using this term since it precluded the common usage of the latter.

Regarding nori paste, discussed in Chapter IV: This paste can also be used by combing with a plastic comb.It is a popular African technique.

Regarding Delta Fabric Dyes,discussed in Chapter IV: Technically speaking, they are a liquid dye rather than a paint. They are, however, catagorized under 'Textile Paints'.

Regarding 'Stamps' in Chapter IV: modeling clay can also be used as a stamp.

Regarding 'Bound Resists' in Chapter VI: with the clamp resist technique, a wooden or metal clamp is used to secure the fabric together.Also an African technique.

Always prewash and preshrink all fabric before painting.

In the interest of avoiding sexism, whether implicit or implied, the pronouns 'she' and 'he' are used interchangeably.

Anyone wishing to paint immediately can skip to Chapter III,'Simple and Beginning Ideas' and to Chapter VII,'Quick and Easy Projects for Beginners'.

"Had I the Heavens' embroidered cloths,
 Enwrought with golden and silver light,
 The blue and the dim and the dark cloths
 Of night and light and the half-light,
 I would spread the cloths under your feet:
 But I,being poor, have only my dreams;
 I have spread my dreams under your feet;
 Tread softly, because you tread on my dreams."

                "He wishes for the Cloths of Heaven"
                William Butler Yeats

1 AN INTRODUCTION TO FABRIC PAINTING

"Nothing to do but work,
 nothing to eat but food,
 nothing to wear but clothes
 to keep one from going nude."
                "The Pessimist"-Benjamin Franklin King

When it comes to clothes, some people echo the pessimist. They happily put on their grey business suit every day, or don blue jeans and workshirt, and go off without further thought as to what they are wearing. For other people, however, every day is a show, a chance to be somebody different, to change personality, to express a different mood. Clothes, with their expressive modes of color,texture, form, and movement, amplify these changes.

Fabric painting leans a little more towards the ostentatious than the drab, but it is a matter of choice for the individual painter. For are not the somber hues of Rembrandt far different from Gauguin's bright colors? Yet both are painters and in their differentness equal in stature. The range and scope of fabric painting is as wide as that of canvas painting, yet different painting techniques are sometimes used due to the greater permeability of fabric over canvas.

Fabric painting is simply painting on fabric. How and why and what are its implications are far from simple. Fabric painting will be discussed primarily for clothing, both manufactured and handmade. Examples of other types of fabric painting- such as for wall hangings, quilts, and soft sculptures, will be given; but I feel that it is clothing which is the greater challenge in fabric painting.

Anni Albers speaks of clothing as a habitat which grew out of humans' need for shelter. Clothing is a type of portable environment. We quite literally picked up our tent and put it on. (Witness the simple forms of early garments such as the poncho, the huiptl, the toga.) Clothing is also our closest environment. We carry it on our bodies, we feel it next to our skin. As our bodies identify us, so do our clothes. In our social environment, clothes can be our camouflage or our communication. (Witness the difference in the grey business suit and the blue jeans and T-shirt.)

Clothing is also an industry. Every process of garment making has become mass marketable, beginning with the garment patterns, through the weaving of the cloth, to the dyeing and printing of cloth, and finally to the sewing of the garment. To balance this industrial process, many people design their own patterns, weave their own cloth, print and dye fabric, or sew their own clothes. Fabric painting is but another catagory of hand expression, yet it is usually overlooked in favour of fabric printing. I suspect one reason for the oversight is the general misconception of what fabric painting is. It is not, although it looks deceptively like, fabric printing, and until it is compared and pulled away from fabric printing, there can be no clear sense of direction as to its development. When people view it as a rudimentary form of fabric printing, fabric printing is seen to be much more efficient as a design technique for lengths of fabric. The approach to painting, however, is quite different from printing, and will be discussed at length.

Fabric painting is relatively little known today in the world of crafts. Most every art form has received stimulation from our technological society with its rapid communication systems, allowing arts and crafts to be influenced with rich sources of information from variant cultures over the world. It is an oversight and certainly a loss for fabric painting to have received no more than scant attention. Fabric painting books were visible in the 1950's and faded again in the sixties. A lack of materials plus a lack of understanding of the basic forms underlying the synthesis of clothing design and painting led fabric painting to a dead stop. For those who love painting, this is unfortunate, for past records even show that fabric painting was not as important a method as fabric printing. Even today, many people interested in crafts are not aware of its existence. When told that a piece of clothing has been painted, the question invariably arises, "but won't it wash out?"

Until quite recently, there were few paints available that were not "washouts". With the discovery of fiber-reactive (Procion) dye in England in 1958 and the continuous improvement of acrylic paints since they were first marketed, the technical problems of fabric painting have greatly diminished. Since both cold water dyes and acrylic paints are less expensive for extensive use than textile paint, there is greater flexibility in materials. Other materials which can be used are indelible (permanent) markers, fabric crayons, embroidery paints, inks, mordants, natural dyes and paints, oil paint with textine, and regular textile paint.

DESIGN IDEAS

Simple design ideas can be used, and can be extended in meaning from simplicity to compositional and psychological complexity. Geometric designs have the advantage of being easily drawn. They also have many moods,ranging from the subdued effect and earthen colours of American Indian designs,to the black and white op/pop art style and its variant,psychedelic art. Painted patchwork squares allow one to experiment with different colour combinations without the extra complexity of form. Sculpture,calligraphy and drawing, watercolour,abstract and realistic designs,Impressionism,Expressionism, Fauvism,and Surrealism,are all sources of design from art history. (Fig.1,2)

Through time,art history has shown a loosening of the definition of painting. Classical painting demanded adherance to strict rules of canvas, oil, and brush. Technique no longer need limit new ideas;technique is created to express them. The disciplines of painting and printmaking even overlap so that there is no longer any sense of "pure"painting. This allows many techniques to be combined and new ones invented.If a design idea cannot be expressed through traditional painting,one breaks out and discovers new methods. The combination of canvas painting techniques and ideas,along with clothing and needlework,creates a new method. One can translate ideas from a two-dimensional surface(the painted canvas) and from a static form(a picture hung on a wall),to a three-dimensional form(the body), and to one of movement within the environment(a person wearing clothing.) (Fig.3)

FIG I:JENNIFER HENSLEY IN MUSLIN SKIRT PAINTED WITH TEXTILE PAINTS AND NATURAL PAINTS.

FIG 2:DYE-PAINTED FLOWER ON VELVETEEN. PORTION OF HANDPAINTED SCREEN BY LENORE DAVIS.

LIMITATIONS OF PRESENT DAY CLOTHING

The combination of painting techniques and ideas with clothing and fabrics is rather exciting in that there are so many possible combinations:patchwork skirts with small paintings on each square;Mexican blouses with painted embroidery alongside thread embroidery,showing differences in texture;skirts which remind one of the paintings of Kandinsky or Modrian or ancient Mayan architecture. If these combinations seem too ambitious,recall Paul Klee, who was trying to pull together painting, architecture, music, and poetry,within his own painting.

To use classical painting as a source for design in fabric decoration is to approach a fabric surface with a fluidity which is not to be found with printed fabric. Fabric painting records the mark of the brush. Painted,as opposed to printed,fabric is farther from decoration and closer to art when it is a surface that can only be hand-painted. And a fabric surface which can only be handpainted has as its idea a design which is equally as fluid as the motion of the brush. This greatly extends the present limitations of clothing design.

When handmade clothing is limited to the kind of material which one finds in a store,and what kind of design is printed on the material,it is nice to have something unique to wear. And when there are so many of us on this planet, when even a name does not insure identity, handpainted clothing can be an expression of one particular person at one particular time.

FIG.A:PAINTED SILK GOWN BY CAROL RACKLIN.ACID DYES & WAX LINES.

Sometimes in the daily routine,the days slip by unnoticed though there are one hundred things worth notice and remembrance. With painting,one can record the small occurences of a day in design and colour,and repeat the mood of that day whenever wearing the clothing. Seeing the body as an environment for design,design a landscape,or figures with backgrounds moving out into their environments, on an arm or leg.

FIG. 3:LENGTH OF COTTON BROADCLOTH HANDPAINTED WITH ACRYLIC PAINT & LARGE HOUSEPAINTING BRUSHES.

4

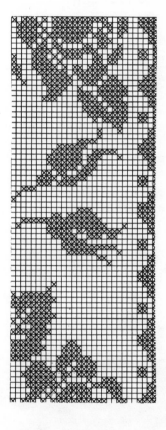

The purpose of this book is to make others aware of the possibilities inherent in the combination of the world of art and the world of needlework and clothing. I have tried to express a variety of moods, sources, interests, and levels of ability. More a needleworker than a painter, I hope to attract the interest of painters who can transfer their ideas from canvas to cloth. Just as the expression of form is inherent in stone, to later be sculpture, so fabric contains colour and form and movement. Free the painted cloth!

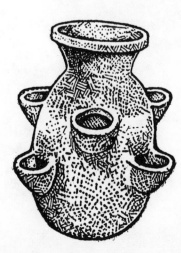

A DEFINITION OF FABRIC PAINTING

Fabric painting may seem to be but a primitive form of fabric printing. It is, and it is not. Designs created by other fabric decoration methods can sometimes be painted,but in order to utilize the unique techniques of painting,it is necessary to know what type of designs can only be handpainted. It is also necessary to know what types of designs would be laborious or repetitious if hand-painted.

A more extensive definition of fabric painting will pull it away from confusion with other fabric decoration methods. Fabric painting as fabric decoration emphasizes painting over other fabric decorative methods,as it is painting rather than decoration. Yet it differs from two-dimensional canvas painting in that it is painting on fabric,a flexible material which is both two and three dimensional. Fabric painting combines the techniques of canvas painting with the function of fabric decoration methods. To see what this combination forms,it is best first to look separately at painting and at fabric decoration.

In a painting, many ideas are pulled together and expressed visually with colour,texture,line,and spacial composition. Much of a painting is composed mentally before the actual painting is done, for the idea is directly expressed via the brush,without the limitations of intermediary devices or tools. The size of a silk-screen, or the number of blocks needed for a block print, can limit a design idea. The directness of painting allows the painter full control and responsibility for the size of the image,placement of images,and placement of colour. The directness of painting also involves making a large number of decisions, because of the wide range of choices to be made. A large painting can be quite complex compositionally as well as taking a long time to complete, whereas with fabric decoration methods,large spaces can be covered in a short time with a repeat motif.

FIG.B:"GALAXY"BY FERNE SIROIS.ACRYLIC STAINING ON RAW CANVAS,OVERPAINTED WITH JAPANESE INK BRUSHES.

FIG.C:WRAPAROUND SKIRT BY
SUZANNE LARSEN.OFFWHITE
INDIA COTTON WITH ACRYLIC
PAINTED SUNFACE.OUTLINED
WITH INKODYE.

FIG.D:WALL HANGING BY
SHANNA SANTOMIENI. TIE-
DYE AND DIRECT PAINTING
WITH OILS AND ENAMELS

It is not the intention of painting to merely fill up space as
quickly as possible. Painting expresses in a visual way what is true
for an artist, and in this sense,
every painting is unique, rather
than a duplication of a former idea.
With fabric decoration methods, one
design idea can be repeated through
space, giving an impression of stasis.
As a contrast,painting,due to its vi-
brancy of color and variency in shape,
can come alive and create just the opposite impression from stasis.The concept of painting changes the traditional approach to fabric decoration,
with its emphasis on covering a large
amount of space with a repeated design,
and therefore leads to a new method,
fabric painting.

FABRIC DECORATION METHODS

Fabric decoration methods include fabric printing, fabric painting, batik, tie-dye, and silk-screen. Most methods approach the large amount of space in a length of fabric by breaking up the space into smaller amounts. The design idea is formed for a smaller space and merely repeated throughout the space of the fabric. Although there are advantages to the idea of the repeat design, the large amounts of space with fabric lengths are not utilized, as they could be in painting.

With the exception of fabric painting, all fabric decoration methods use some intermediary substance to control capillary action. Capillary action is the tendency for paint or dye to spread from fiber to fiber unless blocked by some substance. Wax, tape, paper, starch resists, wood, and string are some common substances used. In fabric painting, capillary action is either used to advantage in the design, or controlled by brush techniques and a thick consistency of paint.

FIG.F:"FLORAL GARDEN"
BY CAROL RACKLIN. BATIK.

FIG.E:BETH BROWN MODELS
CANVAS BACKPACK PAINTED
IN ACRYLICS WITH AFRICAN
DESIGNS

Fabric printing involves transference of a previously formed design via woodblock, linoleum block, silkscreen, to the fabric. In fabric painting, however, the design is directly painted onto the fabric. Batik is closer in idea to fabric painting in that the design is directly formed on the material rather than being transferred, but the design is formed in reverse with wax, with the dye baths forming the actual design.

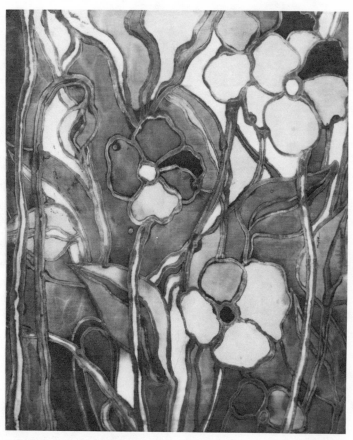

FIG. H: " STAINED GLASS"-CAROL RACKLIN
WAX RESIST WITH DIRECT DYE PAINTING

FIG. G: BATIK WITH DIRECT
PAINTING-SHANNA SANTOMIENI

FIG. I: (BELOW) TIE-DYE WITH
DIRECT PAINTING-JOETTA UMLA

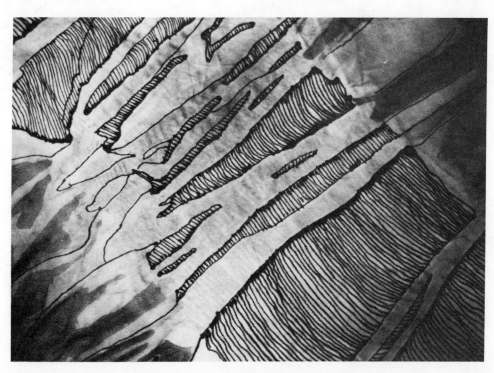

FIG. 4: AUTHOR MODELING
HANDPAINTED CAFTAN.SPONTANEOUS
PAINTING STYLE.

Fabric is tied to block out the patterns of the design in tie-dye,a
method which also utilizes the
three-dimensional aspects of fabric.
Silkscreen is a method of fabric
printing which uses a fabric screen
and tusche, a blocking out substance,
to transfer the design onto the fabric. In all these fabric decoration
methods,with the exception of fabric
painting,the design is formed before
the interaction of paint and fabric.

Fabric painting omits these intermediary steps and paints the design
directly on the fabric.(Fig.4)

FIG. J: (LEFT)"ALHAMBRA WALL"-
FRANCES BUTLER . SILKSCREEN

Fabric painting has many effects,
techniques,and methods which cannot be created by any other method
of fabric decoration. The sponteniaty
of painting allows for the blending
of colors on the fabric, emphasiz-
ing the pure color, form, and texture

11

FIG. 5: TED COTROTSOS MODELING
SPATTER-PAINTED T-SHIRT

FIG. 6: HOPE FOX MODELING PAINTED
CAFTAN. EARLY AMERICAN FLORAL DESIGN.

rather than the transference of a preplanned design. The interrelationship between these colors, forms, and textures can intermingle throughout the length of fabric, changing and growing with the flow of the paint brushed, dipped, pushed, and spattered onto the material. (Fig. 5) In this way, fabric painting transcends painting a design, and becomes painting, an action.

ADVANTAGES OF FABRIC PAINTING

Painting directly has many advantages. For example, no part of the fabric need be exactly alike, yet all areas can be tied together with a certain theme. (Fig. 6) A length of fabric can be painted with flowers, no two alike. A variety of shapes can easily be drawn, whereas in other methods it would be necessary to make different block prints or different screens for various shapes. Also by painting directly, each color can be easily applied. Much preplanning must be done with other methods of fabric decoration; in batik, one must carefully preplan the sequential dye baths in order to have the correct blending of colors; in silkscreen, separate areas of color must be mapped out. Color applications can also be built up with glazes of underpainting, which is quite different from the flat color of a blockprint. With painting, designs and motifs are easily enlarged or reduced; color application is direct.

12

involves the use of space both two and three dimensionally. The composition of a canvas painting of various colored abstract shapes must be much tighter than a similar fabric painting, as the three dimensionality of fabric can change the original composition through draping, gathering, and pleating. A painting which is not extremely well composed when looked at flat could be very interesting when viewed from the various angles at which one can view clothing. There is simply a much greater leeway in the usage of space due to the flexibility of cloth being both two and three dimensional. At the same time, it is true that composition is more difficult when considering not only the flat plane of a painting, but what happens to the designs when they are molded by the shape and movement of the body. The combination of the free or open use of space in painting, and the restrictions or limitations of space due to the garment form, and some of the problems therein, leads to the necessity for an understanding of holistic design.

FIG. 7: INSTALLATION AT SEATTLE ART MUSEUM-PHYLLIS RICHARDSON. (LEFT) DENIM. BLEACHED, WOVEN. (RIGHT) CANVAS, ACRYLIC.

The use of space is totally open in fabric painting. (Fig.7) This is both exciting and difficult. The large amounts of space in lengths of fabric require that you be somewhat comfortable with composition. It may be helpful at first to limit space the way a silkscreen does (Fig.8) with arbitrary size. Fabric painting

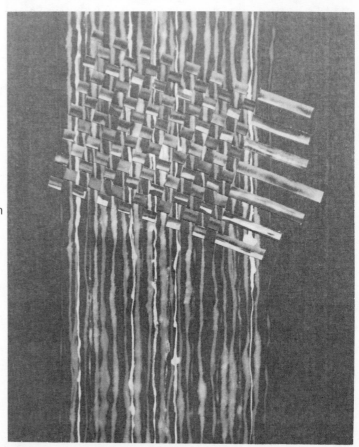

FIG. 8: CLOSE-UP OF ABOVE LEFT. COLOR IS "SUBTRACTED" BY USING VARIOUS BLEACHES.

Holistic design refers to wholeness much in the same way as the word gestalt refers to many parts fitting together in a meaningful way. Holistic design in fabric painting refers to the design idea interrelating in a meaningful way,both with the technical processes of fabric painting, and with the design and form of the garment or fabric.Too often,both of these ideas are avoided or ignored,and the resulting painting looks as if it has been laid on,rather than being a part of,the fabric. The design idea must be suitable to the technique of painting,otherwise it would be better to use another fabric decoration method. A repeating shape in the same colour would best be blockprinted, while one with shadings of colour could work efficiently with stenciling.

If the design and form of the garment is not considered as well when forming a design idea, the shift of the design from two to three dimensions will be ignored,and therefore what the design really will look like will not even be considered. In some cases, there is not that much difference in a design in its two and three dimensional state.(Fig. 9) An evenly spaced design,for example,will be less vulnerable to the change in position from two to three dimensions than a design with a delicately balanced composition,since a painting spread out flat will appear radically different from the same in three dimensions.

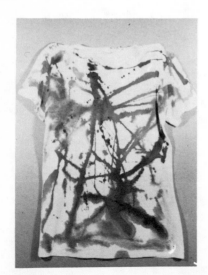

FIG. 9

In order to plan for these two dimensions,one must understand the basics of design and composition for two-dimensional painting,the basics of design and composition in garments, and the successful combination of the two. These are the many parts of holistic design which must be fitted together in a harmonious and meaningful way.

FABRIC PAINTING AS ART AND CRAFT

Fabric painting entails many subdivisions. Do you want to paint on fabrics and hang them-use them in their total space without making them into clothing? Are you interested in costume?clothing?making fabric lengths and letting others use them in clothing? Are you interested in selling what you make? All these need different approaches.

These many subdivisions can be separated into fabric painting as an art,and fabric painting as a craft. As an art, fabric painting emphasizes the uniqueness, rather than the repetition of an image. The painting is a visual idea to be realized,and the process or technique involved is subservient to the idea. A craft,however, stresses technique,and the desired image is shaped through the discipline of the technical process. A roughly formed carved wooden bowl,as an object,reveals the process of its making, records the passage of knife over wood,time over time. As objects they are marked:there is the imprint of the potters' hand upon the clay. As a craft,fabric painting concentrates on repeating a basic form yet amplifying it through individual expression. The potter who specializes in goblets expresses various design ideas through one basic form. By approaching fabric painting as a craft,a large number of similarly styled items can be produced-yet retain their individuality.(Fig.10)

FIG.10: QUILTED AND NON-QUILTED SHELL PILLOWS. DIRECT DYE,INKO DYE FOR LINES, ACRYLIC PAINT.(L TO R) COTTON VELVET SUEDE,ANTIQUE SATIN QUILTED SCALLOP IN BACKGROUND. OTHERS,COTTON MUSLIN. ALL BY SUZANNE LARSEN.

Fabric painting as an art is different in that there is no repetition of a basic form. Five skirts painted in this way are five different works of art, five "moveable paintings". This is important to remember as most clothing is printed and capable for reproduction. Fabric paintings cannot be reproduced. The time necessary for an intricately painted and designed piece of clothing may be many times over that of even a handprinted garment,but then,it is a unique piece of clothing.(Fig.11;Fig. 12) A painting is not just a representation of some object in reality;but an expression of a feeling,an idea,or a visual representation of an idea.

When is fabric painting best approached as a craft rather than an art? For selling,the repetition of a basic form makes it easier to paint in quantity and fill orders on time. If there are variations of a design idea,

they can be spread out over many different garments,yet retain an identifiable connection. When making fabric yardage,there are ways to paint the material so that it is identifiable as one piece of cloth,yet go beyond the repeat design. The amount of space in a wall hanging makes it ideal for art fabric painting,as one can develop the composition on a two dimensional space without having to also deal with the three dimensional. More complex composition similar to canvas painting can be explored. Clothing utilizes fabric painting both as an art and as a craft,ranging from clothing which may take several months to design and paint to a simple border of flowers on a blouse.

15

FIG. 11: DRAWING- BY PHYLLIS THOMPSON.AFTER
MIAO/CHINESE WOMAN'S COSTUME IN COSTUMES OF
THE EAST,BY W.A.FAIRSERVIS,JR. 1971

   Thus far, fabric painting has been discussed primarily as it differs technically from other fabric decoration methods or from canvas painting. It is important as well to understand fabric painting as an idea, for the idea of what something is contributes to how it is used. The most important thing that I would stress is that fabric painting is expression rather than decoration. The design is integrated with the form, rather than being "put on" the form and unrelated to it.

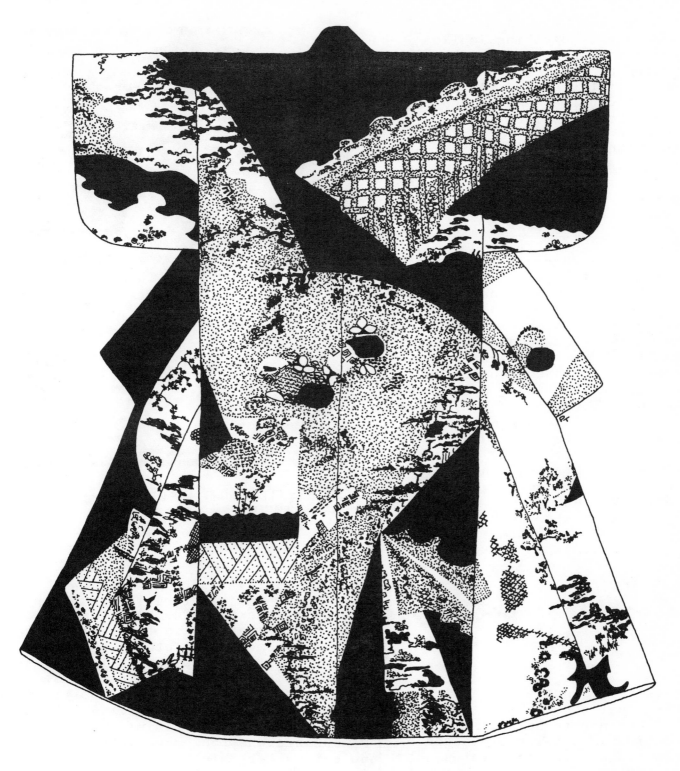

FIG. 12: DRAWING-BY PHYLLIS THOMPSON.
KOSODE IN SATIN(16TH CENTURY JAPANESE-
MOMOYAMA) FIG. 101 JAPANESE COSTUME
BY NOMA

To decorate something implies relieving the monotony of a background with ornament or embellishment. Rather than being interrelated, the design and the background are seen as separate entities. Some T-shirts look as if the design were pasted on the shirt in the way one might stick a piece of tape on paper. To express something, on the other hand, is to directly state in a clear manner what one thinks or feels. Expression is a form through which thought, feeling, or the quality of something is manifest. When the fluidity and spontenaity of painting is combined with the form of the garment, the visual idea can be manifest through painting.

Fabric painting as expression rather than decoration echoes holistic design. There is no separation between design and background. There is the interrelationship of paint, cloth, and brush, with the garment form. North American Indian fabric painters were familiar with this idea. In 1880, due to contact with white culture, Indians in the great plains began depicting phases of their ceremonial life on muslin and canvas. Many of the Plains Indians' clothing were designed so that when worn, the decorative aspects could be visually appreciated.

FIG. 13: ELLEN ROSS MODELING PAINTED SKIRT WITH AFRICAN MOTIFS

DESIGN INTEGRATED WITH FORM

It is very important in painted clothing that design be integral to form. There has to be some meaning to a design idea being expressed through clothing, which relates not only with the body but also with the surrounding environment, and the reactions of other people in that environment.   If the question be asked, "why is this design painted on this piece of clothing?" and there is no answer, then perhaps the next question to be asked is, "as a public moveable painting, is it worth being seen?" The idea of painted clothing is not to have a design painted on a piece of clothing. The idea is to interrelate the paint, cloth, and brush with colour, texture, the body, the movement of the body in the environment and the movement of clothing through the action of the body, as well as the composition of colours, patterns, and textures through various positions of clothing when being worn. (Fig.13,Fig.14) It is reminiscent of the Cubists, who took a variety of subject matter-things such as bottles, winding staircases, paintings or photographs-and unified them into a harmonious whole.

Painted clothing, then, is different from clothing made from woven cloth without a pattern, and even from printed clothing. There needs to be an exploration of what designs on clothing mean, regardless of their technical application. The images created interact, and interact differently, with the

18

environment of the body, the physical environment, and the social environment. Perhaps because of the lack of thought concerning this, there have been very few <u>painted</u> clothes, in comparison to printed clothing. Even batik and tie-dye are used in clothing far more frequently than is fabric painting. Susan Springer, an artist from San Francisco, feels that fabric painting "is all very interesting...especially because it is such a unique field to be part of as awareness blossoms."She handpaints silk scarves, as well as creating unique, one-of-a-kind hand-painted garments such as quiana blouses with large floral designs.

Another reason for the scarcity of painted clothes stems from the diversity of fabric painting. There are so many different painting techniques-all aimed at so many different levels of skill-that it creates confusion for the beginning fabric painter. And since fabric painting encompasses the entire spectrum between simplicity and complexity,it becomes necessary to find design ideas inbetween painting the repeat motif,and working in large spaces with highly abstract problems.

FABRIC PAINTING AS TECHNIQUE

There are some techniques which are very efficient to fabric painting,and especially fabric painting aimed towards painted clothing. Watercolour, Expressionism,collage,painted squares, and drawing are all suited to fill a variety of needs for the beginning fabric painter. Techniques which can be learned easily are preferred in the beginning as there is,at the same time,much to learn about the inter-action of painting materials and clothing composition.

FIG. 14: ELLEN ROSS IN KENTUCKY LANDSCAPE, MODELING HANDPAINTED SKIRT WITH AFRICAN MOTIFS

Watercolour is technically simple,
and watercolour bands or stripes either on fabric lengths or on clothing,
is also compositionally simple. Expressionism is well suited for fabric
painting as fabric painting emphasizes
expression over decoration. Broad
splashes of colour, and free form
painting maximize the spontenaity of
paint and brush. Collage is an exciting approach to fabric painting as it
divides the space as part of the technique. Torn paper,when used in creating a design,can be utilized to draw
a design that would usually be pasted.
More durable materials are used for
the actual pasting or glueing of collage. Painted squares allows one to
focus on testing out a wide range of
mixed colours as well as the juxta-
position of one colour with another.
And drawing can emphasize the expression of shape and form without totally ignoring colour,colour shadings,
and textures. Drawing is also the
basic framework of a large amount of
painting, and by focusing on form, one
can solve problems that might arise

with more complex painting methods.
    These techniques work best for be-
ginning fabric painting as they isolate one approach and maximize its
efficiency,rather than trying to deal
with all possible factors in fabric
painting. Watercolour and collage emphasize a practical use of space. Expressionism and drawing are two different ways of painting. Painted
squares utilize the possibilities of
colour.

In all these techniques, the composition mixes unity with diversity, and it is this which is the key to successful fabric painting. Just as in music or literature,painted clothing and painted cloth must have a central theme,a unifying idea, a focal point. At the same time,there must be some diverse elements needing to be drawn together into a unifying idea. Without this interchange,there is neither unity or diversity,there is only sameness. Some examples of this combination could be :random scattering of flowers or starlike shapes with no two alike;leaves,paint splotch clusters,little geometric boxes,motifs both large and small,torn paper strips; African,Indian,Norwegian,Precolumbian motifs. Arrange these along a larger gridwork or organic sense of wholeness.

The essential unit of cohesiveness is the similar shape or mood of the motif. Try pottery examples, bird tracks, birds flying, pens, alphabets, etc.

Composition which mixes unity with diversity must as well have other characteristics. It must be suited to the technique of painting in terms of the types of effects possible with painting. Therefore the approach to composition must spring from sources other than unilinear repetition of shape. Composition must as well be capable of using the space unique in fabric painting; unique either because through clothing it is a shaped three dimensional space, or because it is an unlimited amount of space. And last, composition must deal with design in movement and motion as will occur with painted clothing.

A definition of fabric painting, as can be seen, includes the <u>technique</u> of fabric painting, the <u>idea</u> of fabric painting, and efficient <u>methods</u> of fabric painting. Perhaps the last question to ask concerning fabric painting is "why do it?" What are its' uniquenesses? Perhaps it is simply the expansiveness of painting glazes, scumbling, thick or impenetrably thin colors over yards and yards of cloth. Perhaps it is the love of painting itself.

Artists have viewed painting in a variety of ways. For William de Kooning, painting was "a way of living". He saw that the act of painting, regardless how others reacted to it, was more important than 'success'. For Adolph Gottlieb, it was necessary to reject established painting styles in order to find his own 'voice'. What is visually true for an artist is more important than how others react to it."..Colors of...light, the feel of flight, the push of birds breasting a morning wind bending the tall flag reeds. He painted the lonliness and the smell of the salt-laden cold". The inner vision can be expressed through the media of paint, cloth, brush, body, clothing, and movement; combining and forming new painting in our populated environment.

In the United States, there is a continuous revolution in clothing. What is in style one decade becomes dated the next, and vintage the next. Whether it be punk-inspired, New Wave fashion or romantically inspired ruffled dresses with lace, the techniques of fabric painting can be used with any particular style. Fabric painting, with its multidimensional variety, is yet another dimension to the clothing revolution. I hope that the variety of techniques presented in this book will allow a greater creative expression in the realm of fabric painting, as well as a higher conscious awareness when we pass each other in the street.

2 FABRIC PAINTING: A HISTORY

◆◆

ANCIENT HISTORY

Fabric is not a durable material. Unlike stone and wood, it is not a predominant artifact gathered from archaeological sites. The record of its passage through time is an irregular one. Histories of fabric are difficult to compile, as the material itself which is to be written about disintegrates after eighty or ninety years, depending upon its condition and where it is stored. The sources which prove to be the most numerous in material are the dry arid deserts and the airtight tombs. The burial tombs in Peru are one of the richest sources for preserved painted cloth, as the Precolumbian Indians wrapped their dead in clothing and fabric. It would seem that there is as much fabric painting found in the dry Egyptian tombs, and it is known that the Egyptians also wrapped their dead in clothing and fabric; yet they were also known to cremate their dead fully clothed. The Egyptian burial sites are a rich source for decorated pottery and we can only infer that similar designs might be painted on fabric. The dating of these fabrics range from the 4th and 5th century B.C., with few examples, to a high interest from 900-100 B.C.

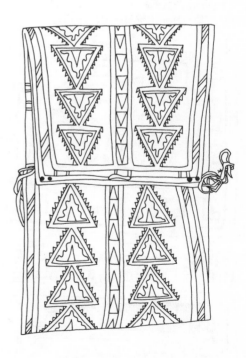

FIG. 15: PAINTED PARFLECHE (GREAT PLAINS) AFTER INDIAN ART IN NORTH AMERICA, FIG. 207, BY FREDERICK J. DOCKSTADER. DRAWING BY PHYLLIS THOMPSON

23

To be accurate in describing the history of fabric painting is even more difficult than with other types of fabric decoration. However, there is still a story to tell, though it must be pieced together, like a quilt, from random bits of information gathered from many fields. Anthropology, historical writings of the lives of various peoples, records of the art of different peoples yield various bits of information. Even the history of economics and trade can give one a lead on the history of fabric painting, as various kinds of dyes and paints were traded in different parts of the world at varying times.

Piecing together the fragmented history of fabric painting may seem tedious, but it is necessary. The history of something serves not only to tell of its past, it also points to its future. Stimulation occurs when one sees where something

FIG. 16: DRAWING BY AUTHOR OF PRE-COLUMBIAN HANDPAINTED TEXTILE

FIG. 17: DRAWING BY AUTHOR OF PAINTED CLOTH, NORTHERN PERU.

has been, and can see where it might
go. The lack of a written history in
fabric painting may be one reason for
its slow evolution beyond the primitive. There are many other reasons
for its remaining prehistoric.

It is possible that fabric painting never really caught on due to the
disparity in older methods and the
methods which we have today at our
disposal due to modern technology.
The American Indians used earth pigments mixed with a glue which was
boiled from the scrapings of the
hide used as a canvas. The painting
was executed with a sharp stick and
was fairly tedious,sometimes taking
several weeks. The pioneers and early
settlers were busy with more practical
matters of survival than decorative
clothing. They were also a different
kind of people,more interested in the
reality of harsh winters and neighbor-
ing Indians,while the Indians were
more involved in mystical and spiritual matters,painting their clothes to
protect them from evil influences-as
well as the white man's bullets.

The Industrial Revolution,begin-
ning in the 19th century,changed the
tenure and tempo of life. Factories
could put together garments much more
quickly than human beings;factories
and technology could also print and
dye materials much more effectively
than could the individual. It may be a
historical leap which caused fabric
painting to go from the primitive
state to the industrial state,bypas-
sing the hands of the common man and
the artist.

A study of modern or industrial-
ized textiles offers some explanation as to this leap,by showing the
different types of effects produced
by hand and machine printing. By
understanding the principles underlying modern textile design,one can
also understand the uniqueness of
these ancient hand painted textiles,
fragmented and faded but surviving in
the museums.(Fig.16, Fig. 17)

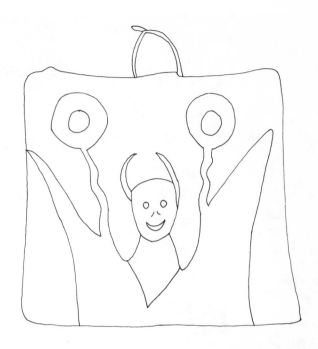

FIG. 18: DRAWING,BY AUTHOR,OF SIOUX
SKIN DRUM.AFTER 200 YEARS OF NORTH
AMERICAN INDIAN ART-NORMAN FEDER

FIG. 19: BETH BROWN MODELING
HUIPTL (SHIRT) WITH PAINTED
PRE-COLUMBIAN DESIGNS

(ABOVE AND BELOW) FIGS. 21 AND 22:
LISA HENSLEY MODELING MEXICAN-STYLE
WRAP SKIRT WITH PRE-COLUMBIAN DESIGNS

(LEFT) FIG. 20: PATRICIA TUBB MODEL-
ING DRESS PAINTED WITH MAYAN DESIGNS

Archaeological digs largely contribute to our knowledge of ancient textiles. Ancient textiles are valuable to the student of textiles as well as to the fabric painter, and yet there are few places where they are known to be found. Until recently, most archeologists did not consider textiles important enough to be written up, so that which was found was ignored. A large number of accounts of fabric painting comes from Precolumbian South American sites, many of which have only been excavated and carefully documented in the past.

FIG. 24: MAN'S COTTON SHIRT WITH REPEATING MOTIF. AFTER INDIAN ART IN SOUTH AMERICA- F.J. DOCKSTADER # 213.

PRECOLUMBIAN FABRIC PAINTING

Precolumbian Peruvian textiles represent the highest achievement of textile production of the ancient world. Not only was there fabric painting, there were fine examples of weaving, knotting, and knitting. Painted cloth and clothing were used in everyday wear, for the dead, and for spiritual ceremonies. (Fig. 24) Many of the patterns of painted clothing were repeated in weavings, and as well it is possible that patterns used for pottery were also used in textiles. Due to a lack of written history, it is difficult to say to what extent fabric painting was used in Precolumbian societies. With the American Indian culture, the importance of fabric painting can be understood more easily.

(LEFT) FIG. 23: PHOTOGRAPH BY MARTIN CHAMBI JR. OF PERUVIAN INDIAN IN TRADITIONAL GARB (1938)

(ABOVE) FIG 25: CHIMU PAINTED GRAVE-CLOTH. AFTER INDIAN ART IN SOUTH AMERICA-FREDERICK DOCKSTADER

(BELOW) FIG. 26: ARAPAHO "GHOST SHIRT" WORN BY PARTICIPANTS IN THE GHOST DANCE RELIGION.

AMERICAN INDIAN FABRIC PAINTING

Although all Indian tribes used fabric painting to some extent, the most examples and usage come from the Plains Indians. Fabric painting was used for spiritual power, for healing, as protection from wild animals and white hunters, and for historical purposes such as recording events, counting time, and the identification of clans. (Fig. 25, Fig. 26)

Painted clothing, as well as painted masks, were worn in spiritual ceremonies, in order to influence the individual towards a certain consciousness. Once a person put on the clothing, he was no longer a person; he became the 'power'. Dreams and visions seen during quests were painted on clothing. The painting was a symbol through which power flowed. Medicine shirts for healing were similar in that the power came through using certain repeating symbols, although each medicine shirt was unique in appearance. Painted symbols were thought to be powerful on clothing as protection against the enemy, both animal and human. In 1880, the Indians of North Dakota painted their shirts as protection against the white man's bullets. The magic did not work, and the shirts were not worn again.

28

FIG. 27: DRAWING OF APACHE MEDICINE SHIRT. ALTHOUGH THESE SHIRTS WERE
DIFFERENT IN DESIGN, CERTAIN SYMBOLS REAPPEAR: SUN, MOON, STARS, RAINBOWS,
SNAKES, TARANTULAS, LIGHTNING, HAIL, AND SMOKE CLOUDS. FROM AUTHENTIC
INDIAN DESIGNS- MARIA NAYLOR. DRAWING BY PHYLLIS THOMPSON.

29

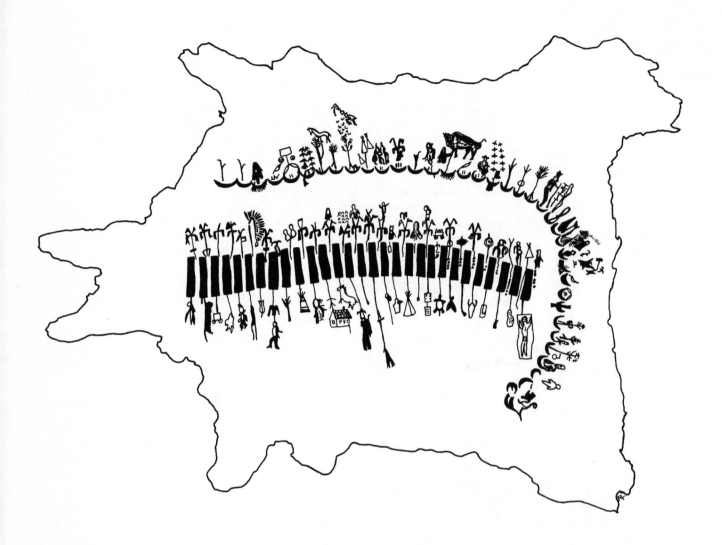

FIG. 28: DRAWING OF PLAINS INDIAN CALENDAR (KIOWA TRIBE) FROM THE 1890'S. A RECORD OF 37 MONTHS IS DEPICTED HERE. FROM AUTHENTIC INDIAN DESIGNS—MARIA NAYLOR. DRAWING BY PHYLLIS THOMPSON.

Painted clothing also had more practical aspects for the Indians. Important events could easily be recorded by painting, as it was a mnenotic device whereby one image would recall a more complex event. As well as clothing, hides, tipis, and saddlebags recorded remarkable events and the passage of time. This type of painting probably evolved from cave painting, where sequented events were recorded. Another practical aspect of fabric painting by the Plains Indians was for identification purposes. Different clans and peoples used certain symbols on their clothes and tipis as identification with a certain clan.

Plains Indians culture lay great stress on the individual personality, so that much fabric painting could express that individuality. Painted robes have been collected dating well into the second half of the 19th century. The Indians living in the Southwest also did fabric painting, but it was an extension of a social order rather than an individual message, and, except for the Navajo, this painting crumbled when the white man dominated the Indian culture. The need for fabric painting as social communication vanished along with that very communication which held the Indians together in a cohesive social unit.

FIG. 29: PAINTED LEATHER HANGING
BY K. LEE MANUEL. FEATHERS, BEADWORK.
THIS IS PAINTED IN A MANNER SIMILAR
TO NORTH AMERICAN INDIAN PAINTED
HIDES. VERSATEX PAINT.

FIG. 30: PAINTED LEATHER GARMENT
WITH INDIAN DESIGNS. BEADED FRINGE.
ARTIST: K. LEE MANUEL.

31

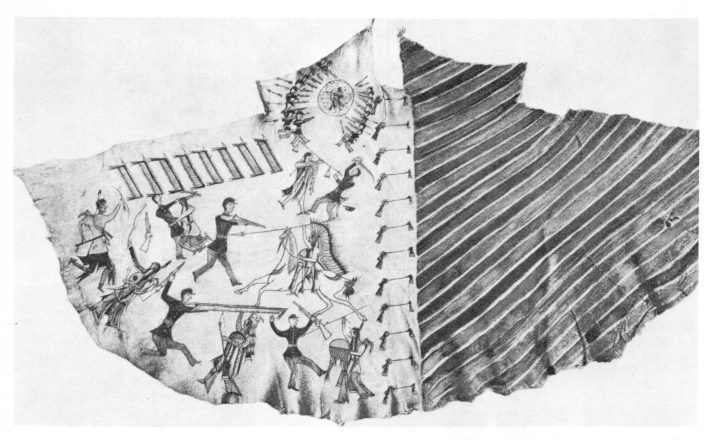

FIG. 31: BATTLE TIPI OF THE KIOWAS.
REPLICA OF HERALDIC TIPI FROM 1872.

Other Indian tribes farther east
and north did some fabric painting,
but we have little record of it.
In 1540, Coronado mentioned painted
bison robes of the Zuni of New Mexico.
Giovanni da Verrazano mentioned finding painted deerskins in New England
in 1524, and in Florida in 1528, Cabeza
de Vaca also found painted deerskins.
Eskimos used fabric painting rather
extensively, on drums and tools, as well
as in clothing.

FIG. 32: WINTER COAT MADE OF CARIBOU HIDE BY
THE UNGAVA INDIANS OF HUDSON BAY. HANDPAINTED
BORDER. AUTHENTIC INDIAN DESIGNS-MARIA NAYLOR.

FIG. 33: NASKAPI PAINTED BUCKSKIN COAT FROM THE EASTERN WOODLANDS. GEOMETRIC AND DOUBLE CURVE MOTIF.

FIG. 35: TSIMSHIAN (NORTHWEST COAST INDIAN) SKIN APRON WITH REALISTIC DECORATION OF PAINTED ANIMAL FORMS.

FIG. 34: DETAIL OF FIG. 32 ON PRECEDING PAGE

FIG. 36: AFRICAN PAINTED COSTUME FROM
THE IVORY COAST. FROM AFRICAN TEXTILES
AND DECORATIVE ARTS-R. SIEBER. DRAWN BY
PHYLLIS THOMPSON.

FIG. 37: DRAWING OF AFRICAN PAINTED CLOTH
AFTER BAMBARA, MALI. AFRICAN TEXTILES AND
DECORATIVE ARTS-R. SIEBER

AFRICAN FABRIC PAINTING

Going from the cold to a very warm
part of the world, one finds fabric
painting included in African textiles.
(Fig.36,Fig.37) They are used in masks
and costumes, for cloth lengths to be
used in wrapped clothing, or as fabrics
for bedding and drapes.A lot of fabric
painting is done with paste-resists,
such as cassava paste, a substance ob-
tained from a starchy tropical plant.
Although the climate of Africa is hot
as is South America, there is not the
aridness and preservative effect of
the caves, and there is dampness which
causes mildew and destruction of some
textiles. In general, wood and stone
art objects are far more common in
Africa than textiles;reeds and grasses
are also used in place of other types
of fiber constructions. In Oceanic
art, the only examples of fabric painting are on bamboo and bark, although
these are sometimes made into clothing, such as belts.

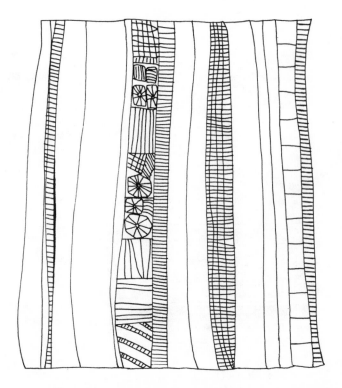

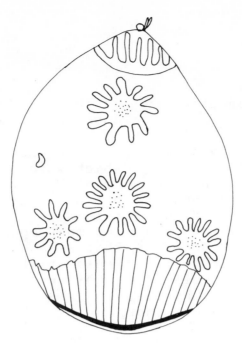

FIG. 38: PAINTED KENYA-TURKANA HEADDRESS.
AFTER PLATE 32, AFRICAN TEXTILES AND DECO-
RATIVE ARTS-R. SIEBER. DRAWING BY AUTHOR.

FIG. 39 AND FIG.40(BELOW): AFRICAN
DESIGNS FROM THE BOOK, AFRICAN DE-
SIGNS FROM TRADITIONAL SOURCES-GEO-
FFREY WILLIAMS.DRAWING BY AUTHOR.

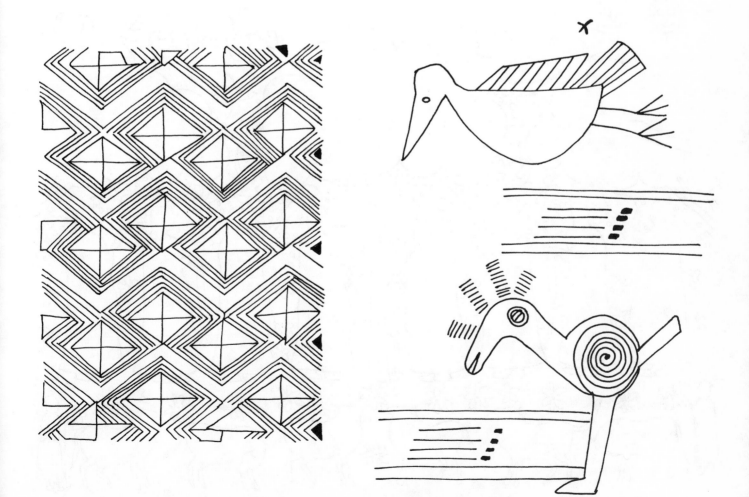

EASTERN FABRIC PAINTING

Farther east,and farther along in history,are examples of fabric painting from Persia,Arabia,India,China, and Japan. A war dress was found in Senegal with Arabic script on it,in 1889. In Persia and India, a number of textiles were painted before hand-printing became more widespread. Hand-stenciling lent itself easily to the repeat motif,but there could be colour variation. The textiles of Persia and India became so popular and their use so widespread that they became a threat to the industry of other nations. A decree in Britian was announced in the 18th century which stated that fabrics of Persia, China, and the East Indies such as calicoes, which were painted,dyed, stenciled, printed, or otherwise marked, could not be imported into Great Britian, nor worn,nor otherwise used. The most popular of these textiles that were banned are the now popular India prints used as bedspreads, wall hangings, and for clothing.

FIG. 41: DETAIL OF PAINTED COTTON HANGING FROM INDIA, 18TH CENTURY. MILKMAIDS ARE SHOWN IN A FOREST. GOLD AND SILVER ON BLACK GROUND. AFTER TEXTILES AND ORNAMENTS OF INDIA-ED. BY MONROE WHEELER.

36

FIG. 42: ONE OF THE EARLIEST RECORDS OF FABRIC PAINTING.
FRAGMENT OF A GESTICULATING MONK, RECOVERED FROM TURFAN,
CENTRAL ASIA, 8TH-9TH CENTURY. PAINTED ON SILK.

There are examples of painting on silk in both China and Japan,ranging from the 8th and 9th century,to an account in the 18th century from a Jesuit missionary speaking of painted Oriental textiles. One problem in accounting for examples of fabric painting in China and Japan is the number of paintings on silk. By look-ing only at a picture,it cannot be always known whether or not the silk was stiffened with glue,as was often the case.

It can be seen that fragmentary examples of fabric painting have been found all over the world. The very earliest fabric painting was found in the 4th century B.C.in Egyptian tombs and in Greek tombs from the Crimea, while the very earliest painting was an Egyptian wall painting in a tomb dating 2500B.C. Records of fabric painting have been found in a German manuscript from the Monastery of St. Catherine Nurnberg(15th,16th century), in Pliny's writings,and probably in numerous other historical records,as yet undiscovered.

MODERN FABRIC PAINTING

There is a large jump from the fabric painting in the tombs of Egypt to what is considered the history of modern fabric painting. Speculations on the gap lead one to consider the advance of industrialization in the 1800's, and the confusion of fabric painting with fabric printing. As well, most paints and dyes used in textile decoration could only be used for industry, not for home use. Materials which could be used at home, such as dyes and natural dyes, were used with hot dyeing, and therefore could not be used very well with fabric painting.

Other possibilities for the fading out of fabric painting had to do with the separation of painting and needlework. In the 1600's, the church ruled over painting with an iron hand. During that time as well, it was necessary for a painter to have a patron, as she could not exist on her own. A painter needed the support of the aristocracy or the academy. In the 1800's, the ideas for painting were more influenced by the general public rather than the church. Still, it was not until the 1950's that the definition of painting began to loosen. At that time, the boundaries between painting and printmaking blurred. Picasso and Braque introduced the Cubist movement, combining collage and painting. Pollack moved his canvases to the floor.

And by the 1950's, in an attempt to get women back into the home and out of the factories, homemakers were encouraged to learn handicrafts(as contrasted to todays crafts). For fabric painting, that meant booklets on how to decorate curtains and other household accessories with simple stenciled designs. It meant decorating all types of clothing: children's smocks, dresses, aprons, neckties, hankerchiefs, scarves, and bedspreads with neatly stenciled designs. A flurry of books appeared, only to go out of print in a few years due to the limited scope of the material presented. The material in these books dealt with design ideas better suited to fabric printing, in my opinion. Handpainting designs which were more easily fabric printed caused the decline and near dead stop of fabric painting by the end of the 1950's.

In the late 60's and early 70's, design industry turned to the art world for ideas. As well, designers and craftspeople had been incorporating tie-dye and batik in fashion and clothing. New offset printing processes made it possible for anything that could be photographed to be printed, and a wide variety of designs were introduced: photographs of movie stars, political figures, famous buildings, works of art. Textile design was no longer limited to geometrics, floral motifs, and nature scenes.

Much more is being done in fabric painting today as more is being done in general in the area of individually designed clothing. Painted clothing can be both a personal aesthetic statement or a social commentary. Just as ancient fabric painting was used in a personally symbolic way, and as a way to establish communication with others, modern fabric painting has the same basis, though disguised and perhaps distorted with time.

An example of ancient fabric painting might be a war dress with special symbols on it, meant as protection to the wearer. In modern terms, this could be a dress with one's favorite images from modern America-a Volkswagon bug, a long winding road, traveling paraphernalia. Many examples of ancient fabric painting dealt with marking time and telling a series of events. Heroic deeds, journeys, and in general changes through time and space, are expressed through fabric painting, both ancient and modern.

By marking time as cyclical rather than linear, it is possible to recycle old clothes as well as old ideas. Many styles of clothing can be combined with many styles of painting. In this way, the concept of clothing can be stretched beyond fashion, with its dictates of time present and time past.

Once clothing is liberated beyond the constricts of fashion, it can be seen as a very flexible environment, lending itself to aesthetic appreciation, costume, social commentary, and social reaction. Clothing is a very personal environment in the sense that any image or symbol in fabric painting is connected not only to the person, but to the body. The meaning of a picture of a political figure on the bottom of someone's pants is quite different from the same picture on a wall. Clothing as the most immediate environment relates it to the environment and breaks down the artificial barriers that keep it from the environment.

THE AESTHETIC ENVIRONMENT

As an aesthetic environment, painted clothing has no limitations. It becomes a visual pleasure of one's creative efforts which can cast a spell, create a mood, heighten an effect. There is a ceremony of clothes which is overlooked in the competition of fashion and status. K. Lee Manuel, a fabric painter from San Francisco, sees painted clothing as a way of relating the body to everyday space, and, for this reason, she creates one-of-a-kind clothing. She has painted brightly coloured capes,

cummerbunds, and dresses. Clothing such as this can be an interference and a distraction; it is not psychologically subdued. It points to who we are. People who wish to be visually or psychologically inconspicuous may prefer mass produced clothing.

Other fabric painters create other effects. Lenore Davis, a fabric artist from New York now living in Kentucky, creates a sculptural effect in painted clothing by padding certain places and then painting them. The clothing becomes very much an environment as it extends into the environment. Aaron Bartell of Eugene, Oregon, uses fabric painting for optical illusions with the shape of the body being manipulated towards this end. The cloth is the vehicle by which the optical illusion can take place. Painted clothing is an excellent vehicle for games and secret hidden messages, due to the curvatures and hiding places both on the body and with certain designs of clothes.

Costume creates a very definite aesthetic environment and mood as the wearer is transformed into a specific "someone". An Indian dress, a Japanese kimona, a cape like a brightly plumaged bird are close to costume and yet allow the wearer his individual personality. Costume is also a vehicle by which many different cultural and historical motifs and images can be expressed which are not included in modern fashion. As well, ancient images and motifs only to be found in dusty books can be renovated through fabric painting and worn on 20th century streets-an interesting time perspective. In wearing painted motifs of a certain historical period or culture, I find it is as if I have gone to that place, having created that environment. Costume leads to psychological travel, changes the immediate environment from its narrow 20th century slot to a multidimensional view of time/space.

THE SOCIOLOGICAL ENVIRONMENT

As well as being an aesthetic environment, painted clothing also creates a sociological environment. It deals with social issues, as well as creating a social commentary and interaction by the use of painted symbols. The sociological perspective of fabric painting is an exciting one, as it deviates far from traditional viewpoints of clothing as "decorative".

(The Plains Indians relied on fabric painting as an integral part of social communication, but most clothing lacked a social dimension apart from that of status.)

Painted clothing can be a sounding board for popular social issues. Ecology, nuclear issues, drugs, sexuality, and other political and social issues and persons are popular with modern fabric painting. (see FIG. 43) Fabric painting of this type can be very close to the effect political cartoons have in the newspaper: they are open to and invite social reaction.

One of the more popular mediums open to social reaction which relates to clothing is the button with a message on it. Fabric painting extends the message of the button to a larger ground, such as a T-shirt. The message is echoed back by those who react. Like a bulletin board, painted clothing dealing with social issues is conspicuous and will guarantee an immediate response from others. (As a painter, this can be rather nice, as you need not try and inconspicuously overhear comments made at a museum as to the quality of your work.) Some caution will be advised both in the designing and wearing of clothing which might provoke certain other people. It is not necessary that all socially oriented painting be dangerous or disruptive, indeed it can be visually aesthetic yet point to a meaning larger than personal aestheticism.

The reactions of others to fabric painting leads it to become an open mural. With social intervention in the creative process, one can decide how to develop a painting through the comments and suggestions of others. In the book, American

SAVE
THE WHALES !

FIG. 43: A POPULAR SOCIAL ISSUE EXPRESSED ON A PAINTED T-SHIRT. DESIGN AND DRAWING BY AUTHOR.

Denim, a New Folk Art-Owens and Lane, Doug Hansen spoke of how he wore his acrylic-painted pants through various stages of painting, which then evolved through the reactions and comments of others.

The open mural effect of fabric painting leads to group painting. As well as being an individual artist selecting and choosing from other people's ideas, you can do group work. An autograph shirt is an example of such a combined effort; it has historical value as well. Children's art often is done with groups of children working on a single project. Although painted clothing done by children may have a personally appealing sentiment, it may not be seen for more than a curiosity to serious designers of painted clothing. It can be edited, however, by someone with a sense of balance and composition who can utilize the raw material and mold it into a visually interesting form. For the children, the clothing would be a public museum, a statement of warmth between wearer and makers.

MODERN FABRIC PAINTERS

Painted clothing can be seen to have a variety of meanings, depending upon the type of painting done, its intent, and its reaction in the environment. There are a number of people today experimenting with fabric painting in a variety of ways. Some people paint spontaneously; others sketch and plan. Linda Nelson Bryan, who airbrushes and stuffs soft paintings and sculpture says, "Although my pieces have a traditional quilting basis, in the trapunto work, they are also painted(and sketched many times previous to the painting), so I consider them works of art." She also uses acrylic paint for an unusual reason: to withstand heat in art galleries. Judy Felgars' woven painted surfaces are also preplanned. "All my work is preplanned. After 'getting' an idea, or a new technique suggests a new approach, drawings are made in black and white. Then I continue with colour studies, usually felt pens. If I decide to do the piece, the drawing is then transferred to graph paper, then woven and painted."

However, Alan Grinberg, an artist/designer/craftsman who airbrushes with found-object stencils, says, "I try not to spend too much time on each piece. It makes me feel freer, and it is easier to take risks without a heavy time investment." Dorothy Caldwell of Canada uses both approaches: "Sometimes a piece is worked out very carefully beforehand through a series of sketches and patterns. Other times, I take a bolt of fabric and just do things to it working completely with what happens and developing something out of it."

Some fabric painters express the practical; others, the abstract. Faith Middendorp, who paints quilt patterns on pillows, says, "In a society where very few people have the opportunity to fashion an object from start to finish in their daily work, I believe there is a profound need for the experiences which would provide a full opportunity to identify in a personal way with the products created by hand, and to give meaning and enduring values to the things we touch and use in our daily lives." Victoria Rivers uses her fabric-painted soft three-dimensional wall hangings as abstract statements of sequential movement in time and space. "They reflect my landscape environment which takes on a spiritual rather than physical presence...(they) symbolize the passing of time and experience and the unfolding of knowledge. The rectilinear pieces symbolize collections of personal experiences, thoughtforms, or memories that compose the person. These vary in colour combinations, often colours remembered from childhood memories of dresses, packages, etc. that are contained by boundaries symbolizing the physical self."

At the present time, there are more fabric painters working in non-clothing than in clothing. Bill Hinz works with fiber-reactive dyes on white velveteen, as does Lenore Davis. Kathryn Westphal works on fabric with an interaction of painted, stitched, and imprinted textures in an exciting composition. Judith Stein uses oil-base printing inks and collographs for fabric painted quilts, while Ann Sams works in the hot Florida sun dyepainting hammocks out of heavy canvas. Other fabric painters are K. Lee Manuel, Valery Guignon, Maggie Kendis, Sue Cole, Carol Racklin, Shanna Santomieri, Phyllis Mufson, Sherry De Leon, Louaine Elke, Michael Foran, Kim and Leigh LaCava, Frances Butler, Jeanne Hillis, Gloria Rigling, James H. Sanders, Joseph Minor, Joetta Umla, Phyllis Richardson, Linda Fisher, Suzanne Larsen, Boats George, Martha Lopez, Ferne Sirois, Eve Zweben-Chung, Cindy Turnbow, Norma Rosen, Susan Springer, Anne Johnston, and Theodora Zehner.

Despite some differences in appearance, modern fabric painting is based on the techniques used by ancient fabric painters. Although the skill level in fabric painting can vary widely from simple brushstrokes (probably used most frequently by ancient fabric painters),to technically difficult procedures(often used today),one <u>must</u> start by learning about three basic elements:the paint,the brush,and the cloth. When these elements are successfully combined,the modern fabric painter can choose to express him or her self in primitive,simple,moderate, or astounding terms!

FIG. 45: CAROL PETRELLI MODELLING PAINTED "PAINTERS PANTS". ACRYLIC PAINT WAS USED WITH WIDE HOUSEPAINTING BRUSHES.

FIG. 44. CAROL PETRELLI MODELLING PAINTED T-SHIRT AND SKIRT IN PRE-COLUMBIAN AND INDIAN DESIGNS. ACRYLIC PAINTS, DYES, AND NATURAL PAINTS WERE USED.

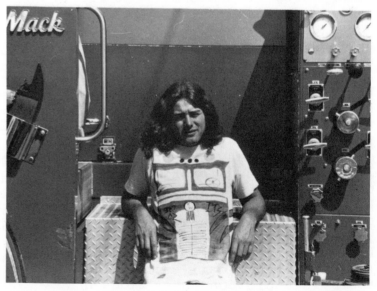

FIG. 46: STEPHEN GARROW MODELLING HIS "TRUCK" SHIRT IN FRONT OF A BIG RED FIRE ENGINE.

3 FABRIC PAINTING: A BEGINNING

TEXTILE PAINT

MORDANT

TEXTINE

PERMANENT INK

FELT MARKER
FELT TIP PEN

BLOCK PRINTING INK

ACRYLIC PAINT

OIL PAINT

FABRIC CRAYONS

EMBROIDERY PAINT

DYE DY

FABRIC DYE

NATURAL DYES & PAINTS

FIG. 47: DRAWING OF PAINT MATERIALS USED
IN FABRIC PAINTING—BY KAREN HAMILTON

In its simplest form, fabric painting is an interaction between fabric and paint which is carried out by the use of a tool(the brush). It is a process:the paint is carried by the brush to the fabric. It is a dance and the hand and the eye are a part of the motion. In its simplest form, what is needed for fabric painting is some cloth, a flat surface, a brush, some paint, and at least one idea. In its complex form, fabric painting extends beyond brush painting and into the use of tools such as sponges or spray guns, and embraces different kinds of fabrics which react in different ways. In its compex form, fabric painting uses natural materials such as rocks and clay and wood as well as many synthetics;it utilizes chemical reactions with dyes to produce various effects, even the making of paint itself.(Fig. 47)

I shall be using the term painting environment to describe what is necessary and what is useful to the fabric painter. With different kinds of paints and dyes, it is necessary to have different sorts of equipment. Ironically, the product which was made for fabric painting, textile paint, is more difficult to use in terms of the demands of the painting environment than other materials such as permanent marking pens or acrylic paints. It is possible to do some interesting work with a minimum of equipment, just as it is possible to do interesting

work with a well-stocked studio. What sort of an arrangement you will need depends upon the materials with which you choose to work.

If you think of the paint, the brush and the cloth as three separate elements forming relationships in various configurations, you may begin to feel the excitement of fabric painting and its range of exploration.

THE PAINT

One has so many materials at hand from which to choose. In the category of paint, there is, besides textile paint; acrylic paint with its many accessories(polymer emulsions such as resin, matte and gel mediums, acrylic modeling paste, matte and gel varnish,

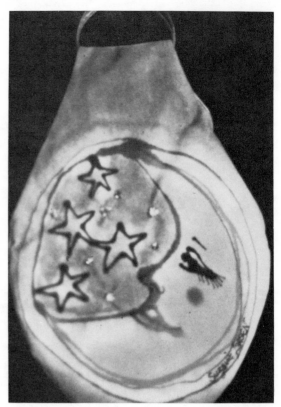

FIG. 48: MOON SIDE OF SUN BRACELET PURSE BY SUZANNE LARSEN. PROCION DYE ON VELVETSUEDE CLOTH. LINE DRAWING IN INKODYE.

and gesso), indelible inks such as Pelican and Koh-i-nor, oil paint with textine, oilbase block printing ink, oil base silkscreen inks, cold water dyes such as Procion, Fibrex, and Dylon with or without thickeners. If you wish to be less reliant upon paint materials found only in stores, natural dyes and paints, mordant painting, and homemade textile paint are all ways to work in a more primitive, less industrial way. Embroidery paints, permanent magic markers and fabric crayons are other materials to use in painting.

These materials can also be mixed with one another or used in combination with each other to create other sources of paint. Cold-water dyes can be used in conjunction with acrylics (with the dye being used in large areas and the paint in smaller, more detailed areas for best effects)as long as the acrylic painting is done after the dye has been set. Jewel-like effects are created with a combination of colour crayons, acrylic medium and acrylic colour. The contrast between aqueous and graphic sections of a piece of fabric is also seen when

44

drawing with a combination of acrylic watercolour,and pen and ink or other drawing materials.(Fig.48)

All these materials can be used as traditional painting media,although their effects will be different due to types of cloth used. Watercolour,collage,oil and tempera effects can be had with acrylics. Textile paints have a consistency and effect similar to tempera. Stenciling,marbling,imprinting,fingerpainting,and splattering of paint are other techniques to be used with fabric.

To fully understand the effects of paint,one must form a relationship with colour. I would like to refer the reader to other books for the technical explanations on colour,the laws of colour and the various types of colour wheels. I would like to give more intuitive ideas for using colour in painting.

Colour is an energy source. The Fauvists loved colour so much that they used it as the main idea of their art,letting line,shape and form be in supportive roles. They were concerned with the painting of colour.

It is a good idea to sometimes limit your palette to one colour and experiment with different shades and tones of that colour,as well as different shapes which seem to fit the feeling of that colour. It is possible in this way to discover a subtle range of effects and materials connected to each colour.

Colour says different things to different people. Everyone has a favorite colour. As you paint,you can begin to form a colour language. This can influence the kind of work you do,by building a unity of colour within the subject matter. It is helpful to understand a colour before working with it, for then there is emotional as well as technical knowledge. As an example,the colours brown and yellow,when used together, make connections in my mind with the smell of dry grass in August,the moist earth, dry autumn leaves on the ground, and the delicate textures of certain grasses.

If colour is frightening or confusing,there are guides which can help you

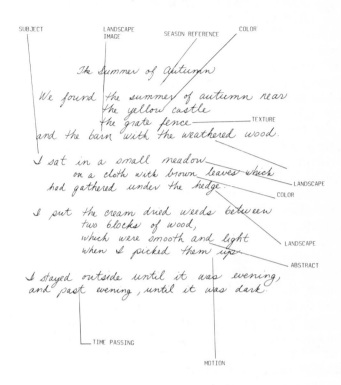

ANALYSIS OF A POEM FOR DESIGN

ABOVE:FIG.49 POEM BY AUTHOR.BELOW:FIG.50: PAINTED T-SHIRT BY KIM AND LEIGH LACAVA.

45

explore your own feelings about them. Take a painting which you like and copy the general areas of colour without copying the entire painting. This is helpful for learning about certain feelings and forms in connection with colours placed next to each other. Take a poem or descriptive passage from a book which you find pleasing and use the colours to form a design. (Fig.49)It is not necessary to use a piece of literature to do this,although sometimes it brings up images and associations that a person would not make on his own. Think of some of your favorite images,put them together and notice their colours and use them. Reverse this idea:think of different names of colours, then find design ideas from the objects created from these names. For example,the colour crayons bittersweet,mahogany,and apricot are all browns and shades of brown. They call up images of wood and flowering trees and thus form a design through mental imagery.

Hans Hofmann and Josef Albers are two painters who harness the power of colour in their work. The power of colour transcends form. They work in geometrics,Albers moreso than Hofmann, and the colour justapositions are what forms the painting.By identifying colour with light, Robert Delaunay used colour as the fundamental building material of his pictures. In modern art,as a whole, the use of colour is a direct and independent language of meaning and emotion, and it can be used in this way for fabric painting.

THE BRUSH

The brush is the next element in this configuration of paint,brush, and cloth. The brush is more than a means of transferring the paint onto the fabric,although it does serve the function of intermediary. The brush is a tool;more than that,it is an idea. A machine can print designs onto yards and yards of fabric very efficiently. A machine cannot capture the spontenaity and originality which can happen when a thoughtful person takes up a brush. The brush creates a fabric or garment which is expressive,rather than merely decorative; just as a painting is an expression rather than a piece of decorated paper.

As well as regular oil brushes to be found in art stores, there are a variety of other brushes to be used-from toothbrushes to housepainting brushes,large and small. The brush, as a tool,extends beyond brushlike qualities. It is a connection between the painter and the paint. In this way,tools such as paint rollers,sprayers,squeeze bottles(Fig.51), palette knives,kitchen utensils,pieces of rope and string("homemade brushes") pine needles,bottles from which to pour paint,and other pieces of cloth, are all brushes. The various types of nibs on drawing pens also function as brushes.

These different types of brushes produce different types of painting effects when used with various types of paint.(Fig. 50 ,Fig.52,Fig.53)It is the interaction between paint and cloth which causes so many different effects, and this interaction comes via the brush. A more static method of fabric decoration,such as blockprinting has less variety,less confusion, but fewer choices. By learning which types of paint interact best with what kind of cloth via what type brushstroke,there are many more choices for expression.

The handling of the brush ranges from the very controlled to free expression and experimentation. Certain techniques which are established today were yesterdays experiments. Handling the brush requires using it and observing how certain procedures will create certain effects. Accidental effects become original,controlled brushstrokes.(Fig.54)

(LEFT) FIG. 51: "LANDSCAPE WITH MOON FIGURE"-LENORE DAVIS. DYE-PAINTED WITH SQUEEZE BOTTLE ON VELVETEEN. DRY BRUSH, BRUSH WASH TECHNIQUE.

(BELOW LEFT) FIG. 52: SILK SCARVES- PHYLLIS MUFSON. DIRECT APPLICATION OF PROCION DYE.

(BELOW) FIG. 53: SILK CHIFFON CAFTAN- SHERRY DE LEON. AIRBRUSH PAINTING USING PLANT SPRAYER, DIRECT APPLICATION WITH PROCION DYES.

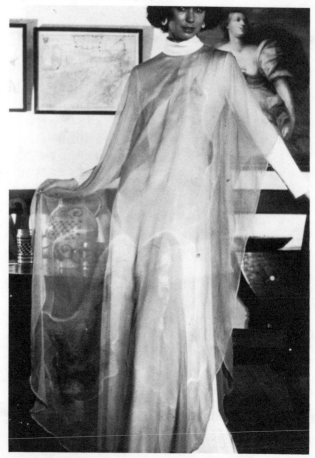

FIG. 54: "THE BRIDGE"-BY FERNE SIROIS.
ACRYLIC STAINING.RAW CANVAS IS STAINED
USING DILUTED ACRYLIC PAINT AND WATER.
IT IS DRIBBLED ACROSS THE CANVAS,WHICH
ALLOWS FOR SPONTANEOUS COLOR MIXING.
WHEN THE CANVAS DRIES, THE ARTIST EX-
PANDS THE DESIGN USING AN AIRBRUSH OR
JAPANESE INK BRUSHES AND ACRYLIC PAINT.

There are certain ways of handling the brush which are standard
and can be learned. The size of the
brush produces certain widths in
line;the shape of the brush produces certain standard impressions.
These basic brushstrokes,when combined with experimental effects,
allow for a flexibility in technique and application. Ideas for
brushstrokes should come from sources other than just painting techniques,as the purpose of a technique is to help the artist express
her   inner vision rather than
having the artists' vision be
limited by technique.

THE CLOTH

Thus far,we have followed fabric
painting from its beginning,the
paint,to its transition of the paint
with the brush. We now come to the
end point of the interaction,the
cloth. The only difference in fabric
painting and canvas painting is the
addition of sizing to the canvas in
canvas painting. Unprimed canvas is
cloth,just as fine drawing paper is
finely ground up cloth(rag linen,for
example). The connection between the
world of traditional painting and the
world of fabric design,as well as the
separation of these two worlds,is
due to one variable:sized or unsized
cloth.

It is very important to be able
to recognize the fiber content in
cloth,so as to know what type of
paint or dye will or will not work
on the fabric. Knowing this can save
you many hours of work,as well as
allowing you to use a combination of
paints and dyes safely on one type of
cloth.

There is a much larger quantity
of synthetic fibers on the market today than there were twenty years ago.
Many materials which look like natural fibers-cotton,linen,wool,and
silk,are only blends,and because of
this,they react differently than do
their pure counterparts. The fiber
content of material sold in stores
is marked on the bolt,so this is a
good way to learn about many fabrics.
Random pieces of cloth laying around
the house may be more difficult to
identify. The burn test for fabrics
is helpful;natural fibers,when burn-
ed,are reduced to soft ashes,while
synthetics smell like chemicals and
melt into a lump or hard bead. It is
also possible to experiment with fabrics of unknown fiber content by
painting them with different types
of paint,and recording the effects.

Experimentation,or testing fabrics,is very important in fabric
painting. It is a necessary basic
rule to avoid wasting time and materials. Most paints or dyes or mar-

kers of a certain brand will all react similarly;however,one could be
the black sheep which could ruin a
work of art-if it is not first tested! Testing materials is very simple.
Label the type of cloth if it is
known. Draw and paint with a variety
of materials:acrylics,textile paint,
oils,permanent markers,embroidery
paints,fabric crayons,dyes. Write
the brand and type of material in
that material(for example,write
Aqua-tec burnt sienna acrylic). Let
the cloth dry,then wash it in warm
water and soap. Give the material
rougher treatment than it would get
in normal wear. Nothing is more dis-
couraging than to see a handpainted
garment fading after a few washings
because you used certain materials
without first testing them!Let the
cloth dry and then press it with a
medium-hot iron.Again,check the vi-
brancy of the colour and how well
the paint or dye has permeated the
fabric. Small squares of different
types of cloth are good for test
pieces,as they can be mounted on
cardboard and used for reference.

A notebook is also handy in which
to keep such information,as it is
portable,and could be used for
filling special orders in fabric
painting.

LISTING AND IDENTIFICATION
OF COMMON FABRICS

NATURAL FIBERS

There are hundreds of different
kinds of cloth. They can be broken
down into the catagories of natural and synthetic fibers;natural
being cotton,linen,wool,and silk;
synthetic being rayons,acetates,tri-
acetates,nylon,polyesters,acrylic,
modacrylic,and stretch(made from
spandex or other synthetic elastic
fibers)fabrics. Due to the many ways
of engineering fibers and yarns,hun-
dreds of different types of fabrics
are derived from each of these different fibers.

Cotton,moreso than other natural
fibers,is a common fabric and would
seem to be easily identifiable. It

is,however, more difficult to identify pure cotton due to the creation
of polyester cotton blends(65% polyester,35% cotton), which keep the appearance of pure cotton without being so. The distinctions between
these similar looking fabrics must
be made, as paint materials will not
react similarly. For example, fabric
crayons work only on synthetics, and
cold-water dyes most always work only on natural fibers.

100% cotton accepts the majority
of dyes and paints easily. It perhaps
is the only fabric to do so, and so it
is a good fabric for beginning fabric
painters. Some of the names of cotton
fabrics are: unbleached and bleached
muslin, batiste, broadcloth, burlap,
calico, cambric, canvas, chambray,
cheesecloth, chenille, chintz,cordu-
roy, cotton knit, crepe, denim, dot-
ted swiss, drill, duck, damask, flan-
nelette, felt, gauze, gabardine, gingham, lawn, madras, monks cloth, needle-
cord, organdy, oxford cloth, percale,
pique,pima,plisse,poplin, sailcloth,
sateen, seersucker, shirting, terry-
cloth, ticking, velour,velvet,velvet-
een, and voile.

Linen is a very crisp and cool fabric. It is not as commonly used as is
cotton, but it is still in demand. It
is woven in many weights, from hanker-
chief through homespun to upholstery.
It is a strong fiber, and takes paints
and dyes well, with less capillary action due to the strength and stability
of the fabric. Cambric, canvas, damask,
holland, huck,momie, and sheeting are
all made of linen.

Wool is the second most popular of
natural fibers, after cotton. The wool
fiber is combed and carded in various
ways, producing wool or worsted fabrics. Some of these are: barathea,ben-
galine, boucle,broadcloth,challis,chen-
ille,Chinchilla cloth,covert cloth,
crepe,doeskin, Donegal, double-faced
fabrics, doubleknits,felt cloth,fleece,
flannel, gabardine,homespun, hopsack-
ing,jersey, lambs wool, merino,mungo,
serge, Shetland,Tartan, tweeds, and
whipcord. Cashmere, camel cloth, alpa-
ca, and mohair are other,more luxurious woolen fabrics.

Wools are the most difficult fabric to use in fabric painting, as not all wools are washable, the drycleaning process may alter the paint, and not all paints and dyes take to wool. Experimentation with different fabrics and dyes is very necessary.

Silk is the last natural fiber to be discussed. Silk is a luxurious fabric, and it is in great use today as a speciality item:fine scarves, kimono-like draped jackets for evening wear or lounging,etc. It must be drycleaned in more cases than not, and therefore it is not well-suited to experimentation in fabric painting. Coldwater dyes which can be used only on natural fibers can be used safely on silk without testing. Silk, produced by the silkworm in spun filaments, has a natural lustre due to the triangular shape of the filament,which reflects light. You can work with or away from this lustre when you are painting. Some names for silk include brocade, broadcloth, chenille, chiffon, China silk, crepe, crepe-back satin,crepe de chine, flat crepe, faille,tissue faille,georgette, habutae,moire, mousseline,organza, ottoman, pongee, satin,shantung,raw silk,silk jacquard,surah, taffeta,and velvet.

VISCOSE RAYON

Viscose rayon is a fabric which is neither totally a natural fiber nor a synthetic. It is a man-made fiber but it is made from pure cellulose which is derived from vegetable fibers. Therefore, as far as fabric painting is concerned, it can be considered a natural fiber. Using dyes on viscose rayon will produce brilliant colors. Some of the fabrics made from viscose rayon are: challis, taffeta, twill, satin, shantung, and chiffon.

SYNTHETIC FIBERS

These,then, are the natural fibers, blending their colors and weaves in historical time. Synthetic fibers were first created in 1889, with a series of discoveries which led up to the production of rayon. Rayon, acetate, and triacetate are three cellulosic fibers which means that they use cellulose,the fibrous substance in plants, in their manufacture. The conversion of cellulose to fiber is manmade,and therefore these materials are said to be synthetic. Viscose rayon, as has already been mentioned,can be considered a natural fiber when fabric painting, as it has not been chemically altered as has synthetic rayon. Rayon is very receptive to a wide color range of dyes. However, it is not always washable. Rayon is processed to look interchangeably like linen, crepe, or silk. It is also combined with natural fibers. Chenille, damask,knits, ottoman, and tulle can all be made of rayon.

Acetate is another of the cellulosic fibers. It is processed in such a way that acetone will dissolve it. Perfume, nail polish remover, textine,turpentine, and textile paint thinner may eat through the fabric, so it is necessary that these materials be tested before painting. Acetate takes a wide range of colors, however, and if care is taken in the type of paint or dye, it can be a highly versatile fabric for fabric painting. It is used, and found, as a dressy fabric with a high lustre, and may appear to look like silk. Acetate can rarely be washed, and,if ironed, it should be pressed on the wrong side. Brocade,cire,crepe,damask,doupion, faille,grosgrain,knits,moire,mousseline, satin,sharksin, and taffeta can all be made of acetate.Triacetate is similar to acetate in its production; its properties,however, are quite different. It can withstand heat whereas acetate cannot. It needs little or no ironing, and can be hand or machine washed.Arnel is a familiar brand name of triacetate; surah, taffeta, and blends of knits and woven fabrics are types of triacetate.

Nylon was created in 1938,and announced to the U.S.by Dupont in the form of nylon stockings. Since then, nylon has been used successfully for quick-drying lingerie,crush resistant travel dresses, and numerous other light-weight items. Nylon is receptive to a wide range of colors, but should be separated when washing due to this receptivity to absorbing other colors. It can be either hand or machine washed. Cire,chiffon, knit and woven blends, matelasse, and velvet can be made from nylon.

Polyesters and acrylics are the next two main synthetic fibers. Polyesters are formed from chemical elements derived from petroleum, coal, air, and water. They must be washed in warm water and ironed on low heat. Polyester is often blended with other fibers to increase general strength and stability. Oil and grease stains cling to polyester, so oil-based inks should wear well in fabric painting. Batiste, chiffon, crepe, gabardine, georgette, knit and woven blends,mousseline, satin, terry cloth, velvet, and voile can all be made from polyester. Another popular use of polyester is in a polycotton blend. Common polycotton blends include broadcloth, corndurory, pinwale corndurory, denim, percale, and sailcloth. Acrylic is another synthetic fiber. It is washable,colorfast, and resistant to chemicals and oil. Acrilan, Creslan, and Orlon are well-known trade names of acrylics. Boucle, fake fur, less expensive wool-like fabrics, and woven and knit fabrics can all be made of acrylic. Modacrylic is a modified acrylic used in fake furs,carpets, and other deep-pile fabrics made up into coats and jackets. Modacrylic is also made into children's sleepwear,since its strength lies in its being flame resistance. (Acrylic,on the other hand, is moderately flammable.)

S-t-r-e-t-c-h fabrics and permanent press finishes are two processes used on both natural and synthetic fibers. The look and feel of the fabric(with the addition of stretchability) will be retained. Spandex and anidex are two synthetic elastic fibers which are used to produce the stretch. When they are spun around the core of elasticity, all the properties of these fibers are retained. T-shirts of 100% cotton are an example of this,as

they stretch a little,yet look and feel like cotton. Stretch fabrics should be washed and dried with cool temperatures. Permanent or durable press finishes keep the garment in one shape.This is advantageous for pleated and shaped garments.It is not so advantageous for fabric painting as dyes cannot be used due to the chemicals used to set the fabric.The dye cannot permeate the finish,and,at best,a rich deep dye will change a white fabric to a very light pastel. Acrylics generally work well on permanent press clothes since they do not need to form a chemical bond with the fabrics as does a dye.

These ten types of fibers can be seen to be quite different in appearance,uses,and washability. It is extremely important to learn to identify these ten fibers-cotton, linen,wool,silk,rayon,acetate,triacetate,nylon,polyester,and acrylic in both fabrics and clothing so that they can be properly used in fabric painting. Chapter VII discusses in detail certain types of garments and their most commonly used fabrics. Chapter IV will go into greater detail as to specific reactions of paints and dyes with these ten types of fibers.

Although it is important to experiment with different types of fabric and paint materials,for the beginner,it is best to begin with materials which are already known to work. There are certain types of fabric which are used extensively in fabric painting. They are: cotton muslin(in both the lightweight and heavier weight grades), cotton sheeting(a plain sheet can also be used), cotton broadcloth,white velveteen,cotton percale,cotton poplin, and cotton sateen;rayon chiffon,viscose rayon challis,viscose rayon satin;China silk,silk chiffon, and silk crepe de chine.If you cannot find these fabrics in stores around you,they can be ordered from the following distributors: Textile Resources/ P.O. Box 90245/Long Beach, CA. 90809; Cerulean Blue,

P.O. Box 21168/Seattle, WA. 98111;
and Testfabrics/P. O. Drawer"O"/
Middlesex, N.J. 08846. For silks,
try Utex Trading/710 9th St. Suite
5/ Niagra Falls, N.Y. 14301; Nikko
Gallery/P.O. Box 71/ Kamuela, HA.
96743; Rupert, Gibbon, and Spider/
718 College St./Healdsburg, CA.
95448; and Thai Silks!/252 State
St./Los Altos, CA. 94022

TEXTURAL PROPERTIES OF CLOTH

The different types of fibers,
as well as fabrics made from
them,have textural variety. This
variety in textural ground can be
well utilized in fabric painting.
Dry-brush work picks up the texture of the cloth and emphasizes
it,whereas a brush loaded with
paint would only clog the interesting texture. In the process of creating a design,learn to observe
the texture in cloth:muslin as fine
grained as sand,homespun like rough
grained wood, silk as lustrous as
oil on water. By recognizing the
personality of different types of
cloth,it is easier to combine the
right fabric with the right design.
(See Fig.55)
    The paint,the brush,the cloth.
These have been examined separately
in order to understand their function. Fabric painting combines the
paint,the brush,and the cloth,in
innumerable ways and for many different purposes. But how to sort
through all these possibilities?
Where to begin? It is best to begin
with some "simple and beginning
ideas".

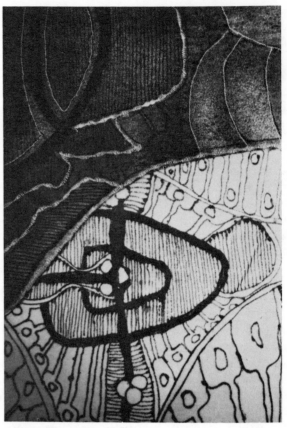

FIG. 55: TIE-DYE AND DIRECT APPLI-
CATION BY JOETTA UMLA. PROCION DYE
APPLIED WITH SQUEEZE BOTTLE. THE
SMOOTH COTTON ALLOWS FOR VARIATIONS
IN METHOD, FROM THE LINEAR DYE TO
THE SUBTLE SHADINGS OF THE TIE-DYE.

(RIGHT) FIG. 56: "NAME SKIRT"-
BY EVELYN BYATT. INKODYE ON
COTTON. THIS IS AN UNCLUTTERED,
ELEGANT DESIGN.

SIMPLE AND BEGINNING IDEAS

Simplicity is not necessarily restricted to "simple"designs. Paradoxically,the greater the simplicity,the greater the skill that is needed to separate the necessary elements from those which serve no purpose in the design.It is a good idea for beginning painters,designers,and workers with cloth to keep the design or the decoration of the fabric within a realm which is uncomplicated.(Fig. 56)New materials and techniques will offer a great enough variety of new and interesting ideas without the added complexity of a complex design. At the same time,I feel that it is necessary for a beginner to be stimulated by a wide range of design ideas so as to not be cramped or uninterested.(Fig.57A-D) Also, it is very important to be able to differentiate designs that would be monotonous in handpainting from those which benefit from it.(Fig.58-59)

(ABOVE) FIG. 57-A: PRE-COLUMBIAN BIRDS PAINTED IN ACRYLIC ON CANVAS BAG. (BELOW) FIG. 57-B: "MONSTER PILLOW"-BY VALERY GUIGNON. PROCION DYE ON COTTON,STUFFED.

FIG. 57-C: LINDA KANZINGER MODELING HANDPAINTED DRESS WITH LACE TOP, TEXTILE PAINTED FLOWERS, AND EMBROIDERY,ON MUSLIN

FIG. 57-D: HANDPAINTED VELVETEEN SCREEN-BY LENORE DAVIS.
PROCION DYE IS USED FOR THIS EXAMPLE OF EXQUISITE AND
LUXURIOUS FABRIC PAINTING.

FIG. 59: HANDPAINTED T-SHIRT BY LEIGH
LACAVA. DUE TO THE DIFFERENT COLORED
BIRDS IN THIS DESIGN, IT IS A GOOD
EXAMPLE OF A SIMPLE DESIGN FOR
BEGINNING PAINTING.

FIG. 58: "WOMAN SHAKING QUILT"-LENORE DAVIS. DYE-
PAINTED COTTON VELVETEEN, 20" TALL. THIS DESIGN
COULD BE MONOTONOUS TO HANDPAINT EXCEPT IN A
SMALL PIECE SUCH AS THIS.

THE LINE

Lines are a simple and effective
way to divide space. Paul Klee
speaks of taking a walk with a line,
to see where it will take you. Lines
can be used as simple designs as
stripes, as bands, as borders. Stripes
can be used as spacing, for colour,
with various painting techniques, and
to show textured effects.(see Fig. 60

Fig.61, Fig.62) Bands and borders
are good in beginning painting as
there is not as much concern with
compositional problems as there can
be in painting, due to the restriction
of the lines. As well, borders can be
placed in many different ways on
clothing.(Fig.63,Fig.64,Fig.66).

FIG. 60:" #67"- BY ALAN GRINBERG.
AIRBRUSHED FABRIC SHOWING LINES
DOWN THE FABRIC. SILKSCREEN PIGMENT.

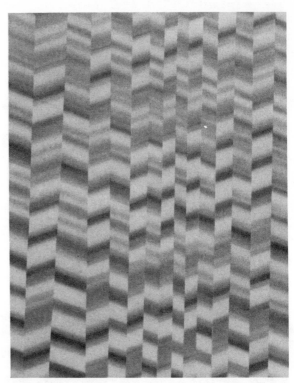

FIG. 61: " #77"- ALAN GRINBERG.AIRBRUSH,
STENCILS,AQUATOL SILKSCREEN PIGMENT.

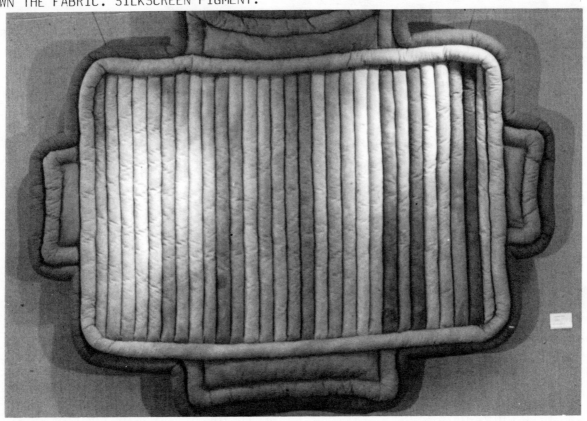

FIG. 62: "COLOR STUDY"-BY DOROTHY CALDWELL OF CONQUEROR
WORM CRAFTS. COTTON WITH DYES.

Many different types of designs can be placed within a band or border. Borders using painting techniques, and borders using motifs are two such ideas. Collage borders are nice as they utilize a variety of materials within one garment, particularly fabrics that cannot be painted, or look strange when painted. Borders are good for collage as the thickness and/or fragileness of the collaged area can be placed in an area of the garment which does not receive heavy wear(for example, the bottom edge of a knee-length skirt.) The edges of sleeves and the bottom of a shirt which is not tucked in are other good areas of placement for collage.

Other ideas of painting techniques for bands and borders include adhering natural materials, using lettering as design, and mixed media. Ideas for borders using motifs include African motifs, 17th century American quilt designs, pottery, embroidery, architecture, needlework, and mosaic work. (Fig. 64, Fig. 65.)

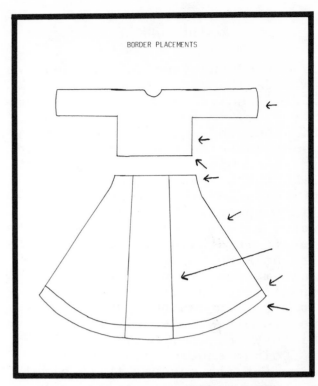

FIG. 63: DIAGRAM OF BORDER PLACEMENT ON CLOTHING

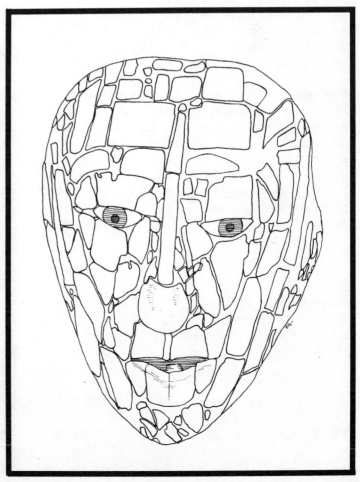

(ABOVE)FIG.64:LAURA DALE MODELING MOSAIC-BORDERED POLYESTER PANTS.(RIGHT) FIG. 65:DRAWING BY PHYLLIS THOMPSON OF JADE MOSAIC MASK AS USED IN PANTS. AFTER MEXICAN ART-JUSTINO FERNANDEZ 1965

THE SQUARE

Beyond the line is the square. As a design element, the square offers endless and untold possibilities. As four lines joined together, the square can contain about anything you wish to put in it.(See. Fig.67   ) The square, like the border, reduces compositional problems as there is a defined space within which you may work. As a geometrical shape, the square foretells of the circle, the triangle, and shapes which blend into masses of colour, with more specific composition. The square is a common design shape used by modern artists as well as in art history.(Fig.68 ,Fig.69)

Colour squares are a basic design for the square. It is simply a square or squares filled with colour. They can be either complementary or analagous colours. Colour squares are good ways to practice mixing colours, and seeing the variations in different brands of the same colour. You can use a ruler and coloured pencils of the same colour as the paint, to mark off the lines before painting. Masking tape or stencils could also be used. Colour squares allow you to see all the gradations, shadings, and the relationships of different colours to one another.(Fig.70)

Colour squares are also good for testing materials. By having a sample of each colour with different

(ABOVE RIGHT) FIG.66: CAROL PETRELLI MODELS HALTER DRESS PAINTED WITH COLOR BORDERS. VERSATEX PAINT ON COTTON.

(RIGHT) FIG.68: SQUARED WORK BY THEODORA ZEHNER. COTTON VELVETEEN IS SPRAY-DYED WITH PROCION DYE. STITCHED INTO SPRAY-DYED RICE PAPER. ENTIRE WORK STITCHED ONTO SPRAY-DYED UNTREATED CANVAS. $4\frac{1}{2} \times 4\frac{1}{2}'$

FIG. 67: "GOOD EARTH QUILT"- BY LINDA FISHER. ACRYLIC TEXTILE PAINT ON COTTON.
EACH SQUARE WAS FIRST DRAWN WITH MACHINE STITCHING, THEN PAINTED TO GIVE IT THE
FEELING OF A SOFT, WATERCOLOR PAINTING.(FROM ARTISTS' LETTER) 6 BY 7 FEET.

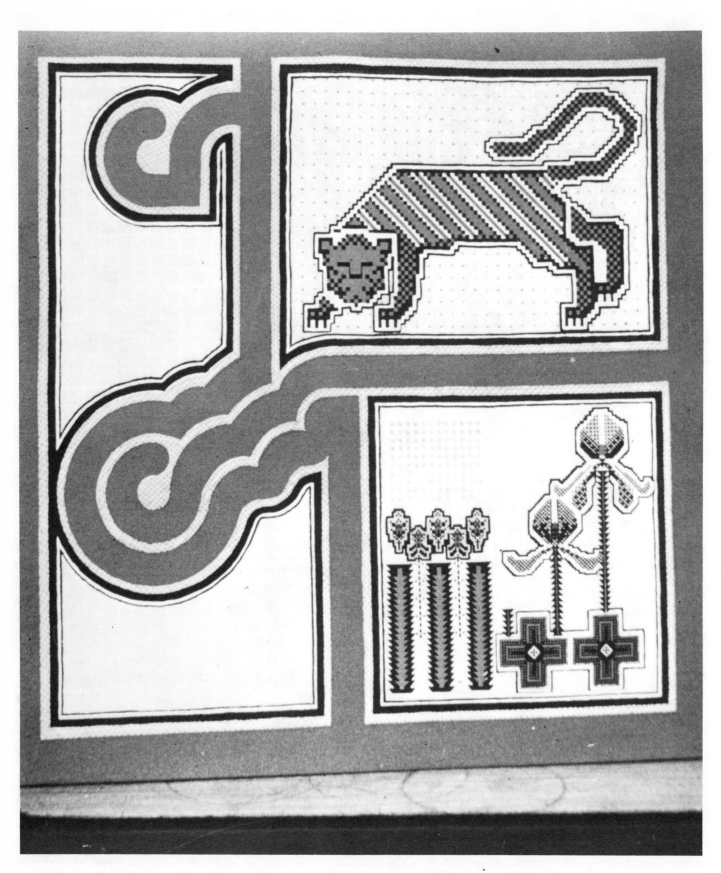

FIG. 69: "CHINA TIGER"-BY FRANCES BUTLER. AIRBRUSHED SILKSCREEN.

FIG. 70: PIECED SILK-BY PHYLLIS MUFSON.
PROCION DYES SHOW COLOR GRADATIONS.

(RIGHT) FIG. 71: CLOSE-UP SQUARE OF A
WATERCOLOR WASH. ACRYLIC ON COTTON.

paint materials,it is easy to see
the durability and washability of
the different materials. By having
this information in one square,it
is easy to choose the type paint or
dye for a certain project.

Besides colour, squares can contain brushstroke techniques,motifs,
and simple basic shapes.(Fig. 71)
Squares containing the same design,
but drawn with different materials
can be compared for clarity and the
general effect of the design. Squares
in general are simple designs in
which to practice other design ideas
before transferring them to a larger working space. Patchwork squares
are another simple yet fascinating
design idea.(Fig. 72) Patchwork
patterns originate in squares. Intricate samplers in needlepoint,em-
broidery,and lace are formed in
squares. Macrame hangings formed in
squares bring out the shape of the
individual knots. Almost any design
can be "put into"a square.

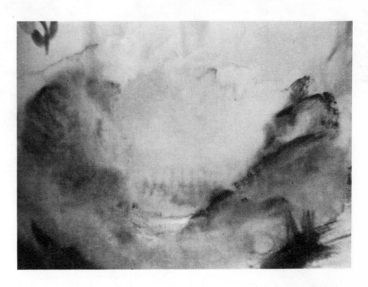

THE CIRCLE AND THE TRIANGLE

The circle and the triangle offer many interesting ideas which are
not difficult for the beginning
painter.(Fig.73-75) Like the square,
the circle is a basic form used
throughout time. There is an entire
philosophy behind these three forms.
The circle has no beginning and no
end. The circle is very important to
the Hopi Indian,as it allows a multiple perspective upon something. (Their
sandpaintings reveal this). It is
the square which is the foundation
for many of our modern cities,per-
haps for our modern problem of iso-
lation. Alternative ways of building
(the tipi,yurt,igloo,and other circular spaces)change as well the way

we relate to each other. The triangle
has also come to be seen as more
than just three connecting lines.
Many books on pyramids explore the
power inherent in this shape. The
connotations of these three shapes
(the square,circle,and triangle)
are many and can be explored and in-
corporated into fabric painting. It
is this connotative meaning which is
one of the strengths of fabric paint-

61

FIG. 72: "PAINT A QUICK QUILT"-BY FAITH
MIDDENDORP. QUILTED COTTON PILLOW PAINTED
WITH ACRYLIC PAINT. CIRCULAR SUN FACE.

ing;it is more than just a decoration of lines,squares,circles,
and triangles.

Getting beyond these defined
shapes,there are more random divisions of space which evolve in
simple and beginning ideas. After you feel comfortable with
defined shapes and spaces,it is
possible to move on-to the scattered motif,lines across the fabric,general layout compositions
from works of art, and freehand
painting.

THE SCATTERED MOTIF

The scattered motif is an excellent design idea with versatility when used with fabric painting. This is due to the great variety within unity possible with
painting. For example, a repeat
motif of a flower,when fabric
painted, can be many different colours,shapes,and sizes,yet all are
considered a flower.

FIG. 73: DETAIL FROM WRAP SKIRT-BY SUZANNE
LARSEN. SUN FACE IN INKO DYE, ACRYLIC PAINT,
OFF-WHITE COTTON. A COMMON CIRCLE MOTIF.

FIG. 74: CHAMOIS JACKET AND COTTON
CULOTTES-BY K. LEE MANUEL. VERSATEX
PAINT. BOTH TRIANGULAR AND CIRCULAR
MOTIFS ARE REPRESENTED.

FIG. 75: WALL HANGING-BY K. LEE
MANUEL.   INKO SILKSCREEN RESIST
IS HANDPAINTED ONTO FABRIC.

Any motif or image which is of one kind or type, that also has great variety <u>within</u> the type, can be used in this way. Shells, birds, plants, trees, microscopic animals, bicycles, and boxes are some possible ideas.

LINES ACROSS THE FABRIC

Lines across the fabric is simply carrying a line from one side of the fabric to another,in a creative and interesting way to form a design. Copying composition layouts from works of art is a good way for beginners to learn the basic rules of composition. By using works of art, good combinations of form, shape, and color, can be used. Yet there is no danger of copying, as only the general layout is used as a guideline. Freehand painting lets go of any preconceived idea of a design. One simply begins painting; lines form, colors appear. Freehand painting can be a delightful loosening of the mind, letting the hand supplant the brain.

As has been seen, beyond the square,the circle, and the triangle are less well-defined forms,as well as masses of shape and color which lend themselves well to the movement of cloth. These are painted with more spontenaity of the brush and less mental preparation, and this approaches the mood of fabric painting,the interaction and movement of cloth and brush. But how to approach fabric painting itself? This we shall examine next.

"The creative artist does not need a direct external influence. The work he has created is for him an internal experience-like a natural phenomemon that has made him internally richer, but externally is not necessary for him. If he does not have it, he will still realize his dream in one way or another, as long as the dream remains alive within him."   So spoke Kandinsky. People approach painting in different ways. As well as technique ,it is a good idea to have some awareness of how you approach painting. Are you calm, excited, sure as to what you will do,uncertain, etc?Being aware of a mood is helpful for deciding what type of painting to approach. Two problems which I have encountered are balancing spontenaity and planning. I need to be sure that I am in the mood for using certain colors, working with certain types of designs. I have struggled with forcing myself to paint, which is not a good idea, as painting is more than good technique, it is expressing feelings and thoughts which form from a certain personal mood. A mood can be harnessed and used, rather than being disciplined into hiding. Another problem which concerns me is dealing with the number of distractions which occur to me while doing a certain painting. One beginning idea inspires many others, and it is difficult to keep a unity about the work.In this case, some planning and discipline is helpful.One practical idea is to do sketches previous to painting. Further ideas can be sketched or jotted down for later paintings.

Being conscious of what you are thinking and feeling while painting allows you to go back to a certain mood if you are in the middle of a large painting. Certain kinds of painting lean more towards definiteness, while others depend upon a fragile equilibrium of mood. Painting,like other art forms, can be approached cognitively or intuitively. As one learns the basics of design and composition, cognitive painting becomes easier; for the beginner, however, an intuitive approach utilizes things already familiar. As well as painting what you feel, you can become aware of certain colors and shapes which are more definite statements of what you are trying to express. This perception is extremely valuable in painting, and its growth will allow you a more direct expression of your feelings. This evolution of perception accounts for a paintings' change and growth. Fabric painting, unlike fabric printing, is re-evaluated over time:the painting can be changed, developed. It grows in its own time, rather than being "preplanned and pasted" on the material.

Painting from music, and from your dreams, are two good ideas for beginners. This type of painting forms as the imagery and symbolism of the mind is yielded up for examination. The most important thing in an expressive art such as fabric painting is that the artist can constantly be aware of the art as expression of her being. One is painting the inner world, and,as is the inner world, so is the interpretation and expression of the outer reality.

THEME AND VARIATION

Another basic approach for a beginning painter is to paint one idea with variations."Theme and variation"is a method much used by musicians, and can be a model for fabric painting. For example, one motif could be the theme,with variations in size, shape,color, and placement. This need not be used only on one particular garment;one idea can be explored in one painting,and further varied and expressed in other garments. Sometimes this will form a set of clothes, much like mix-and-match clothing. I find the idea of theme and variation very valuable in fabric painting, as it is possible to keep growing with an idea through various pieces of clothing. For example, in working with a pottery motif, I want to explore it not only on pants and top, but on a skirt, fancy shirt, shorts,etc. As well, I want to experiment with it in various places on the garment to see which gives the best overall effect.

A question which is very important for the beginning fabric painter is"fabric painting for whom? and what?"Unless you understand this, fabric painting could be an unfocused experience. In Chapter I,we spoke of painting as an art, and as a craft. It is helpful when approaching fabric painting to decide which type you are going to do. As well, a fabric painting could be catagorized into fabric painting for general sewing, or for a clothes designer/artisan. Each of these categories emphasizes certain features of fabric painting, and so will be described.

SELLING AS CRAFT

If you wish to paint T-shirts and sell them to friends or at a craft fair, the type of design ideas useful for this would be quite different from a one-of-a-kind garment sold at an exclusive store. Yet both of these could be construed as selling in bulk-in that you are the supplier of painted clothing. To try and paint a design which is intricate and time-consuming, to sell at a craft fair(with the usual price range of medium to low),is to not sell, either because the price is too high, or you have too few garments for a selection! It is helpful,then, to sort out the type of painting done for crafts and the crafts market, from that which will demand a higher price, and is usually construed as the art(or professional crafts) market.

Painting done for simple craft selling should be able to be executed in a few hours. For some people, this might be brightly striped clothing in watercolor with wide brushes, for others it might be abstract shapes,for others it might be rather intricate drawings. Some types of designs are much easier for some people than for others, and this should be noticed, rather than the type design.(For example, neatly formed patchwork squares takes me much longer than a large intricate drawing) Painting for crafts should be either compositionally simple, or a repetition of one basic type of composition. Again, this does not mean compositionally simplistic design, but rather that the design is independent from the garment form,or less involved with the design of the garment form, and therefore a more simple composition. The repetition of one basic type of composition means that it is easier not to jump around from one type of composition to another. If you are working with intricate designs around the collar and frontispiece, vary the type design from garment to garment, remain with the basic placement. This is a good learning device as well, for only by painting on different types of garments (shirts, skirts, pants, etc) can the most effective design and garment form be discovered. Other good ideas for crafts painting are the theme and variation, which has been mentioned before, and making fabric yardage.

Fabric yardage entails painting a large pice of fabric which can be cut up into different pattern pieces. It is important that the design idea be such that the material can be identifiable as one piece when it is cut up, without it being as repetitive as a printed piece of material. To do this, similar type designs or certain groups of colors can be used over a large piece of fabric. Think of the characteristics of other types of fabric;muslin and cotton, creamy and white like sand, rougher homespun like sand and sawdust, cloth like the bark of trees. Paint is liquid color, and beautiful fabrics can be made, with bright colors, liquid flowers, flowing greens. When considering painting fabrics, think of the relationship of cloth and air; the way air moves across a dress could be painted as the way air moves across a field of wheat. Fabric yardage allows one to concentrate only on design ideas without con-

sidering how the design adapts to the garment form. Some themes for fabric yardage could be stained glass window fabric, fabric for earthdresses, circle fabric, wooden fabric.

Special orders are another aspect of crafts selling. If you have difficulty thinking of good ideas for fabric painting, but have good painting technique, special orders can be a good learning experience, as you are executing other peoples' design ideas. However, if you have difficulty in visualizing anothers idea, special orders may become a burden and a disappointment both to you and to your customer. One possibility is to have a notebook with samples of designs, which you would be willing to make in a larger or smaller size, or in a different area, on someone's clothing. Many people have favorite clothing which they would like to have painted, rather than buying a whole new garment.As well, it is not then necessary that the fabric painter also be a good sewer.

SELLING AS ART

Very professionally done fabric painting is in great contrast to fabric painting for simple crafts. Time, cost, prices, and customer ideas are irrelevant,as the painting is done for the paintings'(and your) sake! Usually this type of fabric painting uses a majority of new and original ideas or combinations of ideas. It means getting the design idea and the design of the garment form in as much congruency as possible.(This will be discussed in much detail in Chapter VII)This type of painting is in total contrast to the squared-off design placed in the middle of a T-shirt.

Fabric painting is also oriented towards those who sew;in fact, sewing is almost as important in fabric painting as is painting,due to the importance of the garment form in the total effect of the painting. Sewing can be divided into general sewing, those who can sew basic and contemporary type clothing;and the designer/artisan of clothing,who does pattern drafting,creating original patterns, and who is capable of sewing intricate and difficult forms. The greater the skill in sewing, the greater the flexibility in fabric painting. People who are limited to T-shirts and manufactured clothing miss the excitement not only of creating original designs in sewing,but in the combination of painting and clothing.(One solution to this is if you can't sew, work together with someone who can!) Tucks, ruffles, big collars, and pockets all lend themselves to interesting painting ideas due to their shape on the garment.To do this effectively, some knowledge of basic design as it relates to clothing and sewing is helpful.

BASIC DESIGN FOR FABRIC PAINTING

Basic design for fabric painting is different from regular basic design in art. There are a number of reasons for this. First of all, the plane in fabric painting is different from that of both drawing and painting in that it is not always flat due to the movement of fabric. In other words, seeing a design on a piece of cloth is a multidimensional experience due to the cloths' flexibility in space. Seeing a design on paper or canvas is usually a one-dimensional experience as it is only in one plane at a time. Also, when fabric painting for clothing, a person is working, simultaneously,on a two and a three dimensional plane. This is due to the fact that, although when painted, the painting is flat, it becomes three dimensional when formed into clothing. This can be a challenging aspect of fabric painting, as it is not always easy to tell what a two-dimensional design will look like in three dimensions. Gathers or pleats also change the two-dimensional flat image in a variety of ways. Last,

the design elements will be viewed at different angles and distances, due to the form of the body and how close or far the viewer is to the body and the clothing. All of these facets must be considered when learning about regular basic design, and changed or modified for basic fabric painting design. It will first be helpful to understand some beginning ideas in basic design.

When we are first learning to see, we don't see specific objects such as a table, or a house. We learn to attach labels, and see things, rather than images. This learning can be replaced with a perceptual sensitivity to elements such as color, shape, texture. The basis for much artistic activity lies in the seeing of images. As well, it is important that ones' painting not be pushed artifically in this direction ,but allowed to grow naturally without being overworked. These are two ways in which basic design is used in painting;to clarify our perception,to balance our painting. Line,shape,space,texture,and color are five basics of design.(Fig.76)

Line can be used as a division of space. Line can be used in and of itself for abstract and representational design. Line can also be used as a space-divider. This is particularly helpful to achieve a better composition on a large piece of fabric. Sometimes it is easier to handle a large area of space by dividing it into smaller areas of space. Line is thin,even at its thickest. Line is thin and running, easily excitable,going places, going through and around and back. Line travels. Travel with a line-see where it takes you!

Shape is not so energetic as line. Shape is slower,bigger. Shape is still movement but it is a more placid movement. Line runs around and where it connects, it becomes shape. Shape is symmetrical or asymmetrical. Line in relation to space is symmetrical or asymmetrical, but of itself it has no symmetry. Shape in relation to space creates more shape.

Space is. It is especially important in fabric painting to have enough space-to spread out and see all the material and all the line and shape at one time. Space connects all the interplay of line and shape; it delineates where there is harmony and balance in this interplay. Space is the invisible material without which there can be no design.

Texture is both one and two-dimensional. Texture can be printed and stamped onto fabric. Networks of line ressembling lace, the veins of leaves, molecular structures, are all textural to the eye though they do not rise above one dimension. Texture is:a raised pattern woven in a fabric and sand mixed into the paint and shells glued onto the fabric. When the shells are painted over with blue paint,we may see shells under the ocean or we may see blue shells. When they are only glued on the fabric, their shape,texture, and color become apparent.

Color as we know it is totally dependent upon the light. And with the light there are far more colors than we have names for.

These are the basic elements in design. They mix and intermingle upon the surface upon which they are placed. One sees the different moods of line- how line has more energy than shape. Shape moves more slowly through this world of space. Line and shape move horizontally over the fabric, texture stretches upward, reaches downward, sometimes simultaneously. Color,though on the fabric ,exists in another dimension, breathes a more rarified air. Color is white light, the focus of the spectrum, the separation into itself(color), the merging of color into light.

Line, shape,texture, and color can all be used as ways to divide space. Shapes which are interesting in themselves as well as interesting in relation to clothing are good divisions of space. Lines can go from one side of the fabric to the other, or loop continuously around each other.(Fig. 77-80)

These are the units of design, and these five elements will be used in various configurations both two and three-dimensionally. It is easiest if they are examined first

FIG. 76: DRAWING BY JUDY BUSK ILLUSTRATING
LINE, SHAPE, SPACE, AND TEXTURE.

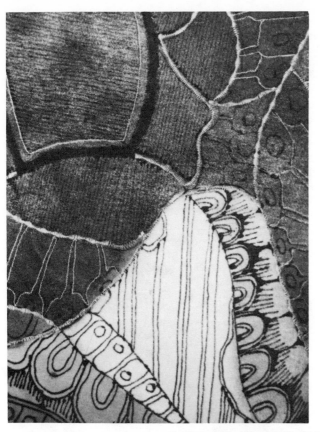

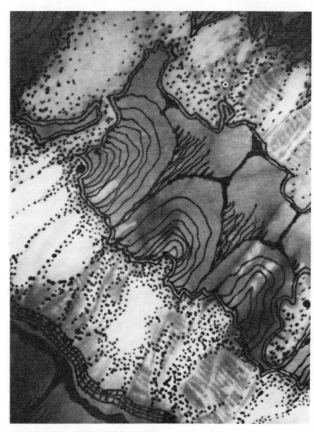

FIGS. 77-80: TIE-DYE AND DIRECT APPLICATION
BY JOETTA UMLA. THIS IS A WONDERFUL EXAMPLE
OF THE CREATIVE USE OF THE LINE. LOOK HOW
JOETTA'S LINE LOOPS AROUND, DOTS, SQUIGGLES,
AND SHADES IN THESE FOUR EXAMPLES.

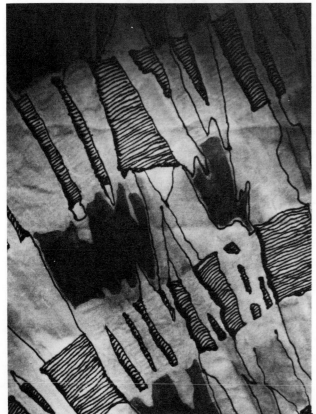

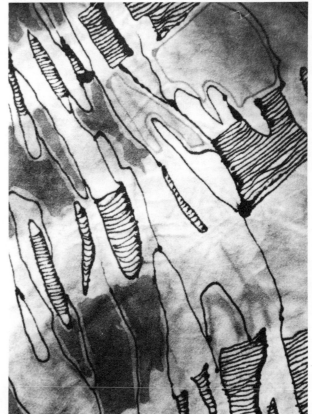

in a two-dimensional way.

One easy way to learn how to fabric paint is by using already printed fabrics as inspiration. Take samples of some of your favorite fabrics and try handpainting their designs. Then evaluate your work. For example: are the designs too small to be painted neatly? Do they need to be drawn first? Is it difficult to keep the edges from bleeding? Magic markers, pen and ink, or colored drawing pencils could be used to draw the designs. If the paint bleeds, make it thicker by adding a medium. This technical knowledge allows you to paint a design which "works" on fabric and which has further interest by being handpainted. Some beginning fabric painters' clothes look like they belong in a circus; the colors are garish, the designs, wild. Using already-made fabric as a guideline, there is less guesswork involved in how the two-dimensional fabric will look when made into clothing. Plus, if desired, you can paint something which looks conventional!

The inspiration from printed fabrics can be <u>direct</u>, in which case the painting copies the fabric. It is also possible to use the printed fabric as a basic guide, and include variations. The <u>repeat motif</u> lends itself well to this, as the gridwork of the repeat motif can be used, but the individual motif can vary. (Fig. 81) Another use of printed material is to actually paint <u>on</u> the printed material. The two can complement each other.(Fig. 82)<u>Modular unit painting</u> refers to a unit of space which is repeated over the fabric, but which has a larger design than the repeat motif. Fabrics with scenes from rural America, racing horses, or other designs with abstract shapes of various sizes and colors, are examples of what I would call modular unit design. The smaller the modular unit, the greater the freedom in cutting shaped pieces. As the modular unit becomes larger, it becomes more dependent upon its placement in relation to the garment form. For example a large splashy design must harmonize with the lines of the garment in order to be effective. (Fig. 83)

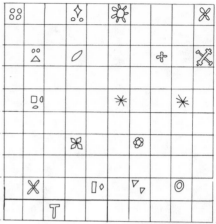

FIG. 81: DRAWING OF THE PRINCIPLE OF GRIDWORK. (BELOW) FIG. 82: KAREN LEEDS MODELING PRINT TOP WITH PAINTED AREAS. FIG. 83: KAREN LEEDS MODELING SKIRT WITH MODULAR UNIT PAINTING.

Beyond the modular unit is the asymmetrical design. This type of design begins to lean in the direction of composition, as it is less dependent upon one variable for its success. Repeat motifs, modular unit painting, and direct copying from printed materials assume some constancy in the design. An asymmetrical design does not balance and harmonize a design in the way a symmetrical one does. When there are many variables in the creation of a design, there is greater dependence upon the rules of composition. Composition as it applies to fabric painting and especially with consideration of clothing is an important aspect of basic design.   There are many things to be considered when designing a garment, as it becomes three-dimensional on the body, but is a two-dimensional piece of cloth while painting. The more traditional ways of fabric decoration, with their dependency on the repeat motif, de-emphasize some of the problems encountered when painting asymmetrical non-repeat designs. However, there are ways of designing such a garment so that it remains primarily a two-dimensional surface.

One of the easiest ways to diminish compositional complexities in fabric painting is by keeping the garment form as two-dimensional as possible; in other words, simple, basic forms. Garments which are well-fitted to the body, made with darts and pleats and shaping, may change the design in unexpected ways. Garments which resemble squares, such as the kimona and the huiptl, are good for compositional painting. Garments which hang two-dimensionally, such as an A-line skirt, an A-line dress, a simple square shirt, a T-shirt, and a straight skirt, are basic conventional garment forms which work well. A gathered skirt, made from a square of material, can be good if the design is not so detailed that it would be lost in the gathers . However, a gathered skirt is a good garment

form to experiment with for more complex composition as the gathers sometimes can, in an unexpected way, change the composition for the better. Wrapped clothing is also good in that it is formed from long rectangles of cloth, and how it is wrapped in part determines the design.

Another approach regarding 2/3 dimensionality is for the fabric painter to use flexible compositional approaches. If composition is based on all parts of the design working together in a fixed way, one mistake is disastrous as it alters the total work. Flexible composition allows for the design to be workable with a greater number of changes, intentional or not. Fabric painting is especially suited to flexible composition, due to the flexibility of fabric and the wide variety in garment forms.

Fabric can be manipulated and its shape be changed by cutting, tearing, and pulling its fibers. Cutting is by far the most common way to shape and form fabric, either by cutting it apart from a length of fabric, or by sewing small pieces together to form a length of fabric. As regards to fabric painting, a length of material can be painted, then cut, either into garment shapes, or into other shapes. These shapes can then be resewn together to form the garment or a length of fabric. If at any point the composition is undesirable, it can be changed by more cutting and more sewing. Fabric can also be cut and glued or sewn over other parts of the fabric if one wishes to change a design. The opposite progression of cutting the fabric, then painting and sewing it, can also be used. In this way, either the garment pattern pieces are cut and painted, or other random shapes are cut and painted. This is much different from painting a large square piece of material, as the design cannot help but be affected by the shape of the material.Sewing is as important a compositional tool as is cutting, and it is as flexible. There is an excitement about taking a group of individually painted pieces, sewing them together, and seeing their effect.

Another flexible compositional approach is taking the garment form and placing other pieces of material on the garment, thus forming a design. This is similar to collage or applique, except that the material is not glued or sewn onto the material. This is a very flexible approach to composition, as you can change the position of the pieces as often as is necessary to create a satisfactory design.

Fabric does not have to be the only material used. Paper is a common and effective design tool. Torn-paper designs have an extra spontenaity about them, as the paper is randomly torn and its edges show the result of the tearing. Cut-paper symmetry is best exemplified by the popular cut-paper snowflake. Other shapes and sizes of paper can be used with folded cut-paper designs. For example, take a rectangular piece of paper, fold it four times, then cut designs(slashes, triangles, curved shapes) along the edges and in the folds with scissors. When you unfold the paper, you can trace the designs onto fabric-or paint through them, using the paper as a stencil.As was described above, paper can be used as fabric was, with paper shapes being laid onto the fabric for the design. Another way paper can be used is as a stencil or template. Randomly cut paper designs are placed on a large piece of material, and moved around until harmony and balance are seen,and the design is complete. They are then outlined with colored pencil, removed, and the design is completed by painting or drawing. These cut-paper designs can also be used like a stencil, in which the area surrounding the template is painted before removing the template. (This is a type of reverse stencil;

regular stenciling will be discussed in Chapter VI)

Regardless of how you approach basic fabric painting design, it is important to understand and remember the principle of organic growth in basic design. Organic, as opposed to synthetic growth, deals with timing. In organic growth there is a regard for the natural evolution of a design. Sometimes you may have the feeling that a design must be completely worked out, under control, before or during painting, in order to be successful. This may be rushing the creative process forming in your mind-which is creating the design. Allow yourself to leave a painting when it does not feel good to be working on it. Psychologically, you may need time to reorganize,rethink out certain aspects.Don't begin with too rigid of an idea- rather give it room for growth.

By understanding what is the core of the design, it is possible to let that core expand and grow. The core of a design may be a certain horizontal-vertical placement, it may be a certain configuration of lines. The core may be expanded through repetition; variations such as enlargement, reduction, opposition, reversal, are also possible.(Fig.84) Most of all, organic growth in basic design is a philosophy, letting elements reveal themselves rather than being forced into awareness. And along this same line, it is important that one's inner vision of a painting or design never be subjugated to hard and fast rules of basic design. Basic design is a tool, meant to help the inner vision be revealed. It must always be subordinate to the creative design idea, in order that the design idea evolve naturally rather than being artificially manipulated.

An artist's sketchbook is a good place to jot down design ideas-fragments which are unformed and which can be synthesized over time into workable designs. A sketchbook is also a wonderful place to try out various design ideas, without taking the time to make up the entire garment or object in fabric. I use a

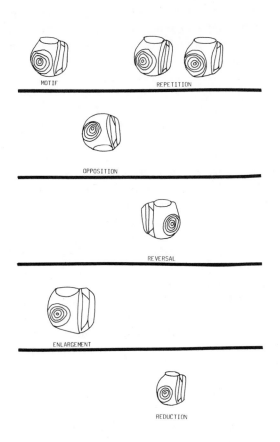

MOTIF   REPETITION

OPPOSITION

REVERSAL

ENLARGEMENT

REDUCTION

FIG. 84: VARIATIONS OF A DESIGN THEME

hardcover empty book and good quality colored pencils which record
my designs neatly and preserve them
for future use. If a particular col-
or scheme interests me, I'll sketch
it out in various forms without
needing to develop it further as a
complete design. Later, I'll look
back and reflect on which combination is most effective. By working over a design in a sketchbook,
the fabric painter can refine her/
his design and therein paint more
satisfying projects!

THE PAINTING ENVIRONMENT

The last consideration for a
fabric painter beginning to paint
is the painting environment. The
painting environment is where you
paint,what you paint with! It is
the physical layout of your painting area as well as the containers
for paint and where to lay your

material. I cannot overemphasize
the importance of a well-planned
painting environment due to its direct effect upon the type and quality of fabric painting done. For
example, if you are painting on a
table that is too high or too low,
your hand will soon tire and that
will effect your painting. Certain
painting techniques will not even
work without the proper amount of
space or a certain kind of table.

There are a number of features
in the painting environment: the
painting surface, space requirements,
the storage of paint, and the per-
manence of a working space. There
are a number of general rules for
the painting environment. The painting surface should be flat and sturdy. It can be fixed or movable. Ta-
bles of various sizes, drawing boards,
large pieces of cardboard boxes(such
as those found behind grocery or department stores)work well. I have
found that the key to good painting
is having a variety of kinds of surfaces. Cardboard which can be leaned
against a wall and tilted at various angles works well for certain
effects, such as long vertical brushstrokes, dribbling paint, and watercolor; it can become tiresome for
detailed drawing. Simple arrangements
seem to work better than adjustable
artist or architect tables- simply
because painting on fabric is rather
messy, and flexibility is needed more
than only one specific surface. The
kitchen table will work well for many
beginning projects. A large work
table is better when working with
big pieces of material. Marking pens,
embroidery paints, crayons, and acrylic paints need less working room
than dyes, mordants, or oil-based
textile paints, since with the latter,
there is a greater need for more
bottles to mix in, separate containers for chemicals, and in the case of
textile paint, a lot of ventilation.

The painting surface should always
be covered(preferably with butcher
paper or newspaper) so that the
paint will not soak through to the
table. In fabric printing, many books

suggest padding the surface with cloth before putting on the fabric, but I find that this is a hindrance in fabric painting and, expecially for drawing, a firm surface is needed to get precise renderings. Newspaper is readily available and works well with all paints except acrylics, which must be watched so that the paint does not dry and stick, along with the newspaper, to the fabric!

Space requirements in fabric painting vary with the type of paint used, the amount of fabric used, and the type of painting technique used. Many things can be made with just small sturdy supports- things such as intricate or small drawings and paintings, with acrylics, marking pens, or fabric crayons,for example. As well, working on small or average sizes of cloth allows one a smaller working space.(Fig. 85)

There are other types of painting, such as spatter painting, painting with large housepaint brushes, or painting on hanging lengths of fabric, which need large amounts of room. Painting such as this needs, first of all, a large painting surface, plus room to move around that surface, plus an area to spread out the paint and brushes, as well as areas to lay large amounts of fabric to dry. A garage or basement with a cement floor is good for this, in that nothing can be damaged by paint. In general, there is enough room in the average house to do most fabric painting, but keep in mind what types of painting need what type of room. (Fig.86)

If you do not specifically plan for it, your paint and equipment can take up more than half of the nice large table you procured from your neighbor for fabric painting! It is necessary to have your paints close by-for convenience, to avoid having to move around a lot while painting, and to avoid dripping paint or dye on the fabric. As well it is nice to have a variety of brushes at hand. A portable surface, such as a plastic tray, is good for materials and paints,as it can be close to the working area without danger of spilling, and it

FIG. 85: DRAWING OF PAINTING ENVIRONMENT IN A SMALL APARTMENT. BY KAREN HAMILTON.

FIG. 86: DRAWING OF THE PAINTING ENVIRONMENT WITH A LARGE AMOUNT OF
SPACE. GARAGE AREA WITH LARGE TABLE AND MOVEABLE TRAY. BY KAREN HAMILTON.

can be easily moved from one area
to another. A moveable cart is
nice when working on larger pieces
of fabric, fabric which is hanging up to be painted, fabric on
an easel, and fabric on any vertical or semi-vertical surface. A
moveable cart allows you to move
around the area with both hands
free for painting.

Areas for drying are important.
Casually draping a nondry garment
across a chair or on your bed gives
you painted clothing and painted
furniture, something you may not
have planned for! You may need:
large flat areas(basement floors
are good) for still-wet dyed fabrics,clotheslines and drying racks
for painted clothes and semi-dry
dyed fabrics, and grass or cement
outdoors for special sun effects
with Inkodye. Be sure to use newspaper beneath the fabric to avoid
painting the living room floor or
the cement patio.

Chairs and stools of the correct and comfortable height are important. Please, do not use a chair
of incorrect height, as it will

cramp your hand, your arm muscles,
and surely your painting.

Ventilation and light are the
last two physical features of the
painting area. Ventilation is especially important when working
with textile and oil paints, as turpentine or a turpentine derivative
is used with the paint. I find it
very difficult to paint at all in
an area without windows or fresh
air, probably due to the connection
between windows and natural light.
Natural light, without being bright
or glaring, is best for painting.
A bright artificial light close to
the painting area will also work.
If you are painting throughout a
whole day, do not paint during and
before sunset as the light changes
so much in that time that you cannot see stable colors.

Most of the above requirements
are easy enough to plan without a
lot of effort. However, the caring
and mixing of paint can be more
challenging, especially the cold-
water dyes. Marking pens, fabric
crayons, and embroidery paints need
no containers and so there is no

FIG. 87 : DRAWING OF SUPPLIES USED IN PAINTING
ENVIRONMENT AND FOR PAINT STORAGE. SPRAY BOTTLE,
TIN FOIL CONTAINER, JARS AND LIDS, BRUSHES. BY
KAREN HAMILTON.

problem there. Textile paint,as well, comes mainly in a jar, so there is no problem with paint storage. Oils come in tubes,and should be mixed up separately each time as they are mixed with turpentine or textine for fabric painting, and those materials are too volatile to be left safely sitting around.

Acrylics also come in a tube, and they are the most difficult material to store. They can be stored after mixing in small glass jars. If you mix the colors on a palette, water can be added to them overnight,and then plastic wrap should be tightly wrapped over the top of the palette. Some people have success with styrofoam cups and plastic wrap, but I find that the paint dries out in a week or so. If you are painting in large quantities,it is possible to buy acrylics in jars with the paint ready-mixed. There are other possible arrangements for storage of paint which may be found out by experimentation. It is important to work out a feasible solution to paint storage in order to avoid wasting time(by continually having to stop and mix up more paint),or wasting paint(by having the paint dry out,)as well as limiting colors due to using only the colors straight from the tube instead of interesting mixtures.

It is also very important to have a variety of shapes and sizes of containers for the mixing of paint,so that you are not limited to certain types of painting techniques with certain size brushes. Large and small bowls,cups,plates, sheets of glass,and the traditional palette are all well used in fabric painting. It is, as I said before, important that the paint does not get in the way of the painting; a work space cluttered with bottles and jars of all shapes and sizes does not allow for free spontaneous painting. A moveable tray or cart minimizes this clutter.

Several other topics should be mentioned. There are a number of supplies and tools that can be used in conjunction with fabric painting. Some of these are especially necessary as they will ensure the artists' safety.

Plastic extruders, metal-tipped applicators, and transfer pipettes are all used to make fine lines with dye. You can buy plastic bottles to store dye, plastic beakers to measure chemicals,and an eyedropper to measure small amounts of dye. A balance scale is also useful to measure out dye and chemicals.Transfer pencils and pens are helpful when transferring designs,while a fine-tipped permanent pen is available for signing your work.

There are many types of palettes which can be used. You can buy disposable mixing trays, disposable waxy paper palettes,muffin pans,egg cartons, as well as a regular oil painting palette. Stretchers are available to help keep fabric taut. Bamboo stretchers, called shinshi, wooden batik frames or just wooden frames,embroidery hoops,and Japanese end clamps, called hariki, are all used as stretchers.Steamers are also very important when working with certain types of dyes. You can buy stovetop models that are either horizontal or upright. Upright ones also come with their own electrical element.Steaming paper is also available.A hot-water bath canner can be used as a homemade steamer.

A number of supplies are extremely important in minimizing hazards of art materials. A NIOSH-approved dust mask is available from many suppliers. Goggles protect the eyes from hot liquids and dye particles.Rubber gloves and a plastic apron protect the skin. Hand cleaning pastes will remove any dye accidently spilled onto your skin. Air respirators and window exhaust fans are very important when working with certain dyes and when airbrushing or spray painting.

A thorough listing of these supplies and other tools need for fabric painting are listed,along with their source of supply, in Appendix B.

The last big question about the painting environment is: how hazardous is it? How safe are the paints, dyes, and thinners that you are using? Do you have an adequete ventilation system? This topic is extremely important,primarily because it has only come to light in the past few years due to certain persistent investigators.

A large number of artists have contracted serious diseases such as kidney disease or cancer because they have been debilitated by the very materials they work with.Two of the basic problems regarding the art materials are that many artists are self-employed and therefore are not protected by regulations that protect factory workers using some of the same noxious products.As well, many art materials come under the catagory of "consumer" goods or professional materials rather than industrial materials. Again, industrial materials are,by law, forced to have warnings concerning their use if they are hazardous.

The third major problem is a political one. The art materials industry is balking at proper labeling of art materials,and hide under the excuse that they "need more information".The artists with chronic lead poisoning, kidney failure, heart attacks, cancers of the lymph nodes or chest cavity,or mercury poisoning,don't need more information about the hazards of working with these materials.What has been needed, and is being provided by activists like Michael McCann(see his book,Artist Beware-Watson-Guptill,for more information), is educational information so that artists can know what they are working with, whether or not it is hazardous,and how to best minimize the negative effects.

One of the problems with a lot of these materials is that they are not particularly hazardous if the body has a resting period to recuperate from the material ingested or inhaled. When an artist is working not just eight hour days,but sixteen hour days and nights, the body does not have time to "bounce back". It's this maximum exposure to many ·of the art materials which causes the hazard to one's health.

Which of this information is applicable for the fabric painter?There are two catagories of art materials which are potentially hazardous:dyes, and the pigments in paint.There are problems with fiber-reactive dyes. The dye particles can react with the mucous membranes and with lung tissue. Allergies, tightness in the chest, asthma, and other respiratory ailments can occur if the dye molecules are inhaled. They should not be allowed to soak into the skin,either. The washing soda(sodium carbonate)which is used with these dyes is also corrosive to the skin and internal organs.Direct dyes(also known as household dyes) are very commonly used. They can be used with a thickener for fabric painting,and some of the colors are highly toxic. The darker shades contain benzidine or benzidene derivatives,which is a known carcinogen. Bladder cancer has been correlated to benzidine. Acid dyes, which can be used on silk and wool with a thickener for fabric painting, are also hazardous. They are a suspected carcinogen as liver cancer has occurred in tests on lab animals.Vat dyes and basic dyes have lesser risks involved,as they only seem to cause skin irritation. Naphthol dyes will cause severe skin irritation;other possible hazards of this dye are not yet known.Pre-metalized and disperse dyes should also be approached with caution,though I do not have specific information on them.

As well as the dye itself, the various chemicals used with the dyes can be harmful.Lye is used with Naphthol dyes with thickener.It is highly corrosive to skin and internal organs. Glauber's salts, which are used with thickened household dyes,is mildly harmful in that it causes diarrhea. Glacial acetic acid is used in the thickener for basic dyes. It is highly corresive by skin absorption,inhalation, or ingestion.Vinegar is an acceptable substitute.Gum tragacanth, a popular thickener, may cause allergies,but is not nearly as harmful as gum arabic(gum acacia). Inhaling gum arabic can cause asthma, other respiratory allergies,as well as skin allergies. Other chemicals, such as glycerin, tartaric acid, urea, sodium nitrate, ammonium sulfate, sodium alginate,and disodium hydrogen phosphate are also used with dyes,and they should be checked out as well for their comparative safety.

Paint pigments and thinners must also be examined regarding their potential hazards to the artist.<u>Mineral spirits</u> and <u>turpentine</u> are moderately toxic by skin contact and inhalation.Turpentine is fatal if ingested,and it can cause skin allergies.<u>Paint thinners</u> used with fabric paint and <u>textine</u>(used with oil paint) are particularly hazardous. If they contain either toluene or xylene,they are highly toxic and can be absorbed through the skin as well as being ingested or inhaled.Inhalation causes heart pain, liver and kidney damage, and menstrual disorders and irritation of nose and throat are other hazards.Textine contains xylene,and should be used with proper ventilation.

Some pigments are highly hazardous. Lead chromate and zinc chromate are known carcinogens. Chrome yellow, zinc yellow, strontium yellow, Emerald green(with arsenic pigments)may all cause lung cancer. So do barium yellow,cadmium red,orange,and yellow,lemon yellow,cadmium vermilion red, lead chromate, Scheele's green, and molybdate orange.Skin cancer is caused by Emerald green, carbon black, and Scheele's green. Other suspected carcinogens are: chrome green,chromium oxide green, cadmium yellow, Hansa yellow, lithol red, phthalocyanine blue and green. PCB's,causing cancer and birth defects, are found in benzidine yellow, flake white,and phthalocyanine blue and phthalocyanine green.

Pigments can poison you, sometimes fatally. Emerald green,cobalt violet(with arsenate), mixed white, and Scheele's green ,if ingested,

can cause fatal arsenic poisoning.

Mercury poisoning, which damages the kidneys, can be gotten from vermilion or cadmium vermilion red.Manganese poisoning,which has symptoms similar to Parkinson's disease, is a possibility with raw umber,burnt umber,and manganese blue and violet. Cobalt yellow, naples yellow,and lithopone can cause acute poisoning.Lemon yellow and manganese blue can cause barium poisoning.Lead poisoning can be caused by chrome green, flake white,molybdate orange and naples yellow.Lead chromate,naples yellow,and mixed white are suspected mutagens.Chromium poisoning is possible with strontium yellow,barium yellow,molybdate orange,and zinc yellow.

Less hazardous problems also occur. Antimony white, barium yellow, lemon yellow, and manganese blue can cause heart problems. Kidney damage can be caused by antimony white,flake white,chrome yellow,chrome green, napes yellow,emerald green,Scheele's green, and cobalt violet.Heart problems occur with antimony white,barium yellow, lemon yellow, and manganese blue. Allergies and asthma occur with cobalt blue,cobalt green, cobalt violet,talc,zinc white,and cerulean blue.Skin irritations and lesions occur with antimony white, barium yellow, lemon yellow,molybdate orange,naples yellow,strontium yellow,vermilion, and zinc yellow. And

reports of children experiencing cyanosis(lack of oxygen) have occurred after ingestion of hansa red pigments.

These horror stories may not give one much hope. However, there are a number of safe pigments. They are: English(or light) red, Indian red, burnt sienna, alizarin crimson,barium white, alumina, ivory black,mars black, mars orange,mars red,mars violet,mars yellow, raw sienna,titanium oxide(white),ultramarine blue,green, red, and violet,venetian red, yellow ochre,and Prussian blue(the last being safe used just by itself and not heated or mixed with another substance.)

It is also important to realize that the so-called organic pigments can be as hazardous as the synthetic ones, as many organic pigments are now made in the laboratory from petroleum derivatives and are therefore suspicious. It should also be remembered that many of the problems are caused by <u>chronic</u> ingestion of very small amounts of pigments.It is the ingestion of materials which causes most cancers and poisonings.

Textile,oil, and acrylic paints all contain these various pigments. As well, acrylics contain small amounts of mercury preservatives, which can be highly toxic by ingestion. The solution to dealing with these hazards in the painting environment is to follow common sense rules and use proper equipment in your studio.

Use rubber gloves and a dust mask when dealing with dyes. A large plastic apron will protect your clothes and you might wish to wear a protective cap on your hair when working with dyes.Goggles will protect your eyes when working around dye powders or when airbrushing.A hand cleanser can be used to remove any dye or paint that gets on your skin,and a barrier cream can be used on your hands to protect them.For spray painting,a fume hood and a window exhaust fan are important because the pigments can remain suspended in the air for up to two hours,and chronic poisoning can occur.

Other important guidelines to fol-

low are: don't eat or drink while working with paints and dyes. Don't let paint get in sores or cuts on your skin. Remember to wash your hands thoroughly after painting. Don't use kitchen utensils for painting and then use them again for food.And certainly don't ingest paint materials!<u>Do</u> use common sense while in your painting environment!

Another question to be asked in considering the features of a painting environment is, shall it be permanent or impermanent? Shall I paint on the dining room table, only to clean it off every night? Or should a special place be made only for fabric painting? If you plan to do a lot of fabric painting, the latter is probably a better idea, as dismanteling a painting environment takes a lot of time. As well, a painting, in contrast with a design, is usually worked on over a period of time, and in this time, the artist reevaluates the work, letting it grow and evolve. By having a place set aside, it is possible to let the paintings grow slowly. Then the artist need not feel rushed to finish them.

Once the painting environment is understood and planned, it is easier to get involved in a greater variety of fabric painting, both in terms of kinds of paints and types of designs. These will be discussed in the following chapters,Chapter IV and Chapter V.

# 4 MATERIALS — AND THEIR MESSAGES

"Each artist who is driven to express and create visual forms realizes the importance that his material has upon his response and his product. Identifying with a material enables him to create those forms with which he is involved. Some artists often feel it necessary to change from one media to another to complete an idea. Other artists,feeling an allegiance to their material,reject ideas that will not comply." Bill Farrell
AESTHETICS AND HISTORY OF ART

"I like to switch mediums.
Each one has a totally
different feel."
Mary Frank,sculptor

'Crafts Horizons'

Materials produce a variety of responses among its users. The importance of knowing the variety of effects of different materials in fabric painting cannot be overstated. Learning how paint materials react with various types of cloth is rather like learning a language; you are learning a"language"of materials. It is possible to have,after a period of time, a certain fluency in this language and you will know what type of effects are possible with a particular paint material.

There are a number of ways in which paint materials can be classified. Many of these classifications have polarities: from most popular and versatile,to limited use and limited exposure;or,high quality and expensive materials versus budget materials producing lesser quality. Materials can be catagorized as those which are simple to use versus those which are complex.

Some of the more popular paint materials used in fabric painting are textile paints,acrylics,and the many fiber-reactive cold water dyes. Dye pastels and fabric markers are also popular. There are <u>many</u> other paint materials which can be used which are more marginal,and limited in use,yet can be perfected within the limits of their usability. These include inks,marking pens,embroidery paints,natural dyes and paints, mordants,fabric crayons,silkscreen inks,linoleum block print inks,and latex or enamel paints.

High quality paint materials, such as some of the textile paints and silk dyes,produce excellent results.Especially when they are used in combination with high quality fabrics, such as silk or some of the mail-order cotton fabrics it,is hard <u>not</u> to create something beautiful.Since the quality of material used affects the end result,it is true that using inexpensive materials will sometimes create slightly lower quality effects. What is important about this is to not expect "designer" effects when using muslin and acrylic paint. Nevertheless, many fine,practical items can be made with these materials.

Paint materials also vary in their complexity or simplicity of use. Fabric crayons,dye pastels, acrylic paints,and some textile paints are relatively easy to use. Dyes,on the other hand, are quite complicated in their usage.There are many chemicals which must be used with dyes,and care must be taken in the handling of these dyes and chemicals.

Some paint materials are used exclusively for fabric or surface design. They include textile paint,fabric crayons, embroidery paints,fiber-reactive dyes,silk dyes,starch and wax resists,mordants, natural paints, silkscreen textile inks,and other printing textile inks. Other paint materials are regularly used in "art" painting,but can also be used for fabric painting. These include markers,drawing inks,pastels and craypas, acrylics,and oil paints.

There are so many types of paint materials for fabric painting that,rather than generalizing, I feel it will be more useful to walk you through each type and give you specifics of each particular brand. There are a number of issues that can be discussed with each paint material. Besides the issues mentioned previously(popular or varied use/ limited use; high quality(expensive) /low quality ("budget"); and simplicity/complexity of use) there are other factors to consider. How does the paint material affect the hand,or feel, of the fabric? What is its washability? Is it best used for clothing or other items? What type of fabrics are best used with it? Is it slow,or fast,to use? Can one be

productive and efficient using the paint material? What kinds of uses are there for the material? What kinds of things can be made with it? How lightfast is the material? How available is it? What are its weaknesses and strengths? Are there any special uses or special effects? And most importantly, how does one use it?

There are so many different kinds of paint materials for fabric painting that it is not possible for the fabric artist to gain expertise with all of them at once. Most artists experiment with them,and then choose several which fit their present needs. Remember also that what the advertisers say about a product is not always true. It helps to experiment with a new paint material to learn what it can do,as well as what it is promised to do!

ACRYLICS

Compared to oils, acrylic paint is a fairly new substance, coming on the market in the 1950's. At first, painters who were used to the slow application and drying time of oils found that acrylics dried too quickly and thus upset their painting habits. As well, some of these painters did not like the brighter colors of acrylic paint,as compared with oils. The industry responded by creating an acrylic retarder, which can slow down the drying time, and by marketing brands of acrylics that had resin bases,dried more slowly, and had colors closer to oils. Today, there is a new type of paint,called alkyds, which combines the smooth, creamy texture of oils combined with the quick drying time of acrylics. (Fig. 88)

Acrylic paint is a polymer tempera. Acrylics are waterbase and water repellant, which means that they are mixed with water before using, and,when dry, are waterproof. It is a plastic-base paint. It may crack if it is twisted or violently rolled (which is why it is not always the best paint material to use with knits) T-shirts painted with acrylics can

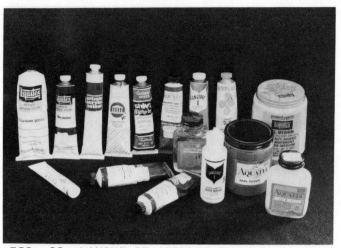

FIG. 88: LAYOUT OF ACRYLIC PAINTS.(L TO R)
LIQUITEX,WINSOR AND NEWTON,CLASSIC, SHIVA,
AQUATEC, VANGUARD,AND HYPLAR.

slowly be ruined if the paint is applied too thickly.

Acrylic paint is a wonderful material for the fabric painter! Especially for the beginning painter,
acrylics are simple and easy to use
with good results. The fact that
they are waterbase is important,for
solvents and thinners which can be
dangerous,needing good ventilation,
are not a consideration here. Since
they are waterproof when dry,what-
ever you paint with acrylics will
last for years and years.(The first
skirt I ever made with acrylics is
still in the same condition ten
years later!) Acrylics are relatively inexpensive,and they are easily
available in art stores. One can
buy a wide range of colors without
spending a lot of money. Since they
are quick drying,painting experiments
and projects can be finished in a
short range of time.Since beginners
have a tendency to be impatient,want-
ing to see the results of their work,
acrylics are a good beginner's paint
material.

The basic drawback of using acrylic paint in fabric painting is that
this plastic based paint does alter
the hand of the fabric substantially.
Depending on the brand that is used,
acrylic can slightly stiffen or greatly stiffen the fabric used. Thinner
fabric is prone to greater stiffening.
As one learns how to more effectively
use the paint,this problem can be lessened,but never altogether eradicated.

I have found that Aquatec acrylic
paint is the least stiffening, Liquitex the most. As one learns to
paint just the correct amount-not
too thin,not too thick, the acrylic
paint will not stiffen the fabric
too much. As well, if you first
paint,and then overdye with a fiber-
reactive dye, the stiffening effect
seems to lessen.

BRANDS AND PAINT ACCESSORIES

There are a number of brands of
acrylics out today. They include
Liquitex, Hyplar,Shiva, Aquatec,
Permalba, and Atelier. Shiva produces a resin-based acrylic called
Signa-Tex, while Bocour produces
another resin-based acrylic called
Magna. Resin-based acrylics have
limited uses with fabric painting,
and will be discussed later. They
are sold in either tubes or jars.
In tubes,they are concentrated, and
last through many paintings,but you
must spend time mixing each color
batch. The jar colors are about the
same consistency as textile paint,
thick and creamy.

As well as the acrylic colors,
you will find many other acrylic
materials in the store. There is:
acrylic retarder,which retards the
drying time of the paint,modeling
paste,for sculptural effects, gloss
medium,for gloss effects, matte medium,for matte effects, gesso,for
application to canvas or wood surfaces, acrylic resin, which can be
shaped into mosaic or sculptural
pieces, and gel medium,a heavy bod-
ied transparent gloss medium used
in impasto work,for better mixture
of colors,and for its adhesive properties. Many of these materials
can be used in conjunction with
fabric painting.

ACRYLIC PAINTING TECHNIQUES

One of the most exciting aspects
of using acrylics in fabric painting
is the many types of painting techniques that can be used with acrylic paint and its accessories.(Fig.89)

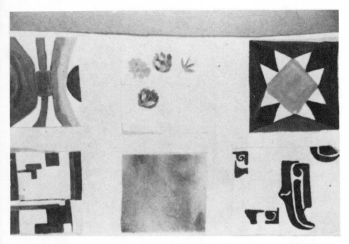

FIG. 89: CHART WITH EXAMPLES OF DIFFERENT TYPES OF ACRYLIC FABRIC PAINTING.

They can be used as an ink, for watercolor effects, as tempera, as impasto, as oil, in indirect painting, for many of the direct painting techniques, and for collage and other adhesive effects. To make an ink, polymer gel is mixed with water, and then the color is added until the right consistency is reached. A regular fountain pen with various ink tips works quite well. Paint that is the consistency of thin cream works well on smooth medium-weight materials. However, painting or drawing on a thin fabric will not make the design diffuse if the ink is made thick enough. The versatility of acrylic paint makes it easy to adjust the consistency of the ink to various types of fabric. In general, the thicker the fabric, the thinner the ink, and vice versa. A wash made from matte or gel medium can be laid down on the fabric (using water to thin it) before using the ink. This will stabilize the fabric and control capillary action.

The basic technique of watercolor is well used in painting fabrics as the medium of water makes it easier to paint large areas of fabric. As well, watercolor techniques with acrylics produce fabrics that keep a fairly soft hand. Acrylic paint is also a good type of paint material to use with watercolor because the paint can be thinned with water to any consis-

tency.

To get ideas for watercolor fabric painting, look at watercolors done on paper. Watercolor is nice on fabrics also because of the melting of one color into another, and the soft, shaded effects of color and tone. Watercolor washes can be used as backgrounds upon which you can draw. The backgrounds can suggest simple drawings such as birds, flying over mountains, subtle landscapes. Watercolor stripes are another easy way to maximize blending of colors.

By adding less water and more paint, acrylics can be mixed to the consistency of tempera; by adding a greater amount of a medium, especially gel medium, it can become very thick and used as an impasto. Acrylic in jars is the consistency of tempera, and you can use it like tempera paint to get flat, smooth paint surfaces. Impasto can be created by building up layers of paint with a brush, by using a palette knife to slab on the color, or by carrying the paint in thick brushfuls to the cloth. Modeling paste can also be added to acrylic color for a very thick impasto.

Some oil effects can be used with acrylics, especially the resin based acrylics such as Magna and Signa-Tex. However, this type of acrylic has a limited use with fabric painting. Drybrush effects work best, as the paint is thick and viscous.

Acrylics are unmatched for their adhesive properties. The gel medium can be used as a glue and will adher to any surface other than an oily one. Fabric, paper, beads, seeds, lace, knitted and crocheted pieces, small pieces of fired clay (to produce mosaic-like structures), wood, bark, twigs, small stones and shells, yarns, buttons, and small beads and sculptures made from acrylic modeling paste can be glued to the fabric. (Fig. 90)

The adhesive quality of the gel allows one many possibilities in the area of collage. Collage, coming

FIG. 90: WALL HANGING WITH NATURE SCENE. PEN WITH ACRYLIC INK.
ATTACHED ROCKS. SAND MIXED WITH PAINT FOR THE "RIVERBED".

from the French word, collere, meaning "to glue", is a good source of inspiration for the fabric painter. Fabrics can be glued to other fabrics and used in wall hangings, curtains, and drapes. The gel can also be used to lift pictures from paper(slick magazine ads on heavy paper transfer well) onto cloth.

The adhesive properties of acrylics make it easy to mix many small things into the paint. Sand,shredded paper or fabric, small rocks, crushed clay or leaves can be mixed with the paint. These ideas are better used for wall hangings than for clothing, as most of these mixtures cannot be washed. However, small beads or buttons made from acrylic modeling paste could be glued onto certain areas of clothing,such as the frontispiece of a dress.

Acrylic resin,like acrylic modeling paste, can be molded into small shapes and glued onto fabric. Acrylic resin needs to be poured into a preformed shape and left to dry. Regular modeling clay can be pressed into shapes on Saran wrap, then the clear resin,mixed with acrylic color,can be poured into these molds. These small plastic pieces are reminiscent of modern jewelry. Jewelry, stained glass,work with precious metals,and stonework in architecture could be inspirations for these techniques.

FABRICS USED

All of the above techniques show the many advantages of acrylic paint. The basic disadvantage is, as mentioned before,that acrylics will stiffen certain fabrics. The worst types of fabrics for this are stretchy knits,polyesters,light-weight cotton and other gauzy or thin fabrics,and fabrics with a heavy finish. As well, napped fabrics, such as corduroy or velvet, or wool, should not be used. Muslin, canvas, polycotton, blue jean fabric, cotton duck, sailcloth, and canvas work well with acrylic paint. Plain white fabric works better than already dyed, or colored fabric. Close weave fabrics also work better than stretchy fabrics.

HOW TO USE

There are several other basic instructions needed for working with acrylic paint. It is very important to keep brushes in water at all times; otherwise the paint will harden and ruin the brushes. A friend of mine calls acrylic paint the insidious brush eater! Watercolor or sable brushes can be used for watercolor and light washes, as well as the lightweight Japanese brushes. All other painting can be done with oil or bristle brushes, and big household or house-painting brushes. Always wash your brushes in soap and water after using them.

Acrylic paint dries quickly; use a palette with a cover, or put Saran wrap over your palette to keep the paint from drying out while you are painting.

Acrylics do not need any setting to make them permanent. However, I like to iron the painted cloth with a warm or hot iron; this often smooths the paint onto the fabric. Acrylic painted fabrics should not be exposed to high temperatures nor rough handling. It can be washed in a washer and dryer, but I would suggest that all handpainted clothing be handwashed.

Acrylics are a popular, flexible medium for fabric painting. They are especially good when painting very large projects, as they are economical and easy to use. There are no fumes, no complex heat setting, and they are waterbased, so that you just have to wash your hands after painting. To sum up their qualities, look at the chart below:

Use: popular and flexible with versatile uses

Quality: medium quality art material

Price: economical

Usage: simple to use

Hand: fair to poor, depending on fabric used and skill of painting

Washability: excellent.

Usage: for clothing and many other items-wall hangings, pillows, sheets, backpacks, quilts, toys, etc.

Fabrics used: Cotton, muslin, cotton blends, canvas, sailcloth, denim, duck

Productivity: Fast results, with good productivity possible

Availability: in art stores, hobby shops, fabric stores-readily available

Lightfastness: Excellent

How set?: no setting needed

TEXTILE PAINT

Textile paint is the next paint material to be discussed. As the name clearly states, textile paint is made especially for use on textiles. Today there are many brands of textile paint on the market, possibly due to the rise in popularity of fabric painting and other methods of surface decoration.

There are a number of brand names of textile paint. These can be divided into waterbase paints and solvent based paints. Waterbase paints include: Versatex textile and airbrush paint, Deka Permanent fabric paint, Createx Poster/Fabric Colors and Createx Textile Pigments, Eurotex Permanent Fabric Color, Sennelier Texti-

FIG. 91: STENCILED LEAVES ON ROCKS. PRANG TEXTILE PAINT ON MUSLIN.

color, Lefranc and Bourgeois textile paint,Gold Label Magic Touch all-purpose paint(including fabrics), Dylon textile paint,Badger Air-Tex Textile Color,and Colortex Fabric paint. The solvent-based paints include Prang Textile colors,Bishop and Lord,Flopaque, and Inmont Textile Colors. Both of these types also carry metallics,fluorescents, pearlescents, and day-glo colors.

The variety of textile paint available today is a wonderful contrast to the situation ten years ago. For many years, textile paint was limited to stenciling projects advertised in women's magazines.With little demand for the product,there were not many products! The crafts movement of the 70's expanded the interest in creativity,and we are lucky today to have so much from which to choose.

The greatest advantage of textile paint is that it can be used on a wide range of fabrics with guaranteed permanency. Unlike acrylics, they do not stiffen or change the fabric upon which they are painted. Textile paint will not wash out or run, although it does fade a little over the years. The colors are comparable to,though a little less bright, than acrylics. In the jar or tube, many textile paints have a consistency similar to acrylics.

Since textile paint is made specifically for textiles,its washfastness and colorfastness is good. There are some disadvantages,however. Unless you are doing small amounts of painting, textile paints can become expensive to use. Certain brands are more economical than others. Also,the solvent-based brands are used with a turpentine derivative;therefore,one must deal with the inevitable fumes.Working outdoors or in a special painting area is needed.

Another limitation of textile paint is that it is best used for a type of tempera painting.In other words, many textile paints have a"flat" hue and it is difficult to produce a variety of tones. Of course,this depends upon the skill of the painter,as well as the brand of paint.Textile paint works very well with stenciling, however,giving sharp clean edges to the design.

Because there are so many different brands of textile paint,as well as accessories, each brand will be briefly described below.

KINDS OF TEXTILE PAINT

Prang Textile Colors is one of the oldest fabric paints around. It has now been reissued as a waterbase,rather than a solvent based paint,and is called Prang Fabric Paint. The Textile Color is used with an extender,and a penetrator-thinner(a turpentine derivative). Both types are moderately priced, with a range of the basic colors-red through violet,with black, brown,and white. The colors can be easily mixed. With the new waterbase colors,one does not have the problems of strong smelling fumes. They are manufactured by the American Crayon Company and can be ordered through Bona Venture Supply Company.

Prang Fabric Paints are of a medium consistency,much like tempera paint. They can be used on both natural fibers,such as cotton, muslin,linen,and silk;and on some synthetics,such as acetates and organdy.The colors are heat set by ironing with a dry iron for three minutes on a cotton setting,or five minutes on a synthetic setting.It can be used on colored fabrics as well as on whites;mix more white with the various hues to make the paint more opaque,if necessary.To achieve a more transparent effect, thin with water.

Versatex textile paint is a popular waterbase textile paint that first appeared on the market in the

FIG. 92:PAINTED DRESS(LEFT)BY MERLIN HORNE. TEXTILE PAINT ON DARK FABRIC.

1970's. Versatex is a more full-bodied paint than is Prang; it comes in a range of 26 different colors.It is manufactured by Siphon Art, in Ignacio, California,and can be ordered through Bona Venture Supply Company and Dharma Trading Company,among others.

Versatex can be used on white or colored fabrics. Mix colors with white to produce an opaque color. The paint can be mixed with an extender to produce more transparent colors,or to merely"extend"the paint. Versatex also carries a binder,which is used with the paint when painting on 100% synthetics. Versatex can be used on a variety of both natural and synthetic fibers, including cotton, polycotton, muslin,linen,silk, rayon, nylon, acetate,and polyester. When painting on 100% synthetic,add 1 part binder to 9 parts color.

Versatex textile paint is heat set similar to other textile paints.Iron on the back of the fabric with a cotton setting. It is a popularly used textile paint,although I personally find the density of the paint difficult to work with.It is moderately priced,with versatile uses.

Versatex also has an <u>airbrush paint</u> which can be used with direct painting. It is not as full-bodied as the textile paint,and is preferred by some artists. It comes in a range of 22 colors. The airbrush paint is more expensive,but it is also a paint with a lot more pigment in it,so you get stronger colors,and can dilute it with water.It includes a binder in it,so working with 100% polyesters or synthetics will not be different than working on any other fabrics.It is heat set the same as the Versatex textile paint.

<u>Deka Permanent Colors</u> or <u>Deka Fabric Paints</u> are another textile paint which is very popular with fabric artists(it happens to be one of my favorite fabric paints). The Permanent Colors were manufactured in Germany and exported to this country;at the present time,they are no longer allowed over U.S. borders. The American version, Deka Permanent Fabric Paint, is almost equal to the quality of the Permanent Colors. Besides carrying a variety of colors-from lemon and golden yellow through the reds,burgundys, and violets, to blue,green,olive,ginger,and white and black, Deka carries a variety of special textile paints: fluorescent,metallic, and iron-on transfer paint.

Deka paints are waterbase. They are flowing in consistency, neither being too thick nor too thin. They can be used on both white and colored fabrics Mix Covering White(a particular white shade) with other colors when painting on colored fabric. Deka can be used on both natural and synthetic fabrics.

Deka Permanent Fabric Paint is now manufactured by Decart,Inc. in Morrisville, Vermont. The paint is available in some art supply stores;and some can be ordered through Dharma Trading Co. in San Rafael, CA. Besides manufacturing the basic shades, Deka carries a nice line of sparkling metallics,called <u>Deka Permanent Metallics</u>. They are available in gold,silver,yellow,red, blue,green, and copper. Also,you can mix Pearl White Metallic with the basic shades for other metallic colors.

<u>Fluorescents</u> are also available with Deka- in yellow, orange,pink, red,blue,and green.The fluorescents are very bright,with blacklight tendencies.Deka paints are heat-set by ironing on the wrong side of the fabric after it has completely dried. Make sure that the heat is dry heat,and use a setting comparable to the fabric.Deka paints are moderately priced,and I find them to be one of the most versatile textile paint available.

<u>Deka iron-on transfer paint</u> is another Deka product. With this fabric paint,one can paint on paper, let it dry,and then transfer the image to the fabric via a hot iron. The colors range from lemon,orange, and pink through the reds to light blue and green, and finally brown and black. The colors are darker in the bottle than they are on the fabric,but much brighter on the fabric than on the paper!

Transfer paint can only be used on synthetic fabrics,preferably 100% synthetic. If your fabric is at least 60%, you will still be able to transfer the design,but it won't be quite as bright.(Read about "Transfer Painting" in Chapter VI for more details on this process)

<u>Sennelier Texticolor</u> is another textile paint which has been on the market for a number of years. It is also a waterbase paint,and is about the same consistency of Deka. At present time,the most popularly stocked Texticolor paints are the Irridescent or Pearlized colors.They are available in turquoise,lemon, yellow,dark brown, pale green, emerald green, carmin,light blue,gold, black,white,violet,and ultramarine. They can be ordered through IVY Crafts Imports,Textile Resources,or Dharma Trading Company.

Texticolor is waterbase,and is heatset with an iron. It is a very nice paint,but slightly expensive if you are painting in any great quantity.Texticolor is manufactured in Paris,by the Sennelier Company.

It is non-toxic, appropriate for all types of fabrics, and is heat set with a warm iron.

In the past few years, an exciting new line of fabric paints has been made available to the fabric artist. Color Craft, Ltd., in Avon, CT. is manufacturing a number of different types of textile paint, including Poster/Fabric Colors, Textile Pigment Colors, Metallic Colors, Hi-Lite Colors, and Pearlescent Colors. They are all water base, with a large variety of colors. The Poster/Fabric Colors are opaque pigments, while the Textile Pigment Colors are transparent. They can be intermixed with each other. You can add an Opacifier to these pigments to make them easier to use on dark fabrics.

These colors can be used on all natural or synthetic fibers, both white and colored. The consistency of the paint is such that it is non-spreading, yet it is not too thick. I find that these paints equal Deka in their consistency and variety of effects. They are somewhat expensive compared to other fabric paints, but they are also a quality product.

You can use an Opaque Extender for the Poster/Fabric Colors and a Transparent Extender for the textile pigment colors. Both extenders will "extend" the paint without thinning the viscosity. The extender will also lighten these colors, something other extenders do not do. The Metallic Colors include pearl white, silver, satin gold, and copper. The pearlescent colors are a new product, and they are very nice. They are similar to the Texticolor Pearlized Colors. They are available in such exotic colors as teal luster, jade green, plum wine, lilac, apricot, electric blue, dusty rose, brown berry, pink gold, candy apple red, and champagne beige. Hi-Lite Colors are very opaque paints with an irridescent base. They will cover colors better than the Poster/Fabric, but I find that most textile paints do no cover colored fabric as well as the advertisements would have you believe.

Color Craft also markets a number of accessory materials to be used with the fabric paints. They include a catalyst, a bond-all, a thinner, a thickener, a binder, a permaseal, and a softener. The catalyst allows colors to become washfast at a lower temperature. The bond-all can be used on knits or loosely woven fabrics to insure wash-fastness. It also helps in alleviating problems caused by fabrics with sizing in them. The thickener, of course, will thicken the paint, while the thinner thins them; the thinner will not cause loss of color, but too much will delay drying time. The perma seal is similar to a Scotchguard type sealed coating; it supposedly does not alter the hand of the fabric. The binder will protect the pigmentation of watered down paint. And the softener will help soften the hand of the fabric.

After painting with any of these colors, let the fabric dry for 24 hours. Then iron on the reverse side at cotton setting with dry heat. Color Craft products are extremely versatile. When I first began painting on fabric, I used to fantasize that there would be a paint that came straight from the bottle, very vivid, bright, and ready to use, with wonderful results. If economics is not a factor, Color Craft paints can fulfill that fantasy!

Eurotex Permanent Fabric Colors are another fine, new fabric paint. They are marketed exclusively by Cerulean Blue, LTD., in Seattle, WA. Eurotex is also a water base paint. It is similar in consistency to Deka and Createx (Color Craft), and is a semi-transparent paint. It comes in 18 different colors; a standard range and three fluorescent colors.

There are several accessory products. Extender base extends the paint when light, transparent values are desired. Eurotex thickener is used to thicken the paint, especially desirable when stenciling. The Eurotex retarder can be used if you are painting large areas of color and want to slow down the drying time so that your brushstrokes don't show.

Eurotex can be used on most natural and synthetic fabrics, such as cotton, muslin, rayon, linen, wool, silk, polyester, and other synthetics. Eurotex, unlike other fabric paints, does not have to be heat-set. It can be air set in five to seven days. (However, I have found that the fabric is not harmed if ironed with a dry iron, like other heat-setting procedures) It can be used with white or colored fabrics; mix opaque white to the various colors to use with colored fabrics. Its price is moderate, and it is also a flexible, versatile fabric paint that is easy to use with good results. It is a pleasure to see good fabric paint being marketed, rather than having to hunt and find only products that are limited in their abilities.

Gold Label Magic Touch Paint is manufactured for a number of surfaces other than just fabrics, but it can also be used for fabrics. It is also a very nice opaque, waterbase paint. It has a range of colors unequaled by other paints: 48 colors, black, white, 32 greys and 11 fluorescents. The only problem I've had with this paint is that it dries slightly scratchy to the touch and a bit stiff. Painting on small areas, rather than trying to cover large areas of fabric, would help alleviate this problem. They are somewhat expensive if you intend to do a lot of painting, but the color range is excellent among the choices of fabric paint.

Gold Label Artist Color, as the paint is also called, is manufactured by Magic Touch of Anaheim, CA. It can be found in art stores, or ordered through them. They are of a medium consistency. They dry quickly and do not have to be heat set. They can be thinned with water for watercolor effects and for use with an airbrush. They can be used on a variety of fabrics; I have had more luck using medium to heavy weight cottons-such as canvas, duck, sailcloth. They are the best paint to use for colored fabric, as they are truely opaque.

Flopaque art, hobby and craft colors are another type of paint which can be used for other materials as well as fabrics. They carry a variety of colors: Flopaque Colors, Flopaque Metallic Colors, Lustre Glaze Colors, and Flo-Glo Fluorescent Colors. They are manufactured by Floquil-Polly S Color Corporation in Amsterdam, N.Y. and can be mail-ordered through Bona Venture Supply Company in Hazelwood, MO. It is a solvent based textile paint, using Dio-Sol, a thinner rather than being a waterbase paint. There are altogether 61 different, intermixable colors; 38 are the regular colors with a flat sheen, and then there are the metallics and fluorescents.

Flopaque is a very thin textile paint. For this reason, I find it has limited use, and is not as versatile as other paints mentioned. It is hard to control the capillary action, and since it is not a waterbase paint, watercolor effects do not work in the same way. Some practice is needed to maximize its benefits. It is good with dry-brush, and it can be used on a variety of fabrics. The manufacturers say that it can be used on all fabrics, but I have found that it dries very stiff on polyesters and synthetics, especially knits.

As stated before, Flopaque can be used on a variety of fabrics (cotton, linen, muslin, nylon, etc) but its hand is very bad. It dries stiffly even on muslin painted with a "light touch". Therefore, it is best used for wall hangings and other items where the soft drape of the fabric is not crucial (as is the case with clothing).

Flopaque has some unusual colors. They include: rose, coral, flesh, dresdan, chartreuse, Paris green, olive, lilac, magenta, maroon, burnt umber, terra cotta, henna, buff, samoa, and sandstone. Flopaque soaks into the fabric, so it is not very satisfactory for painting on dark fabrics. It does not have to be heat set, and it is important not to iron with anything hotter than a warm iron. Flopaque is a moderately priced textile paint.

There are quite a few other textile paints available on the market. Some of them I have used, others I have not. There are also textile paints that are a combination of oil paint and turpentine, or oil paint, enamel paint, and turpentine.(This last method is used by Marge Wing in her book, How to Paint on Fabric).Bishop and Lord is a solvent based textile paint I used a number of years ago. I have not seen it on the market recently. Dylon textile paint (Color-fun) is a waterbase paint with very good hand. It is manufactured by Dylon International Limited in London, England,and can be found in some art stores. It is heat set with a hot iron,and can be used on a variety of fabrics.

Other fabric paints have been used by other fabric painters;these include Colortex, Inmont Textile Colors, Delta Fabric Dye, and Water Tex textile paint. Colortex can be mail-ordered through Sax's Arts and Crafts in Milwaukee, WI. It is a waterbase paint,with a base, pigments, and a binder that you mix together. It is heat set with an iron. It is moderately priced. Inmont Textile Colors are highly recommended by Patricia E. Gaines, author of The Fabric Decoration Book. They are available through the Inmont Corporation in Clifton, N. J. Delta Fabric Dye is used by Serene Miller, author of Painting on Fabric. Delta also manufacturers Delta Stencil Dye and 'Starlite' Fabric Dye,a metallic dye. These Delta products are heat-set with a dry iron. The regular dyes(or paints)have 20 colors; the'starlites' have 12. The 'starlite' colors are especially good when painted on dark fabrics. The Delta Fabric Dye Extendor can be used instead of water for a slightly thicker paint. The extendor also acts as a retarder,allowing the paint to dry more slowly.The stencil dye is a thicker dye product especially made for stenciling. It comes in 22 different colors. These waterbase textile paints are colorfast and all are intermixable.

Rosco-Haussmann products are recommended by Deborah Dryden,who wrote Fabric Painting and Dyeing for the Theatre. There are several available fabric paints: B-2 Latex Colors, Sprila Glazing Colors, Fabric Colors, and Polydyes. B-2 Latex Colors are waterbase, can be used on cotton, viscose rayon, as well as other fabrics.By using the Latex Fabric Color, Extra White Opaque with the other pigments, one can paint on dark fabrics. Sprila Glazing Colors are solvent based; a thinner is used with the colors,and alcohol is used for cleanup. There are nineteen colors in the Sprila Colors. The Fabric Colors are waterbase,with 25 colors. A thickener and a resist are available. Fabric colors can be used on silk,wool, and stretch synthetics. Polydyes are used on polyesters and synthetics.They do not need steam-setting. The basic problem for these products is that, unless you would be using them in large quantities(such as is possible in theater work)they are not available any other way.

Speedball Textile, Britex,Goodstuffs, Aqua-set, and Fashion Paints are other textile paints which I have read about, but have not been able to locate.

Another catagory of textile paints are airbrush textile paints. They include Deka PermAir, Air Waves airbrush fabric paints, Badger Air-Tex Opaque Textile Colors, and Hot Air Textile Artist Pigments. All the airbrush paints are naturally thinner than some of the textile paints. Deka PermAir is waterbase,with 30 different shades. They include metallics and covering white,for use on dark fabrics. Air Waves is also waterbase, with 12 colors, plus a covering white. Badger Air-Tex has 12 opaque colors also and is waterbase. It is heat-set by ironing. Hot Air Textile Pigments have 11 colors, and opaque white for covering dark fabrics. As well, it has a binder,which helps the pigment adher to the fabric,and a thickener, CP-X Printing Clear.You always use the binder and the color in equal amounts. Cotton, muslin, cotton blends, silk, rayon, and acetate can also be used with Hot Air Colors. For handpainting, add 60% of the Printing Clear to 20% of the Binder, then add 20% of color. Watercolor effects can be achieved by working on slightly damp fabric. Hot Air paints are very versatile, and a good airbrush paint to use for fabric painting. Most all airbrush paints come in smaller amounts than other fabric paints; they are not as cost effective as other fabric paints. Versatex also puts out an airbrush paint, called Versatex Textile Airbrush Ink. It was discussed in the section on Versatex products.

There are several other materials that I am going to mention here. While they are not called fabric paints, technically they are closer to fabric paints than any other paint catagory mentioned. One such material is Aritex mineral dyes, the next is Caran D'Ache Gouache, and the third is Pentel Watercolor Dyes. Aritex Mineral Dyes are a very nice product. They come in tubes, and can either be used like a liquid embroidery paint, or they can be used with a brush. I prefer the latter, as the paint flows out of the tube fairly quickly. Aritex is water soluble, with bright vivid colors. 11 colors are available from Aiko's Art Materials Import, Inc. in Chicago, IL. Aritex can be used on cotton, linen, silk, nylon, and synthetics. It does not need to be heat set. It can be thinned if desired, or used as it comes out of the tube. I find Aritex a high-quality product that is easy to use. They are reasonably priced.

Another very similar textile paint is Pentel Water Color Dyes. They are available through Bona Venture Supply Company in Hazelwood, MO. There are 12 colors which come in a tube, just like Aritex. They can only be used with natural fibers, however. A handy plastic palette comes with the set. They are a waterbase paint, with no heat setting required.

Caran D'Ache Gouache, a Swiss product available through art stores, can be used in fabric painting. It is advertised as being used as a batik dye. The watercolors are available in sets of 8 or 15 colors. They are waterbase paints, and work very well with watercolor techniques. They can be heat set with an iron and are washable, although since they are not technically a fabric paint, it is best to gently wash them in water with little soap. One of the best aspects of Caran D'Ache Gouaches is that they in no way alter the hand of the fabric. They can be used on both natural and synthetic fibers. Although these paints are limited in their use, they are a very nice material, being both delicate with vivid colors. They can also be used in conjunction with the Caran D'Ache Neocolor sticks, which will be discussed later under fabric markers.

Another possibility with fabric paint is to make your own. Some artists still like to practice the traditional craft of mixing their own paints. This can be done with fabric paints as well. Dry pigment powder is mixed with glycerine, a thickening agents such as tragacanth gum, a binder or varnish, and oil of wintergreen. Mineral spirits are added as a thinner.

Making your own paint is an adventure. Patience, experimentation, and careful record keeping are important. Check The Textile Arts-Vera Berril for more specific instructions for textile paints.

QUALITIES OF TEXTILE PAINT

As can be seen, there are a great variety of textile paints available today. They range in consistency, use, and price. Many are waterbase, a few are solvent based. Most are heat set by a dry iron, some need only overnight drying to be set. They are all washable, especially those truely classified as textile paints. Those that are available in larger quantities are best used when one is painting a lot. Those manufactured in small quantities can be very good when one is painting small motifs. Most can be used on dark fabrics, although in my experience, painting on dark fabrics does not always give good results. Many times it is preferable to paint on white fabric, and then overdye. Hi-Lite Textile Colors, by Createx(Color Craft, Ltd) are the best overall paint for use with dark colors. Caran D'Ache Gouaches are also good, although their washability is more delicate. One technique which is possible is to first paint a pastel color with an opaque white mixed with a pure color. Then lightly paint over the design with just the pure color.

To sum up the qualities of textile paints, refer to the chart below:

Use:very popular,flexible with versatile uses for most brands. Some brands have limited use.

Quality: a medium to excellent range quality material

Price: Varies from moderately priced to some expensive,high quality textile paints

Hand: very good for most all brands. Flopaque being the unusual exception

Washability: good to excellent, especially with the technically true fabric paint

Usage: especially good for clothing and other wearable items.Excellent for delicate fabrics,high quality items.

Fabrics used: All cottons, linen, silk, rayon, acetate, synthetics,polyesters, blends,knits, canvas.

Productivity: Fair to good.Some textile paints require a long drying time.

Availability: Fair to good in art stores. Best to mail-order through a surface design or fabric decoration supply house.

Lightfastness:Good to excellent.

How set?:Most heat set with a dry

iron,some are air set

OIL PAINT

Oil paints can be used as a kind of textile paint. It can be mixed with a number of different thinners and materials. In the older books and pamphlets on fabric painting, oil paint is a major paint material. Some books recommend squeezing the oil onto a glass palette to drain off the oil,then adding turpentine to the paint before using. Another product which can be mixed with oil paints is textine, a thinner specifically manufactured by Grumbacher for use with oils on fabrics. In her book, How To Paint On Fabric, Marge Wing uses a mixture of oil paint, enamel paint, and mineral spirits.

When oils are mixed with any of these other substances, it becomes a type of textile paint.The colors blend easily, and Impressionistic types of work can be done easily. Anyone who has already worked in oils would find it easy to transfer their skills to this technique. However, this type of textile paint needs good ventilation,for there are a lot of fumes with either the turpentine,and especially the textine.It is not a good paint material for children.

HOW OILS ARE USED

Any type of oil paint can be used: Shiva, Grumbacher, Permanent Pigments,etc.(See Fig. 93) Turpentine, mineral spirits(or turpenoid) and textine can all be added to the oils.Working with oils and turpentine or mineral spirits works well on small areas or for detail work. Colors blend well when using oils. They also appear "soft" on the fabric,and do not disturb the hand of the fabric. I have painted successfully with them on a variety of polyester blends,textured fabrics,cotton knits, as well as cotton and muslin. Some cottons will stiffen a little when painted with oils, but the synthetics don't.

Don't thin the paint down too much or the turpentine will stain the fabric. On the other hand,too much overpainting or painting with thick paint is not desired either.

Use a disposable waxy palette, and dab a bunch of different colors on your palette. Thin them with either turpentine or mineral spirits.Then begin painting,using a firm brush,such as one used for oils. You can blend such minute amounts of color that your painting can have many many different tones very easily. The oils contrast most with the flat areas of color of some textile paints. Try flowers, landscapes,using a variety of colors.Stenciling also works well with oils,as the edges come out sharp and clean with the paint.

The main problem when using oil paints with thinners is the fumes. Textine,mentioned above, contains xylene, a very dangerous chemical. Heart problems and menstrual problems can occur if one ingests this chemical. You need a good ventilating system such as a window exhaust fan. If this is not possible, at least use a face mask and work outdoors, if possible.

Oils can be used on dark or colored fabrics.A method is used similar to that described with textile paints. Opaque white is mixed with a color and applied. Then,if desired, the same hue without the white can be added,lightly though,so as to not stiffen the fabric. A variety of fabrics can be used,but do not try to cover large areas of fabric with oil paint. Use it for small designs.

Oils can be mixed with enamel paints,with turpentine or mineral spirits added. How to Paint on Fabric,by Marge Wing, gives a thorough explanation of this process. Generally speaking, the same methods are used as mentioned earlier. You can paint with just enamels and turpentine, as well.

Working with oils and thinners is moderately expensive.It depends,of course, on how much you paint. The following chart enumerates the various qualities of painting with oil and turpentine,textine, or oil with enamel paint and turpentine:

Use:not well-known except among certain craftspeople.Limited use, yet good effects within limits

Quality:medium to good quality

Price:moderately expensive

Hand: good to very good,depending upon the technique of painting used

Washability: good

Usage: can be used on clothing if small painted areas are used rather than trying to cover fabric.Good for curtains,lampshades,wall hangings

Fabrics used:cotton,muslin,cotton knits, polyester blends,synthetics, canvas, and denim

Productivity: Good to very good. Oils do take some time to dry,however

Availability: Excellent. All paint materials can be purchased at art stores and the enamels can be purchased at hardware or department stores

Lightfastness:Good to very good

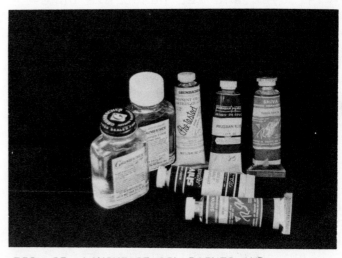

FIG. 93: LAYOUT OF OIL PAINTS AND ACCESSORIES; TEXTINE, TURPENTINE

How set?:heat set with a dry iron, for oils with turpentine;also oil with textine; with enamels added air dry is sufficient

NATURAL DYES

The above fabric paints,acrylics, and oils,are all manufactured paints. The next group of paint materials are made from the raw materials of paint ingredients and include natural dyes, natural paints, and mordant paints.

Natural dyes have been used for many hundreds of years. The American Indians and other indigenous cultures used natural materials in the form of dyes, paints, and inks for coloring matter. Chemical substances in the earth, in plants, and in some animals can be used for dyes. Today natural dyes can be found in the trees, flowers, and plants which grow in the city or the country. They can also be found in your flower or vegetable garden,as well, and some of them can be found in the grocery store. For example, coffee, tea, tumeric, curry,paprika, and wine can all be used for natural dyeing. Vegetables such as the peelings from eggplants, tomatoe vines, carrot tops, red cabbage leaves, red onion skins, and pickle juice can also produce colors such as silver blue, yellow-green, and purple. Edible berries such as the blackberry,huckleberry, blueberry, and elderberry are potential dyes,and the nonedible pokeberry is an excellent dye. Potter's clay becomes a dye; so does clay from the earth. Wood ash, when combined with lye, forms a soft black dye. Mushrooms, lichens, dandelions,grass, rose hips, and sunflower seeds are other surprising sources of dyes.And there are many more.

In the woods, one finds roots,twigs, leaves, and bark of many trees which can become dyes. Madrone bark produces a dark brown, as does walnut bark or hulls. Apple, alder, birch, hemlock, maple, pear, sassafras, white oak, and willow bark can be used. The roots of the Osage orange, bloodroot, beet, and waterlily can be used. Goldenrod, morn-ingglory blossoms, marigolds, sunflowers, and cotton flowers all produce a dye when boiled. Among hundreds of other possible dyestuffs there are mullein leaves, wild mustard, seaweed, sagebrush, horsetails, cedar berries, dock, sumac leaves, pricklypear cactus, the Oregon grape, and mistletoe. These are all substances which have been tested and written up in books. To discover other dye-producing substances, when you are gathering known materials, pick up a few on the side and experiment. Dyes are not always obvious to the eye. For example, a bright red rose will become a drab greenish/brown dyebath, while the dark skin of the eggplant becomes a lovely silver blue.

In general, to make a natural dye from any of these materials, take the gathered material and boil it in water for one hour, or until you can see the dye seep into the water. In order to have maximum strength, most natural dyes act like hot-water dyes; that is, the material to be dyed must be boiled in the hot dye for approximately one hour.However, a less strong dye can be made by boiling the dyestuff in water, then cooling it and using it with or without a thickener directly on the fabric. Mordants also strengthen the durability of the dye. In regular natural dyeing, the material to be dyed is often treated with a chemical which helps keep the dye fast. Alum, chrome, and tannic acid are common mordants, or chemicals, used.For natural dyes to be used in fabric painting, it is possible to add the mordant to the dye bath near the end of its hour boiling period.Or,the cloth that is to be painted can be boiled for one hour with a mordant to insure color fastness. In order to learn the specific amounts of the mordant needed, as well as what types of dye materials need which type mordant and which type of cloth, it is best to look at books on natural dyeing. Gentle Dyes-Cheryl Brooks and Carol Higgins, and Mother Nature's Dyes and Fibers-Will Bearfoot are good sources.

To paint with natural dyes, you simply use a brush and paint to create designs with blendings of color and soft-edged, as opposed to hard-edged forms. An ink pen can be used for detail. Natural dyes vary in their strength. Some are very strong and remain so even when thinned with water. Others may need a thicker solution, with less water and more dye-stuff. After painting, let the dye dry,then heat set it by ironing with a dry iron. Handle delicately,and do not over expose natural dyed items to direct sunlight for long periods of time.

NATURAL PAINTS

Natural dyes can be thickened to make a "natural" paint. To do so, merely add a thickening agent to the cooled dyestuff. Gum arabic or tragacanth gum can be used for thickeners, and can be found at some art or drug stores. Try corn starch or carrogeen moss. Carrogeen moss is used in the marbling process,explained in Chapter VI, and can be ordered through Colophon Hand Bookbindery in Seattle, WA. Sodium alginate is another thickener which is used with cold-water dyes. Dylon's Paintex, Procion dye thickener, or Fibrec's dye thickener can be used. (Fig.94)

Natural paint is thicker than natural dye; therefore there is more control with the brush. The paint can be applied directly, with medium large brushes,for a large amorphous design. Or they can be painted around a blocking out medium, such as starch-paste resists. Painting with natural dyes and paints is somewhat experimental, and should be approached in this manner.

There are several household items which can be used in connection with natural dyes and paints to change their color. Some of the mordants mentioned above can be used to darken or change the color of a dye. Copperas, for example, turns any dye a darker color. Household items such as baking soda, vinegar, cream of tartar, and ammonia can be used in combination to effect color change. Vinegar and cream of tartar work together, as do baking soda and ammonia. Just add a small a-

mount of these to the natural dye and see if you like the new color!

I have enjoyed experimenting with natural dyes and paints in connection with fabric painting. One afternoon in the fall,I remember making "sycamore soup",a mixture of sycamore leaves, wood, mud, twigs, and bark gathered from a field behind our house. I had never seen sycamore leaves mentioned in any book on natural dyeing, and so was curious to see whether or not it would react with the other substances, including alum, to form a dye. It did not, and the beautiful deep goldbrown sycamore leaves,to this day, remain on the ground-and a mystery to me.

MORDANT PAINTING

A step away from experimenting with homemade paint is the process of mordant painting.Mordant painting is probably the oldest form of fabric painting known. It has been mentioned in the writings of Pliny and was used by the ancient Egyptians in their clothing. Records state that fabric or clothing was smeared with chemicals and then thrown into vats of various colored boiling dye. The cloth was multicolored because of the reactions of the different chemicals to the different colored dyes.

Essentially, mordant painting is

FIG. 94: THICKENING AGENTS AND OTHER CHEMICALS USED IN NATURAL PAINTS. CARROGEEN MOSS, GUM ARABIC, IODIZED SALT, CORN STARCH.

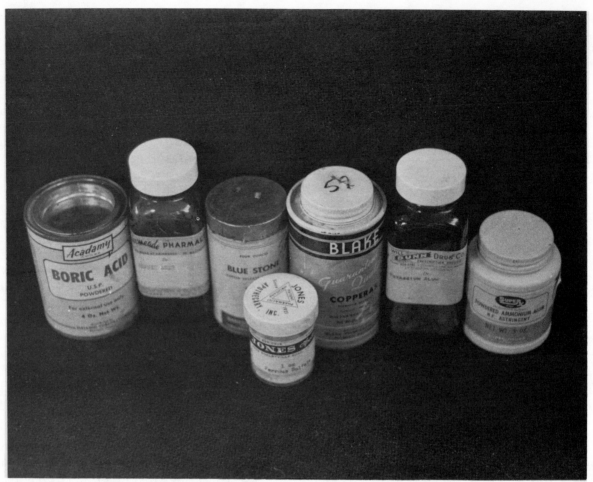

FIG. 95: LAYOUT OF MORDANTS:BORIC ACID, TANNIC ACID,BLUE STONE,
COPPERAS,POTASSIUM ALUM, AMMONIUM ALUM,AND FERROUS SULFATE

using chemicals to both block out areas of the cloth and change the colors of the dyes used. A cloth dyed with only one color of dye could have four or five different contrasting colors due to the type of chemicals used.The most popular ones today which are used for mordants are alum, copperas, chrome, tannic acid, and blue stone.(Fig. 95)(Some of these chemicals are extremely dangerous;use them with adequete protection,and never let children use them or be around them)

In ancient days, muds and clays were smeared on clothing and used as a dye. Both tannic acid and metal salts are in muds and clays,so that the resulting dark brown colors were fast. Even today, the Japanese press leaves inbetween a piece of cloth to force the tannin in the leaves into the fibers of the cloth.

Designs which do not detract from the blending of colors are good to begin with when experimenting with mordant painting.

As well, you can paint more representational forms although they may be rather indistinct, and will probably not have hard edges. If these shapes are planned out in terms of color, a nice design can emerge from the different chemical reactions in a way similar to the process of batik, with one color bath influencing another.

The basic instructions for mordant painting are as follows: mix the mordant or chemical with some water and then dip the brush into the chemical and onto the fabric where you wish to have a color different from your dye or paint. When you have used all the different chemicals you wish, paint over the fabric with dyes, inks, or textile paints.

98

DYES

Dyes are the next group of paint materials to be discussed for fabric painting. Although there are many types of dyes which can be used, only dyes which can be applied directly,with or without a thickener, will be considered. In other words, dyes which must be used with immersion techniques will not be considered. Since fabric painting, not dyeing, is the subject of this book, direct application of dyes with a brush or other tool can be considered painting.

There are, nevertheless, many, many different types of dyes which can be used in this way. Fiber reactive dyes are a popular and versatile type of dye. Other classifications of dyes which can be used include disperse, direct, acid,naphthol, household, pre-metalized, and basic.There are also liquid dyes, such as fiber-reactive liquid dyes and liquid dyes for silk.

The use of dyes is so extensive and its history so vast, I will only focus on one aspect of using dyes-and that is in a thickened "paste" form for handpainting,and in a more liquid form for use with spraying,watercolor techniques, or as a drawing ink. These applications have also been described as either "thin" or "thick" applications.

The dyes are used primarily with cold water,and are not ever boiled or used in a hot dyebath.

ADVANTAGES

What are some of the advantages of using dyes? Dyes are readily available,with many choices. There is a wide range of colors from which to choose,and you can intermix colors to create your own. Dyes are a versatile product, with many effects possible. They are inexpensive to purchase,and will last a long time if properly stored. Their washfastness and lightfastness varies,depending on the type and brand. They can be used on a variety of fabrics,and most importantly,they do not disturb the

hand of the fabric.Unlike some paint materials, dyes will never stiffen the fabric.

Some beginners may find working with dyes overwhelming. Because of the variety of types of dyes,plus the various chemicals which are used,working with dyes is certainly more complex than just opening up a bottle of textile paint and beginning to paint! I have always had a certain block towards using dyes, due to a certain amount of impatience;I just want to jump in and start painting. Once a person has learned about a certain type of dye, how it works,what chemicals are needed, much of the complexity of working with dyes is removed. Still,there are certain disadvantages of the material.

DISADVANTAGES

The greatest hazard in working with dyes is that they are a hazard. I would not recommend that children be allowed to use them,except for Inkodye,which is a premixed vat dye,and can be used safely from the bottle.A mask should be worn while mixing them,as small particles can be inhaled and cause health problems.(Refer to Chapter III,pp. 78-80 for details of health hazards of paint materials).Rubber gloves should also be worn while handling dyes.Most companies that stock dyes now list the precautions on their instructions.

The other disadvantage in working with dyes,is,as I have stated earlier,they are complex to use.One must assemble a number of small containers in which to mix the various colors.I use plastic egg cartons for small amounts of dye. An eye dropper can be invaluable for adding small amounts of thickener or color to a certain color.For larger amounts of dye,it is best to use a separate container for each color. Certain distributors carry plastic bottles for this purpose;I use whatever is convenient from the amassed bottles in our pantry.If you plan to do a lot of painting with dyes over a period of time, try to store the mixtures in dark-colored bottles away from the light. They will last longer this way. I find empty vitamin bottles good for this.

Other problems with using dyes concerns staining and water usage. Some dyes, no matter how careful you are, will inevitably stain your surroundings. Or, you are constantly washing up, finding more dye particals, then washing up. Fiber-reactive dyes especially need a lot of water, since they must be rinsed out until the water runs clear. It's best, though not always possible, to work in an area away from living quarters. Bathrooms can be cleaned; don't work in your kitchen-the dye particles can too easily get in food and on cooking utensils.

Since each type of dye has particular effects, other advantages, disadvantages, and ways of usage will be discussed under each classification of dye.

FIBER-REACTIVE DYES

Fiber-reactive dyes are one of the most popular types of dyes used in all surface design techniques today. One reason for this is that the dye molecules bond chemically with the fiber molecules, creating a very washfast and lightfast dye. The colors are also quite brilliant for a cold-water dye. Although there are many brand names, it is Procion dye which is most synonymous to the concept of fiber-reactive dyes. There is Procion-M, Procion-H, and Procion-MX. Other brands include Fibrec, Fabdec, Dylon, Cibacron F(Ciba), DyeHouse, Putnam Color Fast, Hi-Dye, Pylam, Calcobond, Remazol, Cavalite, Levafix, and Reactone-Geigy. These dyes are in powder form. Createx fiber-reactive liquid dye is produced by Color Craft Ltd. They also carry an "R" series for silk and wool. PROChem Liquid Reactive Dye is also a fiber reactive dye. And Cerulean Blue now carries a Liquid Procion H dye.

PROCION DYE

Procion dye, the original fiber reactive dye, was produced in England in the mid-1950's. Many brands, such as Dylon, Fibrec, Fabdec, Putnam Color Fast, and Hi-Dye are actually packaged Procion, sometimes with additives. While the packaging makes for an easier time mixing the ingredients, experienced painters will find the bulk Procion dye much more economical. All these dyes are readily available, either in an art or fiber/needlework store, or through a distributor. Procion dyes can be ordered through Textile Resources, Flynns, Earth Guild, Cerulean Blue, Dharma Trading Company, Pro Chemical and Dye, I.C.I. Organics, and Mayborn Products, Ltd., among others. Dylon can be ordered from Dylon International, Ltd. in London, England; while Fibrec and Fabdec can be ordered from their respective companies(Fibrec and Fabdec) in the U.S. Putnam Color and Dye produces Putnam Color Fast.

Colors vary on the type of Procion dye used. Procion MX dyes have a wide color range, with 52 colors available from Flynn's.(These are also called Flynn's Cotton Dyes) They have 6 yellows, 4 oranges, 7 reds, 8 purples, 8 blues, 7 greens, an interesting shade called havacado(between the olive drab and the rust brown), 7 browns, and white, grey, and black. Flynn's carries the most colors, and they are sold in large volume(8 oz-100 lbs)or 2 oz also. Pro Chemical and Dye Inc. carries 32 colors, starting with 2 oz. packages. Actually, they are packed in screwtop jars, which minimizes health and storage problems. Procion-M has around 15 standard colors, while Procion-H has 16 different colors.

Generally speaking, the two different types of Procion dyes are the Procion-M and MX and the Procion-H. The latter is used only for painting or printing, and is used with a"thin" or"thick"application of chemical water. It cannot be mixed with the Procion M's. With Procion-M and Procion-

100

MX dye,the descriptive name and the product name are not always the same (for example,the Procion-M dyes distributed by Cerulean Blue have product names of,for example,Procion Brown-MX-CRA,the same as the descriptive name of Flynn's Procion-MX Dark Brown. Keep this in mind when ordering dyes from various distributors.

Procion dyes can only be used on natural fibers,such as cotton,linen, rayon,silk,and wool. They cannot be used on synthetics,polyesters,nylons, etc. They are a reasonably priced paint material,especially when purchased in bulk. They are extremely versatile in their use,and very popular with fiber artists and fabric painters. Since there are so many different brand names of Procion dye, with different accessory chemicals,I will discuss each one separately under its brand name and distributor.

Procion-M dyes are distributed by Cerulean Blue,Ltd.They are a cold-water dye,and can be used for immersion techniques as well as for direct application.Certain chemicals must be added to the dye for direct painting. (Some distributors stock pre-packaged chemicals;others offer the bulk chemicals for you to mix.All Procion dyes follow the same procedure that I will now describe.)

The standard "chemical water" that is the base for both "thin" and"thick" applications is made from Calgon(also called sodium hexametaphosphate),urea, and Ludigol(Also sold under the names Resist Salt L,Sitol, and Nacan). To thicken this mixture, sodium alginate is added.

To make a quart of chemical water, add 1 tsp. of Calgon and 10 tbsp. of urea to 2 cups of hot water. Mix and then add cold water up to 2 cups.This mixture can be used when one wishes a thin application of dye,either by using a brush,or a spray bottle or other tool. Take a small amount of dye(several teaspoons are adequete) and add a small amount of the water. (I do this by putting small amounts of dye in various containers that will hold the finished dye product-jars,yogurt containers, etc.)Then continue adding the chemical water until you have

used all of it.(One quart can be used for up to 8 teaspoons of dye, so you can divide up your colors and the chemical water.)

Baking soda and washing soda (also called sal soda,soda ash,or sodium carbonate) are added last to activate the dye. After they have been added, the dye will be useful for only a few hours;at the most,four hours. This is because the dye will be reacting with the sodas.4 teaspoons of baking soda plus 1 teaspoon of washing soda are used per 1 quart chemical water.(This translates down to 1 teaspoon baking soda and ¼ teaspoon washing soda per cup of water.) Mix the washing soda in a little hot water before adding it to the mixture.

Working with dyes is not an exact science. There are various opinions upon measurements for dyes and how long they will last. The Procion-M series is said to last for up to 2 days if refrigerated(after having added the soda). The chemical water can last indefinitely if refrigerated,and the dyes(without the soda) are said to last up to 4 days if refrigerated. I have tended to use these dyes within a week's period with good effects.

How much dye should be used is another area with wide opinion.I have always judged the amount visually rather than measuring it.However,for those of you who are more comfortable with precise measures, use ¼ teaspoon per 1 cup of water for pale shades,1 teaspoon for medium shades,2 teaspoons for deep shades, and 4 or more teaspoons for very deep shades. This is only for the Procion-M series;there are different measurements for the Procion-H dyes.

There are an infinite amount of colors possible by mixing the standard shades. Ann Marie Patterson and Ron Granich of Cerulean Blue have created a very interesting system of color mixing. For those of you who are interested, it is clearly explained in Surface Design for

Fabric-Jennifer Lew and Richard Proctor(1984), a wonderful book that was recently published. Colors such as salmon, coral orange, apple green, and copper brown are possible to mix, using three colors:Magenta, Cyan, and Yellow.

As well as the "thin" application of dye, a "thick" one can be made by adding sodium alginate, also called Keltex, Lamitex, or Manutex.Sodium alginate is extracted from seaweed in the form of a gum.Two types can be ordered in bulk from Cerulean Blue: a high viscosity mixture(Type"H") and a lower viscosity one(Type "L"). The higher viscosity mixture makes a very thick paint mixture,using very little of the alginate.With the lower viscosity type,one still gets a thick mixture,but it is not as stiff or bulky to stir,and it washes out more easily from fragile fabrics.Other names for the high viscosity product are Keltex S, Lamitex H,Manutex RS,plus Pro Chemical and Dye's PRO Thick SH. PRO Thick F,Kelgin LV,Lamitex L-10, and Manutex F are other types of the lower viscosity alginate.

The"thick"application is useful for direct painting,for the sodium alginate controls the dye,and it works very much like a fabric paint in terms of application.From the finest brush to a big housepainting brush, the thickened dye works equally well. Hard-edged shapes,wavy lines,rubber stamp prints-many techniques are possible.And you can vary the thickness of the solution by adding more chemical water.

Sodium alginate is added to the chemical water in the ratio of 4 teaspoons to one quart of water.Agitate this mixture,either by hand or with an electric mixer, until it is well blended and smooth. This mixture is now called the "stock paste". It can be refrigerated indefinitely,available to be mixed with dye whenever you are ready to paint!Store it in a closed glass container for maximum shelf life.

When you are ready to add the dye, simply pour off an amount of the stock paste. Add dye(in the same proportions as for the "thin application")to the paste, first blending it with a little hot water. Then add your sodas,again,1 teaspoon baking soda and ¼ teaspoon washing soda per cup stock paste. Mix these also with a little hot water before adding to the mixture. Now your thickened dyepaste is ready for use!

With the color added, the Procion-M dye mixture will last 3-4 days if refrigerated between use. With the sodas added,the longevity drops to between 1-2 days.

After using the dyes, let your fabric dry for 24 hours.It must then be steam set by one of several various methods:atmospheric steaming,using a canner or steam cabinet, pressure steaming in a pressure cooker, steam baking in an oven, or steam ironing. The first two methods are discussed on p. 120, under"Notes on Steaming".I have found the next two methods adequete for most projects.

Steam ironing is the easiest way to set your fabric. Simply iron the fabric at its appropriate temperature for five minutes.It is preferable to iron on the wrong side.For delicate fabrics, do not bear down on the iron too hard. Steam baking in an oven requires rolling the fabric in butcher paper,muslin, or paper towels so that no painted surface touches any other. Place this wrapped fabric on the rack of the oven, with a container of boiling water beneath.Bake for 30 minutes at approximately 285 for fabric up to one square yard. Larger pieces should be rerolled and baked an added 30 minutes. Be sure to keep adding water in the container,so that there is an adequete amount of steam.

After steaming,unwrap the fabric, and rinse it in cold water until the water runs clear.Then increase the water temperature until the water runs clear with hot water.If desired, the fabric can then be boiled in a mild synthetic detergent(Synthrapol is being distributed by many dye suppliers especially for this purpose).

Boiling the fabric in the detergent helps to wash away any migrating dye molecules that may have bled into white areas of the fabric. Rinse your fabric in cool water, then dry it.

Rinsing out fiber-reactive dyes in a home work space can be challenging. Quite a lot of water is needed to thoroughly rinse out all the excess dye, and it is preferable to work fast to avoid dye migrating to other areas of the fabric. I find using a shower area for a large piece of fabric and a large wash basin for smaller pieces adequete.However, be sure and wipe up dye that will surely spill on the shower walls and bathroom floor.Use an apron as well to protect your clothing.

The following chart may help you with the basic principles of dye-pastes,chemical water, "thin" and "thick" applications.

DYEPASTES:a dye-paste is a mixture of dye, in this case Procion-M, and a number of chemicals which is used as a painting medium.

CHEMICAL WATER:Chemical water is made by mixing 1 tsp. Calgon,10 tbsp. Urea,2 tsp. Ludigol and adding this to 2 cups hot water.Stir well.Then add 2 cups cold water. This will make 1 quart of chemical water.

Calgon is a water softener.It is also called sodium hexametaphosphate. It chemically reacts with any minerals in tap water that might interfere with the dyeing process.

Urea is synthesized from ammonia and carbon dioxide. It is a fertilizer and retains moisture in the dyeing process.

Ludigol is a sodium salt which helps to achieve maximum color yield. It is especially crucial to use with dark colors, such as navy blue and black.

DYE AMOUNTS:For thin application, add the following amounts per quart:

pale shades-1 teas.
medium shades-4 teas.
dark shades-8 teas.
very dark shades- 16 or more teas.

The same applies for "thick" application.

THIN APPLICATION: Pour out appropriate amount of chemical water into small bowl. Add appropriate amount of dye which has been blended with a small amount of water.Then, per quart, add 4 teas. baking soda and 1 teas. washing soda,having first blended the sodas with a little water.

LONGEVITY: Chemical water can last indefinitely(try and use within a month) if refrigerated.
Thin applications of Procion-M dyes last 4 days when refrigerated. This is without sodas added.
Thin applications of Procion-M dye with sodas will last 1-2 days if refrigerated.

THICK APPLICATION: Add 4 teas. of sodium alginate to 1 quart of chemical water. Agitate. Then add appropriate amount of dye which has been blended with a little water.4 teas. of baking soda and 1 teas.of washing soda are then added,again being blended with a little water.

LONGEVITY: Longevity of thick applications are the same as for the thin.

DRYING:Let all painted fabrics dry for 24 hours.

SETTING: In most cases, set by steaming. Iron with a steam iron for 5 minutes at a temperature appropriate to the fabric.Oven steaming,pressure steaming,and atmospheric steaming also possible.

RINSING: Rinse with cold water, then increasing temperature to hot, until water runs clear. Boil with a synthetic detergent(Synthrapol is good)5 minutes,using 1/8 cup to 3 gallons of water.Rinse again in cold water. Let dry.

SODA SOAK APPLICATION

There is a "short-cut" method which can be used for both thin and thick applications. Prewash your fabric, then soak it for 15 minutes in a solution of 1 gallon of water and ½ cup of washing soda. Let the fabric dry if desired,or use it damp. Apply the thin or thick dye-paste,but omit the baking soda. After painting,let the fabric air dry for 24 hours. No steam setting is needed, simply rinse out the fabric as with the other methods and let dry.

PROCION TIPS

As can be seen,there is quite a bit to learn about using Procion,or fiber-reactive dyes.Here are a number of other ideas which may be useful.

1. Use synthetic,such as nylon, brushes when working with dye-pastes. Natural-fiber bristles absorb too much water and soon become unmanageable.

2. Always prewash your fabric.If you suspect the fabric has a permanent finish on any other type of finish,it can be removed by doing the following:

REMOVING PERMANENT PRESS FINISH

Prepare a solution of muriatic acid (a 30% solution of 30% hydrochloric acid available from Pro Chemical and Dye Company)by adding .5 liquid ounces of muriatic acid to 2 gallons of cool water. Add the fabric,putting it in an enamel or stainless steel pan. Heat over a stove to 185 degrees F and stir the fabric occasionally up to 20 minutes. Remove from heat,rinsing thoroughly.

3. The color black has some special considerations. Often it is difficult to get a true black with dyes. Procion-M does have a good black-use it up to three times stronger for desired results. Or, mix 3 parts scarlet, 3 parts yellow to 6 parts navy for a good strong black.

4. The washing soda in the grocery stores has been cut with additives which interfere with the dyeing process. It is best to order your washing soda from a supplier.

5. Painting on silk with dye-pastes requires special awareness. Procion-M dyes will only dye the silk in light to medium shades. Also, don't steam-bake or use a pressure cooker to steam silk.It can be ironed or used with the atmospheric steam technique(canning kettle or steam cabinet). Another consideration with silk is that only the low-viscosity sodium alginate should be used with it.It is much easier to wash out of the fabric. Cerulean Blue markets a Print Base Kit "L" for both silk and wool. Pro Chemical and Dye uses the PRO Thick F rather than the PRO Thick SH.

PROCION-M SUPPLIERS

As mentioned in the beginning of this section, Cerulean Blue carries Procion-M dyes. As well,Textile Resources carries the Procion-M dyes.

In the Procion-M series of dyes are included the Procion-MX dyes. These are carried by Flynns, Pro Chemical and Dye Company, and Earth Guild. There are some slight differences in each line of dyes. As well, each company has excellent literature on their products with extensive instructions for use. Always refer to these instructions as well as following what you may read in books.

The Procion-MX dyes are exceptionally brilliant. They come in about 52 different shades,and these are intermixable.They can be used on cotton,rayon,wool, and silk.They do not have to be steam set;instead of this process,replace the adding of sodas with the "soda-soak" method, described earlier in this chapter. After following this process, let the fabric set overnight,covered in plastic to prevent evaporation.

Pro Chemical and Dye,Inc.also carries Procion-MX dyes. Some of their chemicals go by brand names, and they also describe several methods of application in their literature. Their instruction booklet is quite complete,and very useful.

They also carry pre-mixed formulas which makes painting with dyes quick and easy.Some of these are PRO Print Paste Mix SH,which only needs water added to make the thick application, and PRO Print Paste Mix F, which is used for silk fabrics. They carry a pure form of sodium hexametaphosphate(or Calgon) called Metaphos. PROchem flakes is the same as Ludigol.They also carry Urea.

PROCION-H DYES

This is another type of Procion dye which is becoming very popular today with fabric painters. It is especially designed for painting and printing, and cannot be used for immersion techniques. Neither can it be mixed with the Procion-M series dyes.Another different with the Procion-H dyes is that they will react on silk with very bright and brilliant colors, rather than just tints or light shades. They are,therefore, highly recommended for painting on silk.

The other advantage of using Procion-H dyes over the M-series is that the dye-paste can be kept for 4 weeks or longer. This greatly facilitates planning and executing a painted work, for one does not have to either continually mix up the dye-paste, or count the available working days.

The third difference in Procion-H dyes is that there is little migration of dye molecules during the wash-off process. This means it is less likely that white areas of the fabric will be stained with dye.

In general, the same procedures are followed when using either type of Procion dye. The same proportions are used when making the chemical water, and the same amount of sodium alginate is used for a thick application. The only difference is that baking soda is used solely; washing soda is not added to the dye. There are approximately 16 stock colors-and they can be intermixed to make many more.If refrigerated,and without the addition of baking soda, some sources say that the stock colors can keep up to 6 months. With baking soda added, these Procion-H dyes will still keep for 1 month.Be sure to label all refrigerated items.

Procion-H dyes have the same characteristics of brightness of color, good light and washfastness, as do the Procion-M dyes. When measuring dye quantities to mix with the chemical water, I find it useful to add approximately 2x the amounts given for the M-series. For example:

pale shades-2-4 teas.
medium shades-4-8 teas.
dark shades- 12-16 teas.
very dark shades-24 or more
teaspoons. These amounts are for 1 quart of chemical water.

Add 1 teaspoon of baking soda to each cup of chemical water used,along with the proper dye amounts. Then you will be ready for painting!

In general, Procion-H dyes must be steam-set. The only exception to this is using Pro Chemical and Dye's PROFix LHF- a liquid alkali which will fix the dyes without steaming. It can only be used on cottons.Fabrics should be steamed by the atmospheric steaming method,which uses either a steam cabinet or a canning kettle.

ATMOSPHERIC STEAMING

Atmospheric steaming is accomplished by wrapping the fabric loosely in either butcher paper, muslin, or paper towel. Be sure that none of the painted surfaces touch. Place this wrapped fabric onto the rack of the canning kettle or steam cabinet.Cover the fabric with an aluminum foil "tent" so that no water or condensation gets onto the fabric. Steam the Procion-H dyes for 30 minutes.

(Refer to <u>Contemporary</u> <u>Batik</u> <u>and</u> <u>Tie-Dye</u>-Dona Meilach for a complete explanation of steaming with a canner)

OTHER STEAMING METHODS

There are alternative choices to atmospheric steaming. If you pressure steam(just like with the Procion-M dyes), steam for 5 minutes instead of 3. With oven steaming, set the oven at 300 degrees and steam for 45 minutes. And with a steam iron, iron for 10 minutes instead of 5.

Other steaming ideas are to wrap your cloth as you would for atmospheric steaming,and place it in a sauna for 15 minutes,at a temperature of 250 degrees. Or, use a shower and run hot water to create steam,but hang the fabric well away from the water source.If you live in a humid environment, you can air dry the fabric for one to two days!

PROCION-H SUPPLIERS

Cerulean Blue, Textile Resources, Flynns, and Pro Chemical and Dye Inc. are four suppliers of the bulk Procion-H dye. Pro Chem suggests mixing the Procion-H dyes with their disperse dyes in order to dye polycotton. Other than that, Procion-H dyes should not be mixed with other dyes.

PROCION-H TIPS

1. With the black dye, substitute washing soda(3 teas. per cup of chemical water) for the baking soda. This is only true for the color black in the Procion-H series. Also,it is helpful to use less urea in the chemical solution-3½ tablespoons instead of the usual 10 per quart of chemical water.

2. When steaming silk,only 15-20 minutes is needed when using Procion-H dyes. After steaming and rinsing, add 1 cup of vinegar in the final rinse to restore the lustre to the silk.

OTHER BRANDS

There are a number of other brands of Procion dye which are packaged for use with fabric painting.Some of them are marked as either Procion-M or Procion-H;others are not. They include Fabdec,Fibrec, and Dylon. There are a number of other fiber-reactive dyes as well, including Dyehouse,Aljo, and Cibacron F dyes.

Fibrec carries a dye thickener which is prepackaged,to be used for silkscreen,printing, and painting. Dylon carries "Paintex" also a thickener for painting. Dyehouse is supplied by Dharma Trading Company-they have 27 different colors and a prepackaged thickener or the bulk chemicals for use. There are a number of other fiber-reactive dyes that I have not used:Putnam Color Fast, Hi-Dye, Pylam, Calcobond, Remazol, Cavalite, Levafix, and Reactone-Geigy.Aljo Cold Process Dye has 20 different colors, and uses a gum tragacanth thickener rather than sodium alginate. They also carry the other needed chemicals in bulk.

These prepackaged dyes are especially good for beginners,since they can easily mix the dyes and focus on design and color.When working with these various dyes,keep organized and everything will go more smoothly! For example, label and date every bottle of dye before putting it in the refrigerator.Make a chart with samples when mixing your own colors-this way you can easily repeat your favorite color mixtures. If you work with one type of dye until you are comfortable with it,less confusion will occur with the great variety of dyes available.

QUALITIES OF PROCION DYES

In order to sum up the vast amount of information about Procion dyes, the following chart may be helpful:

Use: Extremely popular and very versatile

Quality: Excellent quality art material for fabric painting

Price: Very economical

Usage: fairly complex to learn how to use

Hand: Excellent hand

Washability: Good to excellent

Usage: used for many items;T-shirts,tops,pants, dresses,pillow-cases, lampshades,curtains,wall hangings,soft sculpture,etc.

Fabrics used:cotton,linen,rayon (viscose),silk, and wool. Only natural fibers that do not have a finish of any sort can be used

Productivity:Good results,once dyes are mixed

Availability:art stores, fiber/needlework stores, many suppliers

Lightfastness: Good to excellent

How set? steam iron,oven steaming, pressure steaming, or atmospheric steaming

CIBACRON-F DYES

Cibacron-F is another type of fiber reactive dye. (It is sometimes called Cibacron Reactive dye or Ciba dye) It is a lower reactive dye than the Procion-M or MX dye,meaning that it takes a longer time for the dye to completely react. 24 hours is needed for it to cure.

There are 20 different colors available from Pro Chemical and Dye; it is also available from Straw into Gold. These colors can be intermixed with each other,but it is best not to mix them with other fiber reactive dyes.

Since these are fiber-reactive dyes,they follow the same process

as do the Procion dyes. One advantage is that they may be stored for up to two weeks(refrigerated and without the added soda) with no color loss. They do not need to be steam set; rather they can be "cold-batched"(the name for the process of letting the fabric cure for 24 to 48 hours under a protective plastic wrap)

LIQUID FIBER-REACTIVE DYES

There is one more type of fiber-reactive dye available to the fabric painter:the liquid variety. There are several brands on the market at this time;Createx Liquid Fiber Reactive Dyes,put out by Color Craft Ltd., Liquid Fiber Reactive "R Series" Dyes,also by Createx, Liquid Procion H Fiber Reactive Dyes, new from Cerulean Blue,and Liquid Reactive Dyes from Pro Chemical and Dye. In general, these dyes are used in a manner similar to the powdered reactive dyes. They are mixed with a chemical water solution,and can be thickened with sodium alginate. One reason for using these dyes in a liquid form is that there is less danger from inhaling the airborne powder of the dry dye.

The dyes can be fixed by a number of methods.They can be air cured if you live in a warm, humid environment. Let hang for 2-3 days. Or put in a clothes dryer for 30 minutes on the highest setting.They can be steamed. They can be treated using the "soda-soak" method described on p.104 . They can be baked in an oven for 15 minutes at 225 degrees. They can be ironed for 5 minutes at a steam setting appropriate to the fabric used. Pro Chemical and Dye has an additional curing method which uses a fixative named PRO FIX LHF. PRO FIX LHF cannot be used on wool, and it should be handled with caution as it contains a strong alkali. Createx products offers a special solution, called 'Fast Fix' which eliminates any type of heat-setting. It works on cotton, linen, rayon, and silk.

Createx Liquid dyes are unique also in that they can be used on some synthetic fibers-nylon and lycra, specifically. Their "R Series" Dyes do not need heat for fixation on certain fabrics: silk, wool, nylon, and lycra. Citric Acid is used as the fixative, and can be ordered through them.

SUMMARY OF FIBER-REACTIVES

As can be seen, there are a great many different fiber-reactive dyes available to the fabric painter. They are a very popular kind of dye,since their colors and bright and their fastness is good.

Procion-MX dyes are the most highly reactive dye on the market.They are followd by the Procion-M dyes, then Cibacron-F(half as reactive as the MX's),then come the liquid fiber-reactive dyes at 10 times less reactivity than the MX dyes,and at the last,the Procion-H dyes. Depending upon your method of work and what you are doing, each one of these types of dye can be your best choice. Just remember that, the more reactive the dye, the faster it loses its full color,and the less likely that you will be able to store it.On the other hand, the dyes that are highly reactive need less complicated forms of fixing or steaming(the MX dyes need no steaming at all)

DISPERSE DYES

Disperse dyes are the next catagory of dyes to be discussed. They can be used in two ways: as a transfer paint or for direct application using chemical water and thickeners. In Chapter VI, under "Transfer Painting" (pp.188-89),directions are given for using disperse dyes as a transfer paint.I will discuss here the methods of direct application.

Disperse dyes are used for synthetic materials. They can be used on acetate,triacetate(Arnel),nylon,lycra, dacron, kodel, fortrel, and mylar,as well as polyesters and synthetic blends. Disperse dye is very concentrated; a little goes a long way.

Disperse dyes are available from a number of suppliers, including Dharma Trading Company (Polydye), Pro Chemical and Dye(PROsperse disperse dye),

disperse dye(from Cerulean Blue, among others) and Aljo acetate-nylon dyes.Color ranges vary,depending on which company you use. A standard range of nine colors, from yellow, orange,scarlet, fuchsia,black, violet, navy blue,royal blue, and turquoise is possible. Aljo differs in that they offer 22 intermixable colors, including lemon yellow,indian yellow,golden brown, dark brown, sky blue,emerald green, hunter green, pink, baby pink, rose, magenta, and pearl grey.

Disperse dyes are mixed with the same chemical water and sodium alginate thickener that is used for the fiber-reactive dyes.To refresh your memory, use 1 teas. Calgon or other water softener,10 Tbsp. Urea,2 tsp. Ludigol,and add 2 cups of cold water to this mixture. Then add 2 cups of hot water, mixing well. For a thick mixture, sprinkle up to 4 tsp. of sodium alginate into the chemical water. Then add ¼ to 4 teas.of dye per cup of chemical water.One important change with the disperse dyes is that,for each teas. of dye used, add 1 Tbsp. of white vinegar.Another change is that monogum thickener is often used with disperse dyes rather than sodium alginate. Add 2 teas. of monogum(available through Cerulean Blue, among others)to 1 quart of water,sprinkling the thickener over the chemical water until it is thoroughly mixed.

After direct application of the dyes, fix in the following ways: steam iron for several minutes at a setting appropriate to the fabric used; bake at 375 degrees for 45-90 seconds(watch carefully-synthetic fabrics can burn easily);or pressure steam at 260 degrees for 30 minutes.Replace the urea with water(10 tbsp) when using this method of fixation.

The fabric should now be rinsed, just like for fiber-reactive dyes. Start with cold water,increasing the temperature to hot.Use Synthrapol or Ivory Liquid to wash the fabric. Follow with a hot water rinse, and you will minimize the problem of "bleeding".

Disperse dyes that are applied directly have a different effect than those applied by heat-transfer. With direct application, the dyes appear very soft,with slight blending into the fibers due to capillary action.Watercolor effects, with blending of colors on top of each other, is possible. By using a greater amount of thickener,hard-edged looks are possible.However, with heat-transfer,textures are possible since the painted paper can be crumpled or torn before being transferred by ironing to the fabric.

QUALITIES OF DISPERSE DYES

To sum up disperse dyes,refer to the chart below:

Use:moderate use by craftspeople. Especially useful and versatile where synthetic materials are used

Quality: Good quality art material

Price: very economical,as it is highly concentrated

Hand: Excellent hand

Washability:Very good

Usage:used especially for dancewear, costumes for the theatre,hoisery and lingerie,accessories such as scarves. Also used for outerwear,dresses and blouses,curtains,etc.

Fabrics used:Polyesters and synthetics such as acetate, nylon, acrylics, plastics,mylar, dacron,etc

Productivity: Good results

Availability:primarily ordered through dye houses and fiber arts supplies

Usage:Fairly easy to learn how to use

Lightfastness: Very good

How set? steam iron,pressure steaming, oven baking.

ACID DYES

Acid dyes are used on silk,wool, and nylon. There are quite a variety of them,including Acid dyes (Textile Resources),Miyako, Ciba Kiton (Pro Chem, Cerulean Blue),PRO Washfast acid dyes(Pro Chem)Aljo Silk and Wool Acid dyes,Fezan Batik dyes,plus Calcocid(Cyanamid),Ciba Acid, and Lanaset(Cerulean Blue).

Some of these dyes are for use on silk and wool, others for wool and nylon. There are different processes for the different fabric types, and various brands have a variety of recipes that are used. Therefore, it can be seen that working with acid dyes is a complex procedure.

There are a number of different chemicals used with acid dyes.These include glycerin(available at most all drugstores), tartaric acid(available at a medical pharmacy),glacial acetic acid(available at photographic supply stores)acetic acid(photographic or dye suppliers will carry this),ammonium sulfate(available from dye supply houses),and ammonium oxalate(also available from dye houses).White vinegar is also used in some recipes. Sodium alginate and locust bean thickener(indalca gum) are also used to thicken acid dyes.

These chemicals should be handled with extreme care,as some of them are poisonous.Wear a mask,rubber gloves, and a plastic apron,and do not work around a kitchen area.

One of the difficulties in using acid dyes is that each color acts individually-there are no hard and fast rules that are true for all colors. Also, the dyes act differently depending on the fiber or fabric used. The primaries red,yellow, and blue do not dye well on silk(of the Ciba Kiton series),as they will only yield tints or pastel shades.Tests must be made in order to be assured of certain colors.

Acid dyes give brilliant colors, and this is one of their best features. Although they are lightfast, some sources suggest keeping them away from direct sunlight. Their washfastness is not good, and it is best to have articles dry-cleaned. The one exception to this is the series PRO Washfast Acid Dyes, which gives very good washfastness and fair lightfastness.

Most suppliers stock between 11-14 colors except Aljo, which carries 30 different colors, including rubine, lily rose, violamine, milling blue, topas yellow, and pearl grey. All the acid dye colors can be intermixed to expand your palette.

ACID DYE RECIPES

There are a number of recipes for acid dyes. Several will be given here; look for others in books on fabric dyeing as well as instructions given with the acid dyes themselves.

Thickened dye for silk, using glycerin and tartaric acid:
Sprinkle ½ teas. dye over ¼ C. water. Add 1 Tbsp. glycerin. Heat this mixture briefly until the dye is warmed and dissolves. Cool. Then add ½ cup of thickener.(See below)Then dissolve 1½ teas. of tartaric acid in 1½ teas. of hot water. Stir this into the mixture to make ½ cup of dye paste.

Thickener for acid dyes on silk

To make 2 cups:
½ teas. Calgon
2 C. hot water
2 teas. sodium alginate
Add together and mix well.

After painting, steam set the fabric. Different weight fabrics use different methods. For example, light-weight silk such as China silk can be steam set with an iron. Heavier silks and light-weight wools can be oven-steamed or put in a steam cabinet. Heavyweight wools and heavy silks must be steamed in a pressure cooker or autoclave. Steam for 1 hour at 185 degrees. Rinse in cold water, gradually increas-

ing the temperature of the water. Wash with a light detergent to minimize bleeding.

Fezan 'Batik'Dye for Silk with thickener
Take 1 Tbsp.(heaping)dye and mix a little hot water with it. Then add ¼ C. white vinegar,Add 3/4 teas. of plain salt,then add 2 cups of hot water. Stir this mixture,then add 2 cups of cold water.Finally, sprinkle from ¼ to ½ teas. of sodium alginate over this mixture and agitate it. After painting,steam fabric,then rinse it until water runs clear. For best results,dry clean fabric to remove thickener.

Here is a recipe for making liquid silk dyes from acid dye. Take 1 teas. glacial acetic acid and mix with 1 teas. acid dye.Mix this with a morter and pestle until it is blended. Then slowly add two cups of hot water.This mixture can be stored indefinitely.

This liquid dye can be used directly on the fabric with the serti method-that is,painting on silk using gutta as a resist.Or,one can use a thickener,such as the ones listed below:

Gum Arabic thickener for acid dyes(for silk, wool, or nylon)

To make 1 cup:
¼ teas. Calgon
1 C. hot water
3 Tablespoons gum arabic(or more if needed)
Gum Tragacanth thickener

To make 2 cups:
½ teas. Calgon
2 cups hot water
2 teas. gum tragacanth

Locust bean(indalca gum)thickener

To make 2 cups:
½ teas. Calgon
2 cups hot water
1 teas. locust or carob bean flakes

With all these recipes, the thickening agent is sprinkled on top of the water, and then mixed thoroughly. Let the solution sit for at least 10 minutes before using.

Thickened dye for silk,wool,or nylon,using Ciba Kiton dyes
Make a thickener by adding 1 teas. Calgon to 2 cups water;then sprinkle up to 4 teas. sodium alginate on top.
Mix ½ teas. dye with 2 teas. glycerin.Add 1/8 C. boiling water. Let cool.
Dissolve 1 teas. ammonium oxalate in 1 tablespoon hot water. Then add ¼ C. of the thickener.Add the dye mixture to this,plus ½ C. water.
After painting, steam fix for 1 hour,under moist steam conditions. Then rinse under cold running water and wash with Synthrapol to minimize bleeding. Rinse again in cold water.

TIPS FOR ACID DYEING

1. If using acetic acid,white vinegar can be substituted. 2 tbsp. of acetic acid equals ½ C. vinegar.

2. Although acid dyes do tend to migrate on the fabric,causing bleeding,and because they are not generally washfast,it is possible to handwash silk in cool water with a mild soap. This will help washability.

SUMMARY OF ACID DYES

Use:Moderate among fabric painters. More popular among weavers and those who dye their own wool.Used a lot by silk painters, however

Quality:quality of acid dyes varies with the type dye;in general,a good quality paint material

Price: very reasonable

Usage: quite complex to use,with many chemicals,some of them dangerous.

Hand: Excellent

Washability: fair to poor,except for PRO Washfast Acid Dyes.

Usage: silk scarves, blouses, dresses;wool clothing,nylon clothing and accessories

Fabrics used: silk, wool,nylon, other animal or protein fibers, some other synthetics

Productivity: fair,since mixing dyes takes time;also complex procedures in applying and steaming

Availability: ordered primarily through dye houses and fiber arts supplies

Lightfastness: good

How set? steaming by oven or pressure or steam cabinet or autoclave

The colors of acid dyes are what makes their use worthwhile for the fabric painter. By testing a variety of colors, one can create a vocabulary of beautiful, brilliant colors.

DIRECT DYES

Direct dyes are in less use today because they have been surpassed by dyes with greater washability. Still,they are inexpensive, easily available, and easy to use, so they are good for the beginning fabric painter.Some of the brands available are Miyako(Aiko's Art Supplies),Calcomine(Cyanamid),Aljo Cotton and Rayon Dye(Aljo Mfg.Co.), Deka-L,(Textile Resources, Earth Guild, Cerulean Blue),and Fezan.
Direct dyes are used on natural fibers and fabrics such as cotton, linen, silk, wool, and viscose rayon. They are available in a range of 33 colors, including antique rose, wine red, cornflower blue,russian green,salmon, copper,old gold,fawn,

mode brown, and deep black. Direct dyes are one kind of dye where it is possible to get a true black on cotton. Direct dyes are attracted to cellulose fibers, and the colors are good. For direct painting, it is suggested that double the amount of dye be used.

Washability varies with direct dyes. One solution to this is to handwash each item separately in cool water with a mild detergent. Another solution is to dry clean all items. And a third is to use a product called Fixanol(distributed by Straw Into Gold). The fabric is soaked in this solution after dyeing and it improves washability.

There are several ways to thicken the dye. One is to follow the procedure for fiber-reactive dyes, and omit the sodas. Or, use the following recipe:

    1-2 teas. dye
    5 teas. urea
    3/4 cup hot water
Mix dye and urea with hot water. Add 1 Cup plus 3 Tbsp. thickener (gum tragacanth) which is made in the following way:
    Sprinkle 2 teas. gum tragacanth over 2 C. hot water. This will make 2 cups of thickener.
    Add 1.5 teas. disodium hydrogen phosphate(available at a pharmacy) and mix well. Then apply to fabric.

Direct dyes must be steamed thoroughly in order to approach fastness. Steam for 1 hour using either a steam cabinet or an autoclave.

Although the washfastness and lightfastness of direct dyes vary, they have very nice colors and are an inexpensive way for the beginner to experiment with dye-pastes.

SUMMARY OF DIRECT DYES

Use: Declining but still available

Quality: only a fair paint material due to dubious washfastness

Price: Inexpensive

Usage: very easy to use

Hand: Excellent

Washability: varies, but generally poor to fair

Usage: clothing and other fabric items

Fabrics used: natural fabrics such as cotton, linen, silk, wool, and viscose rayon

Productivity: In terms of time, good, but not recommended for salable items

Availability: readily available in fiber/needlework stores and dye suppliers

Lightfastness: fair to good

How set?: by steaming

HOUSEHOLD DYES

Household dyes are a blend of a variety of dyes, most commonly acid and direct. They are very good to use with blends of fabric, such as poly/cotton or synthetic blends, for more of the dye will "take". A cotton fabric will only use the direct part of the dye, while the other dye molecules will wash off in the rinse. The same is true if you are painting on silk or wool; the acid dyes will react, while the direct dyes will wash off. One way to get deeper colors is to double the amount of dye used for hot dyeing when painting with dye-pastes.

Household dyes can be used on cotton, linen, silk, viscose rayon, wool, acetate, nylon, and synthetic and polyester blends. They are readily available in grocery stores, drugstores, or dimestores. They are sometimes called 'union dyes'. Some of the brand names are: Rit, Tintex, Putnam All Purpose, Cushings, Dylon Multipurpose, and Union.

Household dyes are not particularly

lightfast or washfast.They can, however, be drycleaned.Or,wash each item separately in lukewarm water.This will prolong their washfastness.

Here are some recipes for dye-pastes using household dyes:

     1 teas. dye
     1 teas. Glauber's salt
     5 tbsp. glycerin
     3/4 cup water
     1 c. thickener(sodium algi-
nate or gum tragacanth)
This recipe is for cotton and cotton blends, linen,other cellulose fibers.This recipe will dye synthetics to a pastel shade.I also found the washfastness of this recipe very good;there was no migration of dye during the washoff as there was with the direct dyes thickened with sodium alginate.

This is a recipe for silk and wool,using household dyes:

     1 teas. dye
     5 Tbsp. glycerin
     1 Tbsp. acetic acid
     ½ C. water
     1 C. gum tragacanth thickener
In both these recipes, mix the dye, Glauber's salt or acetic acid, and glycerin together and heat briefly until the dye is dissolved.Cool, then add thickener.After painting, steam fabric by atmospheric steaming, pressure steaming,or oven steaming. Small test pieces can be steam-ironed.Rinse and wash with a mild detergent.

Household dyes can be usedful for beginners as they are easy to find and their washfastness is fair. However,fiber-reactive dyes are far superior for long-term use.Another use of household dyes is for over-dyeing of fabrics. Certain painted works using white fabric can be overdyed with no change in color. Household dyes are good for this.

SUMMARY OF HOUSEHOLD DYES

Use:used primarily by beginning fabric painters

Quality: fair to good

Price: moderately expensive except for use in small amounts(due to high packaging costs)

Usage: Fairly easy to use

Hand: excellent

Washability:moderate but varies

Usage: good for beginner's projects, small samples,casual clothing such as T-shirts

Fabrics used: natural fibers and synthetic blends-cotton,linen,viscose rayon,silk, wool, and synthetic and polyester blends

Productivity:good

Availability:readily available

Lightfastness:fair to good

How set?:by steaming-atmospheric, pressure, or oven-steaming 45 minutes

BASIC DYES

Basic dyes are known for their brilliant colors.They can be used with a thickener on cotton,linen, wool, silk, and synthetics,but the cotton and linen fabrics must be mordanted,either before or after applying the dye-paste. There are several brands available,including Aljo Alcohol/Water Dye(Aljo Mfg.Co.), Batik Tintout Dyes(IVY Crafts),Astrazon(Mobay Chemical Corporation), and Calcozine (Cyanamid). These last two suppliers only carry bulk amounts(100 pounds and up),and require repackaging charges. The first two suppliers are recommended for most craft purposes.

Up to 22 different colors are available, including gold,dark brown, red, pink, black,fuchsia, sky blue, and turquoise.The colors are intermixable for a greater variety of combinations.The washfastness and lightfastness of basic dyes is not good;therefore it is best to make items that will not receive direct sunlight.Basic dyes can,however, tolerate artificial light. They should be drycleaned,if possible since their washfastness is poor.

There are several different procedures for using the thickened dyes. For cotton or linen,the fabric must be mordanted either before or after the painting process. In the following recipe,the mordanting occurs afterwards.

BASIC DYE-PASTE ON COTTON

    1-4 teas. dye
    5 teas. glycerin
    4 teas. glacial acetic acid
Mix these ingredients together.Add:
    1/3 C. hot water.Mix together with this
    2 teas. tartaric acid
Let this mixture cool and then add:
    1¼C. of thickener,either gum arabic or gum tragacanth)
(see pg.110 for thickener recipes)
Then mix 5 teas. of tannic acetic acid by mixing 2/3 teas. tannic acid and 2/3 teas. glacial acetic acid with 4 teas. of water;add this to previous mixture.

After painting,steam fabric for 1 hour.Then immerse the fabric in a bath of 1 teas. of tartar emetic mixed in 2 cups of hot water. Immerse only for 30 seconds,then rinse fabric in cold water.

Tannic acid,tartar emetic,glacial acetic acid,and glycerin can be purchased through a pharmacy.

BASIC DYE-PASTE ON SILK AND WOOL

    1-2 teas. dye
    2½ teas. glycerin
    2½ teas. glacial acetic acid
    2½ teas. cold water
Mix these substances together.Then add:
    3/4 C. hot water. Mix well.
Then add a gum arabic or gum tragacanth thickener(pg.110).Add 1C.plus 1½ tablespoons thickener.
    Dissolve 5 teas. tartaric acid in 5 teas. of water.
Mix this into the dye mixture. Apply to silk or wool fabric.After the fabric is dry, steam for 1 hour. Rinse in lukewarm water.

BASIC DYE-PASTE FOR SYNTHETICS

    1-2 teas. dye
    2½ teas. glycerin
    2½ teas. glacial acetic acid
    3/4 C. plus 4 teas. warm water
Mix these ingredients together. Add:
    1 C. thickener(gum arabic or gum tragacanth)
After painting, steam fabric for 1 hour. Rinse in warm water.

Basic dyes are not widely used by fabric painters. This is due primarily to their poor washability and lightfastness.However, they are effective for painting on silk and they are considerably less in price than the liquid silk dyes. Their bright,brilliant colors are their "selling point".

SUMMARY OF BASIC DYES

Use: limited usage

Quality: fair to good

Price: reasonable

Usage:easy to use on silk,wool, and synthetics;slightly more complicated on cotton and linen

Hand:excellent

Washability:generally poor;dry cleaning recommended

Usage:good for silk clothing and accessories;other synthetics such as scarves,acrylic knits

Fabrics used:natural fibers are possible but best results on silk, wool and synthetics

Productivity:good

Availability:not easily available

Lightfastness:good on synthetics but not natural fibers

How set?:Steam set

PRE-METALIZED DYES

There are several pre-metalized dyes in use for fabric painting.They are Cibalan and Irgalan. Cibalan is available from Cerulean Blue;however,they are stocking a new dye,Lanaset,and their Cibalan dyes are being discontinued.Pre-metalized dyes are very lightfast and good in their washfastness.While their colors are not brilliant, I find them to produce deep shades on most types of fabrics.

There are only 10 different colors,but they can be intermixed. Certain shades are deeper than others, and are called super milling dyes. Pre-metalized dyes can be used for silk,wool, nylon, and certain synthetic blends. When used as a dye-paste,the dye does not spread or migrate. This gives hard-edged,clear images,a desirable feature of the dye.

RECIPES FOR DYE-PASTES

The following recipe can also be used with acid dyes. However, with pre-metalized dyes, the recipe will work on synthetic blends as well as the standard silk,wool, and nylon.

1-4 teas. dye
5 teas. glycerin
2/3 C. water
Mix these substances together and heat briefly,until dye dissolves. Cool. Then add 1¼ C. of thickener, either gum arabic or gum tragacanth. (See pg.110 for recipes for thickeners)
  Mix 2½ teas. tartaric acid with 2½ teas. water. Add this to the thickened dye paste.

Note: When painting on silk,add only 2½,rather than 5,teas. of glycerin

After painting fabric,let it dry and then steam for 1 hour. Rinse,wash in a mild detergent,and rinse again in cool water. When rinsing nylon fabric first rinse in a mixture of 3/8 teas. washing soda per quart of water.Then wash in a mild detergent. Then rinse again with 2 teas. of white vinegar mixed in 1 quart water. This will minimize "bleeding".

Pre-metalized dyes are especially good for use with direct painting. They can be used on a wide variety of fabrics,and they do not bleed. Their washfastness and lightfastness are also good. Here is a summary of their qualities:

SUMMARY OF PRE-METALIZED DYES

Use:a somewhat popular paint material

Quality: a high quality dye

Price: reasonable

Usage:fairly straightforward some mixing of hazardous chemicals

Hand: Excellent

Washability:very good

Usage: particularly recommended for synthetic blends,silk,and wool; scarves,dresses,other clothing and accessories;also wall hangings,curtains,quilts,etc.
Fabrics used:silk,wool,nylon, and some synthetic blends

Productivity:Good

Availability: not readily available

Lightfastness:very good

How set?: steam-set

LANASET DYES

I want to mention briefly the new Lanaset dyes that Cerulean Blue is substituting for both their Ciba Kiton Acid Dyes and their Cibalan Pre-metalized Dyes.These dyes have good washfastness and lightfastness;they are available in 15 intermixable colors. These colors produce more stable results on different fibers,such as silk and wool.They are a wool reactive and 1:2 metal complex dye.

VAT DYES

Although there are a variety of vat dyes, only Inkodye will be discussed here as it is a soluble vat dye with the quite hazardous chemicals already mixed in.Inkodye is available from Screen Process Supplies Mfg. Co. in Oakland, CA.

There are 14 intermixable colors and an extender, called Inko Clear. Inkodye,like other vat dyes, appears clear or pale until sunlight develops the colors.Therefore,color mixing cannot be done by dye,and making test swatches is extremely important.Colors are mixed like pigment-red and yellow make orange;yellow and blue make green; and red and blue make purple. The simplist way to make tests of colors is to use a hot iron to develop them quickly.

Inkodye is sometimes called a "sun dye" as it is most common to develop the colors outdoors on a sunny day. This type of paint material is also popular with children as it is premixed, easy to use, and fun to apply!The colors are exceptionally light and washfast.

Inkodye can be used on natural fibers such as cotton,linen, and viscose rayon(Inko Silk Dye,which is used on silk,will be discussed under "Liquid Dyes"). It can also be

FIG. 97: A CAFTAN BY SUZANNE LARSEN. POLYCOTTON-WRINKLE GAUZE DYED WITH CUSHING DYES.LINES DRAWN WITH INKODYE.

FIG. 96: JUDY HANKIN IN EUGENE,OR. USING INKODYE TO PAINT A SILK PARACHUTE

116

used on certain synthetics and fabrics with a finish.

To use Inkodye, simply use from the bottle,with or without a thickener. Sodium alginate can be sprinkled on top of the dye and left to sit for 10 minutes or so. Sunlight will develop the colors in 30 minutes. Some artists like working under a sunlamp,for they can see the colors as they develop.While still damp, the fabric can be ironed,and the colors will develop this way as well. If you prefer to let the fabric dry, steam iron the fabric.Another method of processing the color is to oven bake at 280 degrees for 15 minutes up to 1 hour. Check the fabric periodically to make sure it is not scorching.

No further setting is needed.Just wash and rinse the fabric. Keep the Inkodye away from the light. Store it in a cool,dry place away from the light and it will last for up to 2 years.

Inkodye is an easy-to-use paint material for all ages. Its results are pleasing,as well.To summarize:

SUMMARY OF VAT DYES(INKODYE)

Use:popular use with versatility

Quality: a good quality paint material

Price:reasonable

Usage: very easy to use

Hand:excellent

Washability:excellent

Usage:Children's projects such as T-shirts,toys,dolls;also quilts, clothing,accessories

Fabrics used: cotton,linen,viscose rayon,some synthetics

Productivity:very good

Availability: available from dye houses

Lightfastness:very good

How set?:by ironing, oven baking or exposing to sunlight

NAPHTHOL DYES

Although naphthol dyes can be thickened and used for direct painting, I am not including them in this book. They require the use of strong chemicals,such as lye, and they are no longer easy to find.

LIQUID DYES

There are quite a number of liquid dyes on the market today.They are primarily for silk,but there are a few other types. They include Inko Silk Batik Dye(available from Screen Process Supplies),Tinfix,Super Tinfix,Tinsilk(all from IVY Crafts Imports),SeriTint Liquid Dyes(Straw into Gold), Seidicolor((Dharma Trading Co.),Princefix Color(Textile Resources and Sureway Trading Enterprises)and Du Pont Silk Dyes(Sureway Trading). Some liquid dyes for other fabrics include Tincoton and Tincoton II (IVY Crafts Imports)and Du Pont dyes for cotton(Sureway Trading Enterprises).Some of the above mentioned suppliers carry more than the one particular dye indicated.

I shall discuss these dyes depending on the type fabric they are used with. The most extensive dyes are the silk liquid dyes.

SILK DYES

Silk dyes are often an acid dye or a mixture of acid and direct dyestuffs. Since they are premixed,they are ready to use without any added chemicals or procedures.They come in a wide variety of colors,depending on the brand,and can be intermixed.Often they are used with gutta, a resist which is used with the French gutta serti method of painting on silk. Most silk dyes require steaming,but there are some brands which bypass this step.

Inko Silk Batik Dye has 8 colors and a clear. This dye is thicker than many of the others,and therefore is much easier to control without using a resist.It is a mixture of acid and direct dyes. Tinfix is an acid dye.They are manufactured in France by the Sennelier Company; if you come across 'Sennelier Silk Dyes',reference is being made to one of the Tinfix dyes. These dyes come in 58 different,brilliant colors. Tinfix dyes can also be used with a Silkscreening Thickener to achieve hard-edged results.(IVY Crafts Imports carries this thickener). Some of the colors include: Chinese Vermillion, Peony Red,Pollen Yellow,Tyrien Pink,Persian Blue,Almond Green,Prussian Blue,Nut Brown, Indigo, Slate Blue,and Rosewood.Both of the above dyes need to be steamed.

Super Tinfix is also an acid dye. It is a concentrated form of dye, and must be mixed with a solution of water and alcohol. There are 22 colors which must also be steamed.Tinsilk varies from these other dyes in that they do not need to be steamed. They are an acid dye,available in 21 different colors. After applying directly,let dry for 48 hours.Some of these intermixable colors include: Anthracite, Tropical Blue,Persian Red, Moss Green,California Poppy,and Cinnamon.Tinsilk,like Tinfix,is fairly liquid; a resist is helpful unless watercolor effects are desired(one of liquid dyes' assets!)

SeriTint Liquid Dye is another liquid dye used for silk. There are 49 colors-Buttercup,Watermelon,French Rose,Blueberry,Holly Green,Blue Spruce, Jade,Curry, Cappuccino,Butternut Brown, Terra Cotta,Champagne,and Eggplant. Fabric painted with SeriTint is machine washable-a unique feature.SeriTint can be used with or without a thickener.Seidicolor Colors are another silk dye that can be used without steaming.After painting the dye on silk,let dry and then brush on a Fixer. Let the fixer sit for 1 hour, and wash off. Seidicolor Colors are often used with the Seidicolor Resists especially the colored resists! These

are unusually nice resists available in 10 colors. This allows you to paint and apply a resist simultaneously. These resist colors will not be removed with either washing or drycleaning.Seidicolor Colors offer a unique silk painting experience with both resist,fixer,and no steaming.As well, the dye can be thickened with sodium alginate.Simply sprinkle a little sodium alginate over a small amount of dye. Agitate, then let sit for up to 10 minutes or until dye appears to have thickened.

I have used all these silk dyes and find them all to be a very satisfactory paint material. The following silk dyes I have not tested,but they are a popular paint material,used by others. Princefix Color Concentrate comes in 29 colors,including Corn Poppy,Geranium, Red Cherry,Pansy Hearts,Petrole Blue,Night Blue,Hazel Nut,and Bordeaux Wine. These brilliant colors require no steaming,only hand washing after painting. The Princefix dye is mixed before painting with a Dilutant-Fixative to make the colors permanent. Du Pont Dyes Par Excellence for silk come in 170 colors!They also carry a thickener for silkscreening and handpainting.Pebeo Nebotatik is another silk dye with 20 colors.It is available from Sureway Trading Enterprises.

PAINTING ON SILK

To paint on silk with these dyes, it is best to have the silk stretched,either with a regular frame stretcher,or a substitute such as an embroidery hoop. Use a light touch with these paints,and use their spreading action to advantage in your design. Watercolor and wash brushes are especially suited to working on the fragile surface of silk.For those paints and dyes which need steaming,a few guidelines may be helpful.

STEAMING SILK DYES

In order for the colors to be fast,

many silk dyes must be steamed. They need dry steam rather than wet steam in order that the dyes do not run.

Pressure steaming or atmospheric steaming are the best techniques to use. To pressure steam, roll the silk in an absorbent paper(steaming paper is available from IVY Crafts Imports and other suppliers). Seal the ends of the paper with adhesive tape. Carefully fold in sections and put into the wire basket of a pressure cooker. Be sure and place the basket on a trivet so that its bottom will not touch the bottom of the pan. Add ½" of water. Cover the rolled fabric bundle with a hood of aluminum foil. This will keep condensation from touching the paper, thus wetting the fabric. In one recipe, the next step is to steam for 45 minutes. Another recipe suggests bringing the pressure cooker up to 3 pounds of pressure before putting in the fabric bundle. Then steam for 20 minutes. With a regular steamer or steam cabinet, follow instructions for its use.

These silk dyes can also be used on wool. Other liquid dyes for other fabrics include dyes for polyesters and cotton. Polydyes are supplied by both IVY Crafts Imports and Roscoe Haussmann. Both brands have 9 intermixable colors and do not require the addition of chemicals or steaming. Tincoton and Tincoton II(available from IVY Crafts Imports)can be used on cotton, linen, and other vegetable fibers. The Tincoton II does not need steaming, while the Tincoton does. They come in 15 intermixable colors. A fixative is used with the Tincoton II dyes in place of steaming. I found that the Tincoton dyes were not especially bright; the colors are subtle. Mli Dyes by Du Pont are another liquid dye for cotton. They are available from Sureway Trading Enterprises. And lastly, there are Fabric Colors by Rosco Haussmann used for silk, wool, and certain synthetic stretch fabrics. They come in 15 colors, with a thickener and fabric resist. They must be steam-set.

DISCHARGE DYES

Discharge dyeing is really a process of bleaching or lightening colors. A thickened paste can be made, or a premixed paste, called Inko Discharge Paste, can be used. In both cases, the areas that are applied with the discharge will, in some cases, totally remove the color and in others will lighten it. Interesting effects can be created by painting, then discharging, then overpainting. The discharge process can be used on colored fabrics to lighten certain areas; then these areas can be painted.

To make a thickener, mix ½ C. hot water, ¼ teas. Calgon, and about 1 teas. sodium alginate. The amount of the alginate can vary, depending on how thick you wish the paste to be. Add ¼ C. liquid bleach and mix well. I have found this mixture to be very effective on cotton and cotton blends, both colored fabrics and painted white fabrics. Do not use the discharge process on silk or other delicate fabrics, as the bleach may weaken the fibers and ruin the fabric.

DYEING ON COLORED FABRICS

No mention was made in the summaries of the various dyes as to how the dyes would react on colored fabrics. This is due to the fact that, unlike paints, which can be made more opaque with an "opaque white", dyes react with the fiber molecules. Most dyes will, therefore, change color when painted on already colored fabrics. The same principle works when under and overpainting with thickened dyes.

OVERDYEING PAINTED FABRICS

There are some instances where overdyeing of the fabric is desirable. Sometimes it is not desirable to always paint on a white background; yet painting on already dyed or colored fabric does not yield the desired results. One solution is to overdye the white fabric after painting. Acrylics work best with this, as there will be no color change. Oil paints also work well with overdyeing. Certain markers or dye pastels may change color, especially the lighter colors. Many times the colors will be more subdued after overdyeing.

Textile paints vary in their response to overdyeing. On a test run using Eurotex fabric colors, Texticolor Iridescent, and Createx Hi-Lite Colors, I found that the last two did not change color with an overdye of household dye-paste. The Eurotex blended with the dye when both were wet, creating a lovely purple color. The textile paint that was not covered with the dye remained blue.

Another instance where overdyeing is desirable is when working with fragile art materials for fabric painting. For example, there are a number of art materials that are not washable, and really are not suited for fabrics. Yet, when overdyed, they can be used for certain types of articles. One example of this is using chalk pastels to draw on muslin. By overdyeing, the fragile pastel is stabilized.

There are two ways of overdyeing pieces of fabric. Small pieces can be painted with a dye-paste, preferably with a large brush. Large pieces of fabric, as for clothing, should be immersed in a dye-bath. Fiber-reactive dyes are especially suited for this.

NOTES ON STEAMING

1) Steaming may look harder than it really is! Reading about it is really more complicated than the actual process.

2) First, wrap your fabric in paper towels. Then wrap with newsprint or in muslin. Be sure no part of the fabric touches itself. This is your fabric bundle.

3) Be sure that the bundle does not touch the edges of the pot used for steaming. Wrap the fabric loosely enough so that the steam can get to the fabric.

4) With a canning kettle, which is atmospheric steaming, wrap the bundle in a "tent" of aluminum foil and steam 15 minutes. Some fabrics will take up to 1 hour to steam.

5) Protect the fabric bundle by wrapping other protective material around the bundle. Do not let this protective material touch the sides of the pan, either.

6) For both oven steaming and steaming with a canner, have the water steaming before putting the fabric bundle into the oven or pot.

7) Look for steamers at a restaurant or hospital supply house. You may be able to purchase them used.

8) Most dyes need 1 hour of steaming between 180 and 210 degrees F. Fiber-reactive dyes need only 30 minutes.

9) Unwrap the fabric immediately after steaming so that the condensation does not cause the colors to run.

CONCLUSIONS ABOUT DYES

As can be seen, dyes are a very extensive paint material. The amount of material about dyes could be seen as overwhelming. It's best to choose one type of dye and learn about it well before going on to another type. Your knowledge from one type will build a foundation and learning about the next type will seem easier. Sometimes ordering the primary colors (in most cases, red, yellow, and blue) and learning to mix them is a good way to "break in" a dye.

The greatest problem with dyes, other than the vast amount of information about them, is that many of them require steaming when they are applied as dye-pastes. Steaming takes time and is a skill which must be learned. Other aspects of dyes can be seen in the following chart:

Use: the most popular and versatile paint material for fabric painting

Quality: a very high quality paint material

Price: very reasonable, especially when ordered in bulk

Usage: somewhat complex to learn how to use, but once techniques are learned, fairly straightforward

Hand:excellent

Washability:varies,depending
upon the type of dye. Some are excellent,others poor

Usage:Usage is vast. Clothing,
both casual and formal,accessories,
quilts,wall hangings,curtains,lamp
shades,toys,soft sculpture,etc.

Fabrics used:Most dyes take either all natural fibers or synthetics and polyesters. Some are for
silk and wool;others for cotton and
linen.

Productivity: fair to good,de-
pending upon procedures used

Availability: very available,
from drugstores to art and fiber
stores to dye suppliers

Lightfastness:good to very good

How set?: generally,steam-set
either by steam iron,oven steaming,
pressure steaming,or atmospheric
steaming with a steam cabinet or
canner

INKS

Inks are the next catagory of
paint materials which can be used
in fabric painting.There are two
different kinds of inks:oil-base
textile printing inks such as silkscreen inks,block printing inks,
etc;and permanent waterproof drawing inks. We shall first discuss
the textile printing inks.

These printing inks are sometimes
known as 'pigment pastes'.They are
more viscuous than regular textile
paint,but in many ways they are similar to textile paint.They are usually a combination of ground pigments,a binder,an extender,a thinner,and a transparent base.Many of
them can be found in art stores,un-
der silkscreen supplies or block
printing supplies. They can also be
ordered from a number of distributors.

Screen Process Supplies in Oakland,CA. supply several types of
fabric inks.One is called Inko-Tex
which is a water-base fabric ink
coming in 17 colors.(Water-base
inks which are textile inks are
suitable for fabric painting).Inko-
Fab is another fabric ink;this one
is solvent based.

Pro Chemical and Dye Company
stocks some very nice textile inks.
They are called PROfab Textile Inks.
They are a waterbase textile ink
that comes in 16 different colors.
They can be used on both natural and
synthetic fibers,and are especially
good with poly/cottons. They can be
used on white or light fabrics as is;
and they can be made more opaque by
adding a White Color Concentrate.They
only need to be heat set for 3-4 minutes with a dry iron.The 16 colors
are intermixable,and a PROfab Color
Concentrate is also available to make
colors deeper,or for you to mix your
own colors.The Print Base Extender
will make the colors lighter and allow you to mix pastel shades.Add a
little water when doing direct painting.

These textile inks are especially nice and easy to use. They are
contained in a plastic screw-top
jar,so they can be easily stored
and used. The hand of the fabric
remains smooth with these inks,
although they,as most other inks,
give a 'flat finish'look(meaning
the dried ink has a matte,rather
than a glossy,look).

Naz-dar Fabric Ink,Hunt/Speed-
ball Textile Screen Printing Ink,
Hunt/Speedball No Heat Textile
Screen Printing Ink, Advance Textile Silkscreen Printing Ink,Hunt/
Speedball oil-base block printing
ink,and Shiva oil-base block printing ink are some of the more popular textile inks that are available
in art stores. Naz-dar Fabric Ink
is used on cotton and other natural fibers;while Hunt/Speedball Textile Screen Printing Ink can be used on most natural and synthetic
fibers. Both of these are also ver-
y nice inks;they are only slightly
rough to the touch.

Colonial Printing Ink Co.,in New

Jersey,carries a large number of textile inks. They are stocked in bulk
amounts,the smallest being l quart.
Perma-Print Ink comes in 15 colors
and can be used on T-shirts and sweat
shirts. Poly-Print Ink can be used on
waterproof nylon garments. Denim Ink
is used,obviously, for denim material;
Aqua-Bright has 24 colors including
fluorescents.Texdye Pigment is used
for clothing,hand and beach towels;
Hydro-Tex D.G.is used for dark fabrics. Stretch Ink has 40 colors and
can be used for T-shirts, sweat shirts,
as well as to make heat transfers.Dy-
no-Print Plastisol Ink is especially
good on polycottons,and Pro Print Wet-
on-Wet can also be used as a heat transfer paint.Mul-T-Print Plastisol is used on woven or knitted cottons.Ad-
vance Process Supply Co. is another
supplier of silkscreen or textile inks.

I find that these textile inks are
most satisfactory on cotton,muslin,
and medium-weight fabrics.On light-
weight fabrics and synthetics they are
apt to stiffen in an undesirable way.
They are also very good in combination with overdyeing,especially when
making fabric yardage.Textile inks are
easy to apply and quite inexpensive to
use. To summarize:

Use: fairly popular

Quality: a good quality paint material

Price: one of the most inexpensive
paint materials

Hand: fair to good,depending on
type of fabric used

Washability:Very good

Usage: Clothing,wall hangings.Esp-
ecially good for fabric yardage

Fabrics used:natural fibers such as
cotton and muslin are good;some synthetics

Productivity: very good,as inks are
quick drying

Usage: easy to learn how to use

Availability:readily available
at art stores and silkscreen supply houses

Lightfastness: Very good

How set?: generally set with a
dry iron

DRAWING INKS

Drawing inks are the other
type of ink that can be used for
fabric painting. In general, drawing inks are not washfast,even if
the ink is described as a waterproof ink.Sometimes,the fabric can
be dipped in cool water without
soap and the ink will not run,but
these inks should not be used for
clothing that needs washing. A
fine-tipped brush or pens with a
variety of pen tips can be used
with these drawing inks.(Fig. 98)

There are a number of different types of ink that can be used
for fabric painting. I have tried
Pelican Drawing Ink,Luma Watercolors,FW Drawing Inks,Koh-i-noor,and
Higgins Permanent Ink,and found
Pelican to be the most washfast.
Lettering pens and drawing markers
can also be used directly on fabric.

When working with pen tips,use
a light touch,and work on smooth,
evenly woven fabric rather than
a stretchy knit or textured fabric.
Drawing and lettering such as is

FIG.98: LAYOUT OF DRAWING INKS AND
SOME TEXTILE INKS

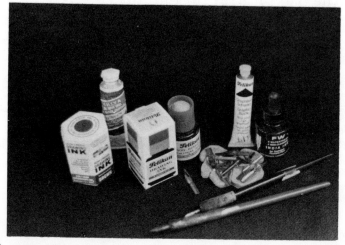

FIG.99:CLOSE-UP OF HAIKU WRITTEN ON NYLON PANTS-SUIT WITH MARKING PENS.

done on paper can also be done on fabric.(Fig. 99) Drawing inks are best used for small,delicate pieces; fabric cards, small pictures that can be framed,dolls and soft sculpture. Their colors are luminous and give a soft look to fabric. To sum up their characteristics:

Use: limited in use

Quality:not a high quality paint material for fabric painting due to poor washability

Price:Moderately priced

Hand:Very good

Washability:Poor

Usage:Small wall hangings or pictures, dolls,soft sculpture,fabric cards

Fabrics used:all types of fabrics such as cotton,polycotton,polyesters, synthetics,silk

Productivity:Very good

Usage:Moderately easy to learn how to use. Always stretch fabric before drawing

Availability:Readily available in art stores

Lightfastness:fair to good

How Set?: No setting needed

MARKING PENS

Fabric marking pens and marking pens are other paint materials that are used with fabric painting. The most permanent markers are those which are made specifically for fabric,but some"permanent"design markers can also be used. In the latter category, I have found Design Marker to be fairly permanent in most colors.Some of the brands of fabric markers include Loving Touch Permanent Fabric Marker, Setaskrib (Textile Resources),Deco-color pens (Textile Resources),Superfine pen (IVY Crafts),Nepo pens,Niji pens,and Glad Rags Marker(Sax's). Sharpie laundry marking pen,though labeled permanent,did not test out for permanency.

Setascrib has 12 colors,and is especially good for cottons and T-shirts. Deco-color pens also has 15 colors,while Glad Rags has 10. The other markers mentioned can be found in most fabric or needlework stores.

Other permanent markers that are generally found in art stores that can be used include Sanford Hi-Impact Intensive Color Markers(Sax's),Uni-Paint Markers by Faber Castell(Sax's) and Sanford Permanent Calligraphic Pens(Sax's). These are permanent markers that are waterproof.All "art markers" should be tested,as some will withstand water but not soap,and others are not really permanent at all.

Markers are the best paint material to begin with for drawing on fabric. They require practically the same techniques as would be used on paper. There is a very good book, called Painting with Markers-Troise and Port, which gives many ideas for using marking pens in a painterly way. As well, markers are good for intricate designs as they come in fine enough tips to execute precise lines.Lattice work, lace, iron wrought fences, sculpture, calligraphy,and embroidery are intricate designs which could be drawn on fabric. Markers are also good for gesture drawing, quick sketches,and cartoons. I also use them for the preliminary drawings for some paintings.

On smoothweave cloth, such as cotton or muslin, markers make fairly contained lines. Any close-weave cloth will produce a consistent line;however, the rougher the fiber,the less consistent the mark or line. Fabric markers and marking pens are easily available,easy to learn how to use on fabric, and come in a wide variety of colors. Their disadvantages are that they are fairly expensive and that they are not very washfast.They are best used on nonwashable items,such as wall hangings,toys,soft sculpture, etc,rather than clothing. They can be used on most any type of fabric.

TRANSFER PENCILS

Another type of marking pen is one used solely for transferring designs onto fabric. In general,the lines made from these pencils wash out.The other type of transfer pencil is used to draw a design on paper,and then transfer the image to the fabric via a hot iron. Deka makes such a transfer pencil. Transfer pencils are good when a design is complex and you wish to get an accurate representation of it on the fabric. Bona Venture carries a textile washout pencil in red, green, and blue.

EMBROIDERY PAINTS

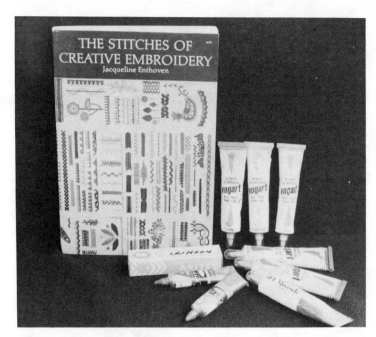

FIG.100: LAYOUT OF EMBROIDERY **PAINTS** AND EMBROIDERY BOOK

Embroidery paints are another type of marking tool that is used in fabric painting. It has been on the market for a long time, and is usually found in needlework stores, in the embroidery section. Embroidery paints can also be mail-ordered,and are often advertised in women's magazines and needlework magazines.Another name for embroidery paints is decorator paints.Some of the brand names of embroidery paints are Cameo Silhouette Designs,Vogart Ball Point Paint Tubes,Minuet,Crafttint Deco-write,Artex Decorator Paints, and Tri-Chem. Tri-Chem is a dealership of embroidery paints which sells their product through dealership parties. Other brands also use this method.

Embroidery paints are applied to fabric by pressing hard on the tip of the tube of paint,and allowing the paint to flow. (This is why they are called paints rather than markers)The tube should be held firmly from the bottom,but never squeezed. Since the paints need pressure in order for the color to show, they do not work very well on stretchy material or on thick textured fabric. They are best used on cotton,muslin, and other smooth-weave fabrics.

There are many embroidery stitches

which can be used effectively with embroidery paint.(Fig. 100)In general, stitches which are composed of long running lines, and those which do not use twisted or overlaid threads to create their pattern, can be drawn so as to look like authentic embroidery.Besides, painted embroidery is not supposed to copy thread embroidery; it is an emphasis on line,whereas in embroidery,there is more of an emphasis on texture within line.

Embroidery paints can also be used for plain line drawing,and for filling in small areas. They work especially well with small delicate types of designs. Certain types of paint give unusual results;the Glolite,metallic, and pearlite paints are especially popular.Embroidery paints can be used on a variety of fabric. They do not need to be heat-set.

FABRIC CRAYONS, DYE PASTELS, AND OTHER ART MARKERS

The last major group of paint materials to be discussed is fabric crayons,dye pastels,and other art markers such as regular color crayons,Stabilotone markers,etc.

Crayola Craft markets a fabric crayon which is used on synthetics. It is actually a disperse dye in a wax base,and works like other transfer paint materials. First the design is drawn on paper,and then transferred to fabric by ironing with a hot iron.Only 8 colors are available, but it is a popular item with children.

When drawing the design, it is important to remember that it will transfer in reverse. If this is not desired, lightly trace the design in pencil in reverse on the paper by recopying the lines of the original design. These lines can then be marked over with the fabric crayons,with the entire design transferring correctly.Fabric crayons are an excellent way for children to wear some of their favorite coloring book characters!For adults, Dover carries a marvelous series of coloring books with many interesting topics:

books on the ancient near east,the middle ages, and a medieval alphabet are some of their many titles.

Although fabric crayons are easy to use,they do require strength in ones arm muscles.And,just like color crayons,they require a certain amount of patient diligence to use!

DYE PASTELS

Another type of 'crayon marker' which can be used is called a dye pastel. (Fig. 101) Dye pastels are marketed by Pentel,and,like the fabric crayons, they are available through Cerulean Blue,Ltd. 15 colors are available,including red,yellow,buttercup,pink,green,turquoise, white,and black.These pastels are similar in consistency to an oil pastel.They are best used on natural fibers,such as cotton and muslin,but will work on some synthetic blends.

Unlike the fabric crayons,these pastels are used directly on the fabric. It is best to stretch your fabric,using either an embroidery frame or other stretching frame. Use short,swift marks.Be careful not to let little flecks of the crayon land on white parts of the fabric. After drawing,set the pastels by ironing with a medium hot iron. Use a soft cloth to cover the drawing and protect your iron.

Overdyeing works well with both these pastels and the fabric crayons.

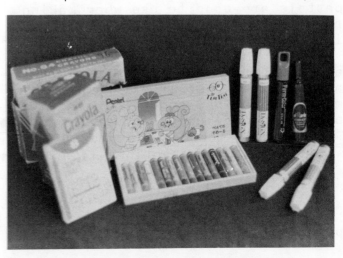

FIG. 101:LAYOUT OF MARKERS AND CRAYONS. DYE PASTELS,FABRIC CRAYONS,CRAYONS,MARKERS.

Or, use an acrylic wash after drawing with these crayon markers.

REGULAR COLOR CRAYONS

Color crayons can be used with limited effects. They can be used directly on certain fabrics,such as cotton or polyester blends,with very nice effects. Wall hangings,soft pictures,or other nonwashable items should be made with the colored fabric. Color crayons can be heated, using a crayon,and drawn in a soft or semi-melted state,onto fabric. This approaches a crude method of batik,and the fabric must be pressed with a hot iron to remove the wax.This method is best used when subsequent overdyeing occurs.Another possibility is to draw with crayon over fabric which has been painted with an acrylic wash.Heat-set all these methods by ironing.

OTHER ART MARKERS

There are a number of other art markers which I have used on fabric for decorative purposes. One is called Stabilotone marker. Its texture is similar to an oil pastel,and it works very nicely using a combination of direct drawing and washes.It is a waterbase marker.

Oil pastels and regular chalk pastels can also be used. For the oil pastels,stretch your fabric as the marker will work better that way.Oil pastels are good to use when making rubbings,or any other textured or relief effect.(Fig.102)

Shiva /Markal Artist's Paintstiks are another interesting marker.They are actually a solid oil paint,in marker form.They can be dipped in turpentine before using,or used straight. Caran D'Ache Neocolor I, a wax oil, is also used with turpentine. To summarize:

Use: Limited

Quality: a fair to good quality paint material

Price:reasonable

Hand: Very good

Usage:Wall hangings,fabric pictures, soft sculpture, dolls, curtains,some washable items

Washability:Poor for all items except dye pastels and fabric crayons

Fabrics used:Synthetics for fabric crayons;all types of fabrics for others

Productivity: Very good

Usage:Very easy to use

Availability:very available

Lightfastness:good to very good

How set?:no setting or by ironing

With so many good paint materials at hand,it is possible to learn a whole vocabulary of 'painterly' techniques for fabric.We'll look,in the next two chapters,for inspiration and ideas for painting.

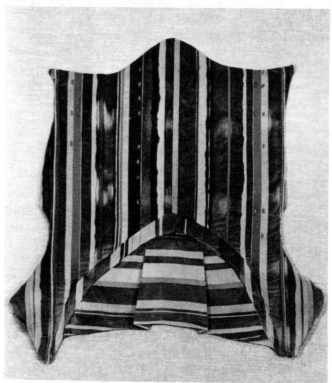

FIG. 102: "REFLECTIONS IV"-VICTORIA RIVERS. PROCION ON VELVETEEN,OIL PASTELS,STUFFED.

126

5 PERCEPTION, INSPIRATION, CREATION

Inspiration for design ideas can be found everywhere! The wider ones' perception, the more possibilities for fabric painting. In fact, sources of inspiration for fabric painting cover a very wide area: ideas can be found in biology books, tree identification books, in a geography or history book, in an auto parts store, in the anthropologists' library, or on a trip by bus into a downtown area; as well as in the area generally called the humanities- art history, music, literature, drama, dance. I want to describe some unusual and unapparent design sources as well as presenting familiar ideas- flowers, colors, lines, etc.

The main question when forming a design for fabric painted cloth and clothing is:1)is the design functional to painting, and 2) is the design functional to clothing? As was explained in Chapter III, there is no use in designing something which would be easier fabric printed. There is, however, such a wealth of design ideas that are unique to fabric painting that it is soon easy to discern what type of design to bypass.

With direct painting, for example, there is no need to use repetition of image or placement, unless it is desired. At the same time, a design with scattered images without any unity is not the aim of fabric painting design. Cohesive variety is the aim. This means that a variety of ideas, images, colors, and compositional devices such as line, texture, shape, etc. are used within a larger unifying structure. A larger unifying structure could be composed of different <u>types</u> of musical instruments drawn on the fabric, with or without a background. This basic idea could be used with any number of images- types of metal clasps, old lace patterns, or words and poems in different languages- any number of <u>types</u> of images can be used in combination to achieve a pictorial unity for fabric painted cloth.

As well as various types of images within a certain category, a theme could be any short subject from which variations are developed. I have been working on a series of designs which evolve from "organic design" where the main theme is nature, both the materials in nature and the idea of natural growing processes. A theme could include a certain type of design motif, a certain garment design from the area or time of the motif, and a way of putting the two together that would not be a traditional pattern.

Another example of this is correlating an archaic design or material with a garment design from the same period. Songs from the ancient troubadours (such as the ones compiled by Raynaud, entitled "Chanson de Richart Coeur" or "Chanson du roi de Navarre") could be combined on a dress with other motifs from that historical period, and, as well, the design of the dress could be similar to those worn by the ancient troubadours. There is an immeasurable amount of unfamiliar design material stored away in library books in the forms of designs, diagrams, photographs, drawings, pictures, music, and words. Research could be combined with fabric painted textile design to create numerous images that would be visually interesting, intellectually stimulating, and rarely seen. At the same time, a beautifully drawn flower is a new design, since arts' capacity-or magic, if you will, can present a new vision of an old idea. Research does not pretend to be original, but it can expose ideas and designs long forgotten.

Research used in connection with textile design is very functional as concerns fabric painting, and in general this approach also works for the design being functional to clothing. For now, we shall focus on design ideas in two-dimensional space, independent of their relationship with the clothing form. (The combination of the design on the surface with the design of the garment form will be discussed in depth in Chapter VII.) Let us then turn our perceptual eye to the world and see what visions we can create for fabric painting.

Since fabric painting focuses mainly on painting, I would like to describe some of the origins of painting, and how the process of painting formed into design. There are three forms of painting: painting as writing, painting as drawing, and painting as sculpture. Early prehistoric painting was a rough form of writing, as the painting recorded events of the hunt, wild animals, battles with other humans, and the general comings and goings of various peoples. From a realistic recording of events, prehistoric painting evolved into symbolism, with medicine shirts which contained powers for healing, due to the symbols and images painted on the shirt. When this primitive "painted writing", or pictographs, began to become more symbolic, painting and writing began to separate. Painting began to be more representational, and writing began to be more abstract, with symbols that were subject to certain rules of usage and capable of being deciphered by other people. This separation has not been quick, nor even complete. For example, just in the past thirty years have the Mayan hieroglyphs been deciphered.

One type of pictograph began evolving towards alphabets: starting with hieroglyphs, such as Mayan and Egyptian, then the cuneiform (a simplified version of the hieroglyph) which was used in the writing of the Babylonian-Assyrian periods), then Chinese characters, and hence to our present day standardized alphabets. Some older languages retain more of the pictorial in their alphabets, such as the aforementioned Chinese, as well as Arabic, Russian, Eskimo, and Tamil. As well, our regular alphabet is modified and illustrated by calligraphy. The divorce of painting

and writing is seen to be slow. Illuminated manuscripts are an example
of the combination of painting and
writing, being as equally pictorial
as written. Even today, alphabets
and words are used both as symbols
for information and as design forms.

The other type of pictograph began
to evolve into drawing, as it became
more representational and less symbolic. Painting as drawing usually concerns the first stage of painting-
the making of a form. When a painting
is of form, rather than formless (or
abstract),drawing is an integral part
of the painting. In many paintings,
the drawing portion remains visible
in the finished painting. For example,
14th and 15th century paintings began
with an outline of the subject matter,
then marked out areas of light and
shade. Only later was color added.

If a painting is solely the application of paint upon a surface, with
no consideration of form, then painting is not involved with drawing.
"Painterly painters" of the 1970's such
as Larry Poons and William Pettet concern themselves with the mechanical
application of paint upon the surface,
yet even they are as concerned with form
(and therefore drawing) as they are with
color and texture.

It is hard to differentiate painting
from drawing. A line could be a streak
of color. A color could be a line.

Painting as sculpture concerns the
interchangeability of the two art forms.
Painting can render three-dimensional
sculpture in two-dimensional space. So,
it is an illusion? It can be done. In
ancient Egyptian and PreColumbian art,
painting and sculpture were combined.
Much sculpture was colored, the Parthe-
non was painted brightly. Certain periods of painting are considered "painterly",others "sculptural". Renaissance
painting is sculptural, while Baroque
and Hellenistic sculpture is painterly.

These,then, are the roots of painting. All three forms are still evident
in todays' modern art, and form the basis for the history of design. We shall
now explore design images, which can be
used in fabric painting, in a somewhat
chronological order, beginning with design images from prehistoric art.

Prehistoric art found in caves
consists of hand silhouettes, animals such as bison, wild horses,
and some deer. Examples of painting and sculpture are found in
caves in France, Eastern Spain,
North Africa, and Norway. Carved
menhirs, which are stone monuments
found in Brittany and Italy, Neo-
lithic pottery with great amounts
of geometric ornamentation, and
Bronze age weapons and utensils
from Scandanavia are other art
objects from prehistoric times
that can be used in fabric painting design. As well, there are numerous examples of pictographs found
in cave paintings. In general, inspiration from the fruits of archaeological digs and anthropological
studies gives the fabric painter a
wide range of subject matter.(Fig.103)

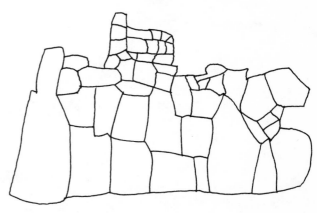

FIG. 103: DRAWINGS OF PREHISTORIC ITEMS:
ROCK FORMATIONS AT SACSAHUAMAN,PERU·
POTTERY FRAGMENTS· POTTERY DESIGNS.

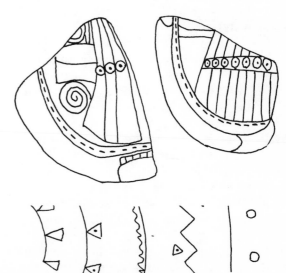

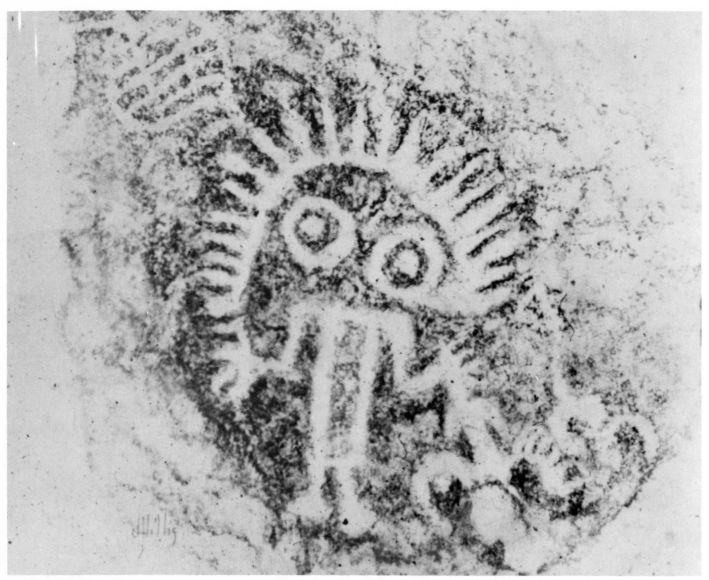

FIG.104:"MEDICINE MAN"-BY JEANNE HILLIS. A RUBBING TAKEN FROM AN ANCIENT PETROGLYPH (1500-2000 YEARS OLD) FOUND ON THE OREGON SHORE OF THE COLUMBIA RIVER.

As well as using images from prehistoric art, one can use the ideas behind the images which are the basis for this art. In other words, one can understand the reasons for ancient peoples making what they made, and then simulate the reasons in a modern context. Probable reasons for painted animals were to appease a dead animal, attract live ones, or record the events of a hunt. Other motivations for prehistoric painting include recording of seasons and time, painting for healing,(Fig.104), painting as magic and power, painting visions and dreams, and painting to record social history. You could paint your dreams(night or day),your visions, or symbols which give you a sense of strength and power. Or you could paint a series of events which mark time.

Very close to design ideas from prehistoric art are design ideas and images from alphabets and other symbolic forms. Pictographs, Egyptian hieroglyphs, Mayan hieroglyphs, and cunieforms are the most primitive alphabet forms. (Figs.105,106, 107,108,109)Occult signs and symbols, such as can be found in The Book of Signs-Koch(Dover),zodiac signs,and musical notations are other symbolic forms used with fabric painting. Foreign languages can be used as a design form rather than a symbol,

FIG.105: TED COTROTSOS MODELING T-SHIRT WITH MAYAN HIEROGLYPHS DRAWN WITH MARKING PENS.

FIG.106: DRAWING OF SIOUX AND ARAPAHO PICTOGRAPHS, BY PHYLLIS THOMPSON. AFTER PRIMITIVE ART-FRANZ BOAS,1955

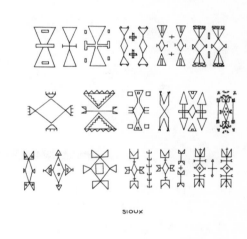

SIOUX

ARAPAHO

FIG.107: DRAWING OF CUNIEFORMS

FIG.108 : TED COTROTSOS MODELING A LONG-SLEEVED COTTON PULLOVER
WITH EGYPTIAN HIEROGLYPHS AND MOTIFS.

thus taking a symbolic form and making it more abstract. Chinese characters are another alphabet form which is easy to use as a design form.(Fig.110) There are a number of good calligraphy books, such as Calligraphy-Baker (Dover), Written Letters- Suaren,Calligraphic Lettering-Douglass(Watson-Guptill), and Letter Forms-Lambert, which show different calligraphic forms of the letters in a large format so that it is relatively easy to learn to paint calligraphic letters. As well, calligraphy and lettering can be done regularly with pen and ink on smooth cloth.(Fig. 108)Illuminated manuscripts, which use a combination of calligraphy and decorative painting, make intricately beautiful painted clothing.

Alphabets in the forms of words can be a very beautiful design form to use in connection with clothing. I find that using an alphabet and a language which is not one in common usage gives me a new perspective on the form and shape of the words, as they are not connected to images and ideas. The following phrases in Eskimo on the shirt were chosen for their poetic nature. They can be pure design to those who do not know Eskimoan, or they can be a word-symbol if translation is added to the design.(Fig. 111 I have seen tops printed with French words that are fairly familiar,which becomes a design that combines pure design with some symbolic meaning. Many languages can

132

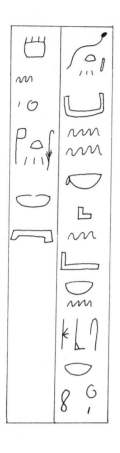

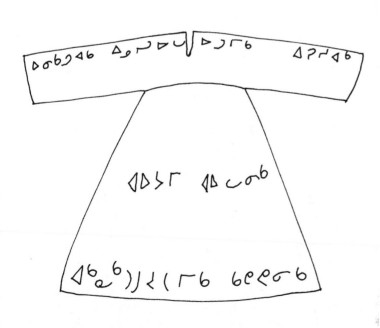

FIG.109: DRAWING OF EGYPTIAN HIEROGLYPHS

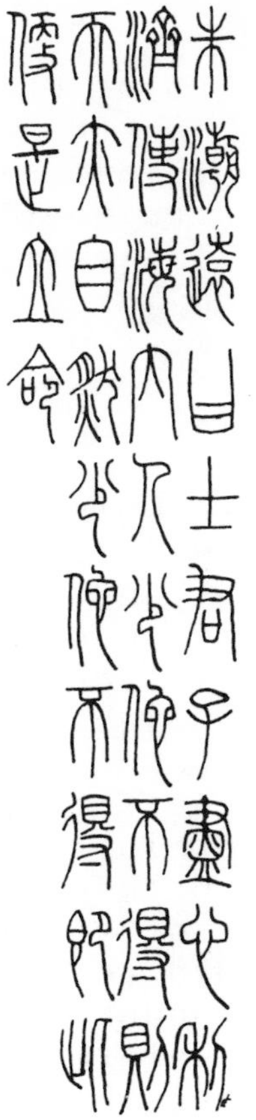

FIG.110: DRAWING BY PHYLLIS THOMPSON OF CHINESE CALLIGRAPHY. FROM CHINESE CALLI-GRAPHY-BY CHIANG YEE

FIG.111:DIAGRAM OF DRESS WITH ESKIMO PHRASES AS THE DESIGN.

FIG.112: NAME SKIRT-BY EVELYN BYATT. COTTON AND INKODYE. AN EXAMPLE OF LETTERING ON CLOTHING.

be used in this way.

When the word becomes less of a pure design form, and more of a symbol, then the painted word and words begin to evolve into literature. Taking the idea of books and connecting it with the idea of clothing can be very exciting. Children's literature is an especially good inspiration as there is a maximum of pictures and a minimum of words. It would be easy to make an Alice in Wonderland shirt or a dress with illustrations from The Little Prince(St. Exupery). The composition of the painting in a garment is similar to the layout of the pictures and copy in a book, with the juxtapositioning of pictures, colors, words. There is also a connection with this type of design to movies, which are a series of pictures which move after each other in rapid succession.The composition for fabric painting can be made in a linear way to show a kind of a picture-movie. As well, these designs go beyond the one-dimensional idea of pictorial decoration; there is meaning in the visual images which accompany stories and myths.

There is a wide range of literature which can become painted literature; it is not limited to certain genres or centuries. In fact, painted literature(although not on clothing) is a historical fact, with epics such as the Ramayana being painted into tapestry-wall-hangings in Persia. Poetry ranging from the long epic to the very short haiku can be used in fabric painting design.

Stories and fiction become design ideas, with or without pictorial elements. (Fig.113)Stories from books are nice; making up your own stories and putting them on your clothing can also be a lot of fun. If you add drawings and pictures, it is like a comic strip, or a walking book!

Real comic strips can be used in a limited way with clothing, by lifting the ink colors from the paper with acrylic gel(see pages 84-85 of Chapter IV for instructions on how to do this) onto some clothing. The comic strip "Peanuts" is fun to wear on clothing.

Titles from books can be a design inspiration. Quotations which form around a general theme are good design material for fabric painting, as the theme unites loosely linked material. It can be seen that painted literature can take many forms, from the very intellectual and sophisticated forms to the comic book and humorous tales.

I find that the idea of using book ideas and clothing ideas together is very exciting in that many ideas for books can be created in clothing; with less expense,and with the same chance for a large number of people to see them. This would refer primarily to short works, although a larger body of work could be painted on a larger piece of material. Fabric can be a walking book-as the pages of the book can be spread out on the fabric. Think of the form of the body as a natural landscape and the character(of your book) adventuring in different parts of the landscape- the points and planes formed by the body in motion and at rest.

There are a number of interesting things which happen when words are put onto cloth, particularly when the words are symbols rather than pure design. For one thing, wearing words in public(as clothes usually are) makes them a stronger message and an identity linked to you. Do not paint what you really do not believe, or are not willing to defend. It is much more personal to wear a sign than to carry one, since clothing is today an extension of personality. As well, words so close to the body change their meaning somewhat, for they relate to the body. Close-fitting garments emphasize the relationship between body and word much more than words on looser parts of a garment(such as ruffled hems). Material which drapes from the body, rather than forming to it, creates a detachment between the meaning of the words, and the body.(see pages 28-29 for more discussion of the social reaction to painted clothing.)

Sizes and shapes of words have varying relationships to the shape and form of the garment. Words can be written small or big,but very small print may cause people to come up close to you to read what is written, unless they only see the visual(rather than visual and verbal) effect. Large print allows others to read the clothing without stopping you or coming close. (See Fig.112) What size letters you use depends partly on what type of relationship you wish to have with other people when wearing painted clothing.

Another variation on this is to write small words small and big words big. This illustrates not only the meaning, but the shape and sound and dimension of the words. The shape of a poem can be integrated with the shape of a garment, as different words go better with different shaped garments. Flowing words need flowing clothes. Poetry which must show every word in order to be coherent should be lettered on a flat sturdy garment which is rather closefitting. The progression of a poem can be graphically shown: action such as running can be lettered on the cloth, running around and through it. Directions such as behind, above, and below can be graphically spaced. The form of a poem and the form of a garment and a body can interact in a more meaningful way without being gimmicky. (Fig.114)

Some of the most successful words to use on clothing for the beginner are images which relate to clothing: images dealing with texture, color, action and motion, either abstractly or specifically. Specific images would be words connected with sports and dance, as they describe movement. In deciding on the composition for painted literature, think of the body as a landscape. This will draw it out of its purely physical and sex-

FIG.113: AVA LAKE MODELING A COTTON DRESS WITH AFRICAN TALE WRITTEN IN ORIGINAL ALPHABET, ORIGINAL LANGUAGE WITH ROMAN ALPHABET, AND ENGLISH TRANSLATION. MARKING PEN AND ACRYLIC GEL TRANSFER.

FIG.114: T-SHIRT DECORATED WITH AN E.E. CUMMINGS POEM,"IN-JUST", WRITTEN WITH MARKING PENS, ADDED PAINTED DESIGNS.

ual meanings, allowing for a larger range of thought in design. The
landscape could be timeless or sur-
real, or it could be a setting
with a specific time and place;such
as the woods in winter, or the city
in the spring. This gives the garment a setting much like our summer
and winter clothes, with certain
colors, material, and styles which
are actors within the setting of
the real weather. To bring time
and place into the garment only
adds another dimension.

Another source of design ideas
comes from motifs from various
cultures, such as Pre-Columbian,
American Indian, African, Chinese,
Japanese, the Far East, Persian
and Indian, Asian, South American,
Russian, Scandanavian, Eastern
Europe, and European. Some of these
cultures or areas are richer in
motifs than others, but all should
be explored for their possibilities.

Motifs from Pre-Columbia include
stylized birds and animals, woven
and embroidered designs, and geometrics in earth tones from pottery.
Sculpture, fabrics, architecture,
and pottery can be explored to find
many interesting design ideas.(Figs.
115-116).There are a number of Dover
books, including Mayan Hieroglyphs-
Morley, Design Motifs of Ancient
Mexico-Enciso, and Pre-Hispanic Mexican Stamp Designs-Field, which include many motifs from Pre-Columbian
America. American Indian motifs are
extensive and can be found in their
fabrics and weaving, painted tipis
and hides, and pottery.(Figs.117,118,
and119).African design holds interest with its mixture of primitivism
and modern awareness. There are a
number of printed fabrics with design motifs and layout inspired
from African design(Figs.120,121,122,
and 123),and Oceanic art.(Fig.124)

Designs from the Far East(China,
Japan, and Korea) and the Near East
(India, Persia) are quite different
from the above, but are equally ap-
plicable. For example, the motifs
can be used on American clothing,
(Fig.125) within a traditionally
Eastern garment form such as a ki-

FIG.115 : LESLIE ALLEN OF LEXINGTON,
KENTUCKY, MODELING A PRE-COLUMBIAN
PAINTED SKIRT. ACRYLIC ON COTTON.

FIG.116 : DRAWING BY PHYLLIS THOMPSON OF
A MOTIF FROM THE CODEX ZOUCHE-NUTTALL(MIX-
TEC)FROM THE CONQUISTADORS BY HAMMOND INNES.

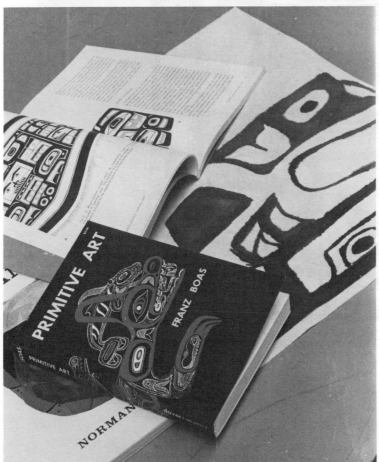

FIG.117: NORTHWEST COAST INDIAN MOTIF PAINTED ON MAN'S COTTON SHIRT. TIM RENN MODELS SHIRT MADE BY CINDY TURN-BALL,BOTH OF EUGENE,OREGON. THE DE-SIGN REPRESENTS A THUNDERBIRD FROM THE KWAKIUTL INDIANS OF SOUTHWEST BRITISH COLUMBIA. VERSATEX PAINT.

FIG.118: LAYOUT OF NORTHWEST COAST INDIAN ART:BOOKS,SHIRT IN PROGRESS.

FIG.119: DRAWING BY PHYLLIS THOMPSON OF A MAN'S SHIRT FROM TLINGIT,
ALASKA. AFTER INDIAN ART IN AMERICA-F.J. DOCKSTADER

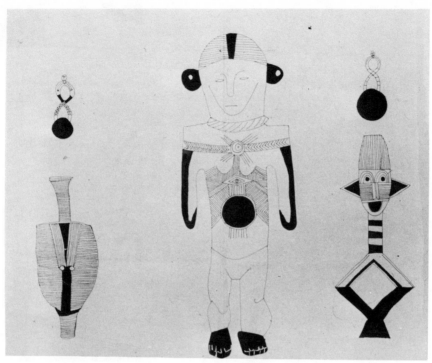

FIG.120: AFRICAN WOODEN SCULPTURE DESIGNS
PAINTED WITH ACRYLICS ON COTTON.

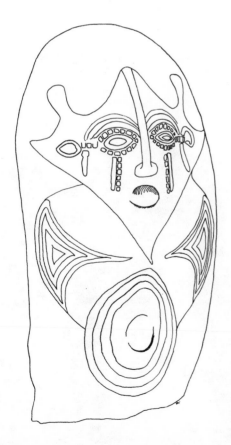

FIG.121: DRAWING OF E. NIGERIAN STONE
CARVING, AFTER AFRICAN STONE SCULPTURE-
BY PHILIP ALISON. DRAWING BY P. THOMPSON

FIG.122: DRAWING OF BAKONGO STONE
CARVING.AFTERAFRICAN STONE SCULPTURE-
P. ALISON. DRAWING BY PHYLLIS THOMPSON.

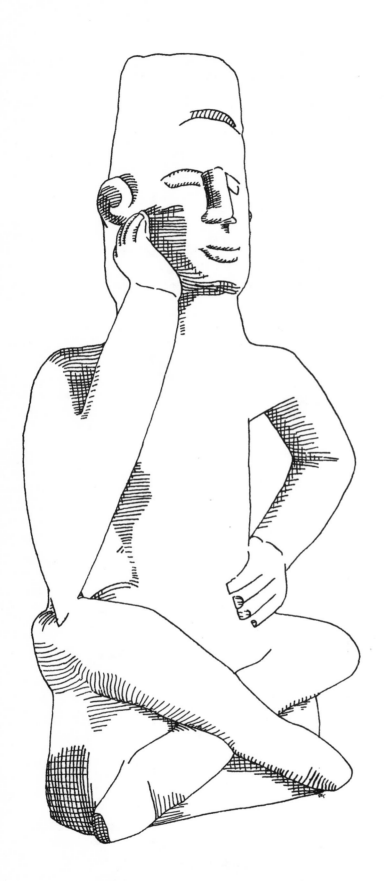

FIG.124: LAYOUT OF MOTIFS AND
DESIGNS FROM NEW GUINEA.

FIG.125: HANDPAINTED T-SHIRT
BY KIM AND LEIGH LACAVA WITH
CHINESE MOTIF.

FIG.123: DRAWING BY PHYLLIS THOMPSON OF A
CONGOLESE STONE FROM NTADI,BAMBONA. AFTER
AFRICAN STONE SCULPTURE-PHILIP ALLISON

mona,(Fig.12)or as pillows.(Fig.126-127)
Rugs, bedspreads, treasures, music,
and literature are other sources
for Persian and Indian designs.
The bright stripes of Mexican,Span-
ish, or Russian clothing(Fig.128),
and the unique layered looks from
Asian clothing and Eastern Europe
are other design sources. As well,
there is the whole of Europe and
Scandanavia to be considered, and
it will be given more extensive
treatment later in this chapter, in
"Design Ideas from Historical Costume and Dress",as well as in Chapter VII, under basic and complex
clothing forms. By working in these
geographic areas, as seen above,it
is possible to experience the atmosphere of that area without necessarily wearing what might be felt to
be a costume. Modern day designers
and manufacturers have been using
this technique for a number of years.
In an ad for Dan River fabrics, the
following types of fabrics are des-
cribed:Persian peasant looks, spicy
Mexican serape stripes and prints,
North African mosaics, light re-
freshing Indian batiks and gauzes,
and potluck patchwork plaids. All of
these fabrics have the vivid interest of costume without the ensuing
nationalism, nor the inappropriate-
ness that a costume sometimes has.

When talking about design ideas
from needlework, one does not intend
to capture the textural interest via
painting to the extent that it can
be created by thread and needle. However,certain needlework stitches can
be copied into the language of painting. It is impossible to recreate the
textures and body of yarn with paint
in knitting, for example, but knitting
stitches can be approximated in fabric painting by their design. Texture
ressembling needlework has been shown
in paintings by Van Gogh("Starry Night"
and"Wheatfields") with the straight,
sharp brushstrokes.

Design ideas evolving from knitting
include painting brushstroke textures
similar to the textures created by the
knitted stitch,or copying the whole
design in a garment, such as the textured patterns in the Ayran or fisherman

knit sweaters. As well, knitted
pieces can be used in fabric painting,for a collage-type effect.

Design ideas from crochet deal
more with the process of crochet
than from the end result. For example, by thinking of the yarn as
a long unending line(which it is)
and the crochet hook as the guide,
director,or seeker, it is easy to
transfer the process of crochet
into other mediums. Drawing and
painting can be approached as well,
as a journey.(see the books,The
Dot and the Line-Juster, and Taking
a Walk with a Line,for inspiration).

There are many new design ideas
concerning crochet. Old patterns
are still used, but new ideas in
construction have come about. Cro-
chet:Discovery and Design-Del Pitt
Feldman, and Creative Crochet-
Edson and Stimmel(Watson-Guptill)
describe many new ways of crocheting. One simple idea with a lot
of potential is to crochet simple
shapes such as squares, circles,
triangles, and loops and then attach them in various ways and
crochet around that area;perhaps
adding on another separate piece
somewhere and crocheting around
more. This type of composition
could also be painted on fabric.

Lace and macrame are two more
fiber structures which can be reproduced by drawing. With pen and
ink, an expert draftster can reproduce intricate lace designs.
(Fig. 129) Needlemade lace with
the many buttonhole bars as anchors
are especially graceful designs
for clothing. There are many types
of lace made in different ways.
Unfortunately, hand-made lace is
becoming a rariety. Yet, for the
purposes of fabric painting, books
on lace can bring lace designs
alive again. The designs can be
copied and worked with pen and ink,
markers, and stencils and paint.
(Fig.130) As well, real lace can
be used as a stamp.(see Chapter VI
under "stamps") Macrame, which is
formed in a manner similar to
lace, can also be used as a design

FIG.126-127: MONSTER PILLOWS BY VALERIE GUIGNON.THEY DEPICT THE FIERCE AND FRIGHTENING VISAGE OF AN EASTERN MYSTIC SYMBOL IN A COLORFUL AND CUDDLY FORM. PROCION DYE ON COTTON.

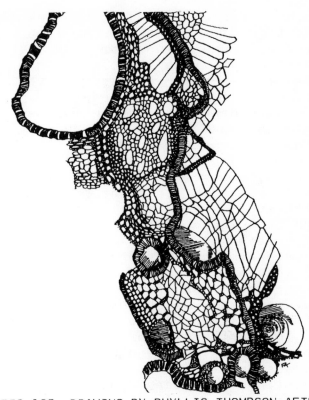

(ABOVE)FIG.128:DRAWING BY PHYLLIS THOMPSON
OF A SPANISH STRIPED SKIRT FROM AVILA,SPAIN.
AFTER PEASANT COSTUME IN EUROPE-KATHLEEN MANN.

FIG.129: DRAWING BY PHYLLIS THOMPSON AFTER
UNTITLED LACE ON PLEXIGLAS BY OTTO THIEME,
IN LACE BY V.C.BATH

FIG.130 : LAYOUT OF LACE AND BOOKS ON LACE.

form. Different kinds of needlework,
point to different kinds of ideas
for fabric painting. For example,
needlepoint, with its limited number of stitches, yet its wide variety of designs, is a wonderful
place to draw inspiration for"painterly" scenes. (Latch-hook rug designs are another good source).Scenes
such as baskets of flowers and farm
scenes, all stitched in one or two
basic stitches, could be painted
with small brushstrokes similar to
the techniques of the French Impressionists and Pointillists. Bargello
needlepoint reminds me of some types
of weaving, and could be translated
into fabric painting by working with
marking pens, oil paint and textine
with small brushes, or pen and ink.

The term "stitchery" is sometimes
described as painting with a needle,
because of its freer design. Many
paintings have been copied into
stitchery, and stitchery ideas can
be used for fabric painting. Stitchery is a more modern term for embroidery, and focuses more on the composition of the design and less on specific intricate stitches.

Traditional embroidery,on the
other hand, has many types of stitches,
with numerous effects possible. It is
easy to copy embroidered designs with
embroidery paints, marking pens, and
with regular textile and acrylic paint
using small brushes. "Stitchery"-type
effects, rather than "painterly",are
likely. Also, painted embroidery designs are much quicker to complete
than sewn embroidery. What is lost in
texture is gained in time.(Fig. 131)

Historical examples of embroidery
give good ideas for the placement of
embroidery on garments. As well, it is
possible to copy the designs without
having to have the technical needlework skills. Erica Wilson's Embroidery
Book has excellent color pictures of
historical embroidery.

Weaving, tapestry, applique, and
patchwork are four other types of
needlework which can be used as inspiration in fabric painting. The design,rather than the technique, of
both weaving and tapestry should be
considered.(Fig. 133) On the other

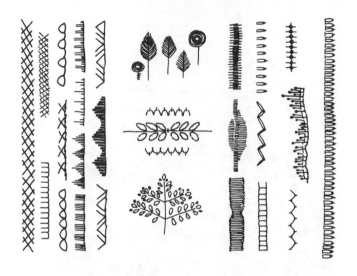

FIG.131 : DRAWING OF EMBROIDERY STITCHES
WHICH CAN BE USED IN FABRIC PAINTING. BY
PHYLLIS THOMPSON.

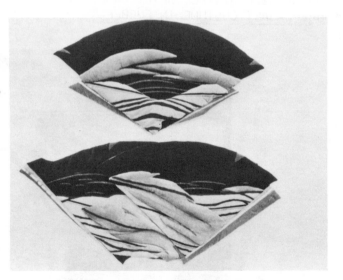

FIG.132:"TIME ENLARGING II"-BY VICTORIA Z.
RIVERS. PROCION DYE ON VELVETEEN, BEADS,
AIRBRUSH, APPLIQUE, HANDPAINTING, QUILTED
AND STUFFED.

FIG.133: (FOLLOWING PAGE) DETAIL OF"ICA-
RUS"-BY JUDY FELGAR. PAINTED WEAVING,
DOUBLE WEAVE PICK-UP IN WOOL, PAINTED
WITH SAX'S COLORTEX.

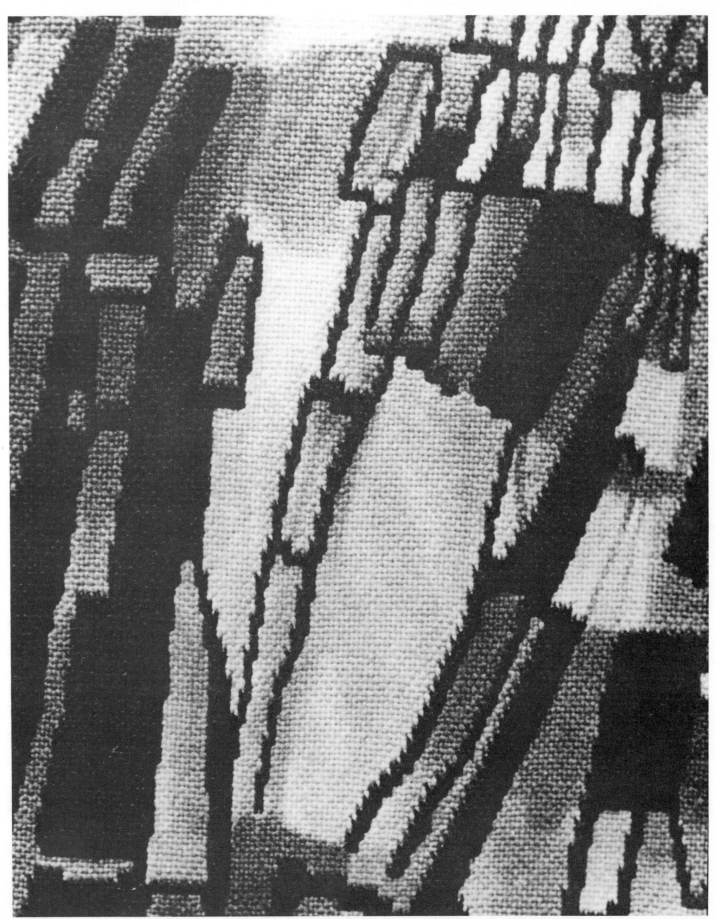

hard, designs evolving from applique and patchwork rely on process as much as design.

Applique, collage, and the Cubist movement in art are all very closely combined. I am using the term "applique" to apply to abstract design which is first cut and then pasted or sewn onto the material. Collage usually has more of a message, either psychological or sociological, and often uses newspaper clippings and lettering in its composition.

Henri Matisse used paper cutouts for some of his art. These paper cutouts were previously painted with gouache and then experimentally composed into a variety of layouts. Some of Ferdinand Leger's earlier work, such as "The Smokers" and "The Woman in Blue", though painted rather than pasted, are very good guides for painted applique. The shapes are geometric with straight edges and look like cut-paper shapes, yet the color-

ings within the shapes have a variety of shadings and texture. This effect can be created in applique with cut shapes of fabric which are painted and composed into a design. (Fig.132)Design evolving from applique and applique processes can be found in the work of other painters and needleworkers.(FIG.135)

Patchwork can be used as design and technique in fabric painting. Chapter VIII goes into detail about painted patchwork as it is such a unique combination. (see pgs.219-221). However, for design ideas from patchwork, two approaches can be followed. Various patchwork patterns can be drawn and painted onto fabric, eliminating the tedium of sewing together small pieces of material. Or, painted material can be cut and pieced in the tradition of patchwork. (Figs.134 and 136)

As well as needlework, there are other crafts, both fabric and non-fabric, which can be a source of design ideas for fabric painting. Batik,

FIG.134: "COLLOGRAPH QUILT"-BY JUDITH STEIN. COLLOGRAPH ON UNBLEACHED MUSLIN, PIECED AND QUILTED. OIL-BASE ETCHING INK USED(GRAPHIC CHEMICAL'S PERFECTION PALLETE INKS) 70 X 70"

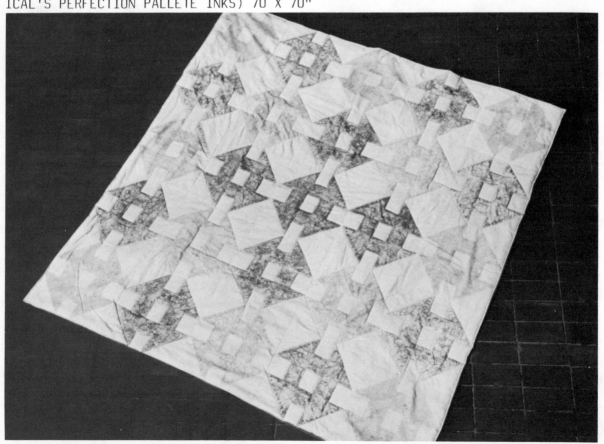

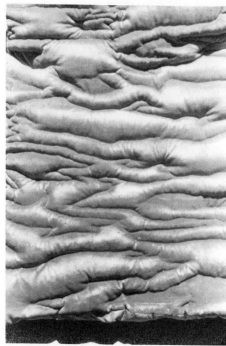

(ABOVE) FIG.135: "HOMAGE TO FURR AUDITORIUM"
BY JAMES H. SANDERS III. AIRBRUSH AND TRAPUNTO
(A TYPE OF QUILTING). (BELOW) FIG.136: LAYOUT OF
PATCHWORK DESIGNS: BOOK AND UNFINISHED SHIRT

pottery, ceramic sculpture, jewelry, wood, glass, enameling, and soft sculpture are some of the many crafts at which to look. Batik, with its emphasis on bright colors, color overlays and swirling lines caused by the motion of the tjanting, is a good design source for fabric painting. Other methods of fabric decoration, explained in detail in Chapter I (pp. 8-11) should also be looked at for design ideas. Ideas from pottery and ceramic sculpture include drawing the three-dimensional forms onto the fabric, thereby translating the medium of clay and fire into color and form. Ancient and modern pottery and ceramics should be explored. Another possibility for design ideas comes from analyzing the methods used in making pottery, and adapting these technqiues of construction to painting and the forming of garments. For example, the coiling method could be transferred to cloth, creating coiled skirts, either with sewn or painted coils. Handbuilding of clay, with the process of adding various sections of clay to a main form, could be used in an approach both to sewing and painting.

Jewelry and metalwork form another category for design inspiration. (Figs.137) Expressions in wood, ranging from a wooden house to a wooden carving, form design ideas. Glass, enameling, fiber wrapping and twining, in fact, any other form of art or craft can be a design inspiration for fabric painting.

DESIGN IDEAS FROM SEWING

The history of sewing, generally known as historical costume and dress, yields up much useful information about how ancient peoples dressed, what types of materials they used, and what type decoration they used in their clothing. There are so many ways to approach design ideas from the category of historical costume and dress. The outline

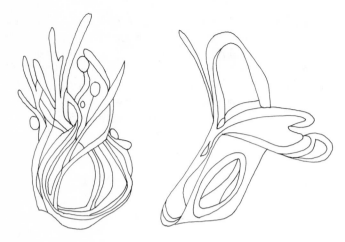

FIG.137: DRAWINGS OF JEWELRY RINGS. DESIGNS FROM SCANDINAVIAN ARTISTS. FROM <u>NEW</u> <u>DESIGN</u> <u>IN</u> <u>JEWELRY</u>-DONALD WILLCOX

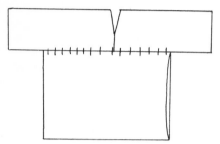

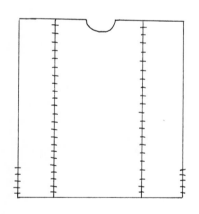

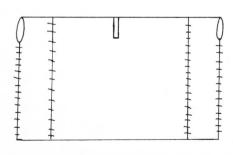

FIG.138: DRAWINGS OF HIUPTLS, A BASIC MEXICAN CLOTHING SHAPE.

of the clothing can be drawn to fit the wearer, and then if there are variations within the garment, they can be painted in. Or, pattern pieces can be cut, painted, and then sewn together to form the dress. Or, just the form of the clothing can be used as inspiration, with a modern design painted in or left plain. Or the design could be decorated in another way, such as embroidery. In general, designers and the clothing industry use historical costume as a base for new designs, but what they can do is regulated by consumer interest, production costs, and available mechanical techniques. The fabric painter has the advantage of considering only the designs themselves, basic painting techniques, and the way in which they themselves would best like to use the design.

Certain historical periods may yield more of interest, but all have possibilities. Greek, Egyptian, Roman, Byzantium, Medevial Peasantry, Early Renaissance, 17th, 18th, and 19th centuries in Europe, Russian, Slavic, and the Far East offer a wide range of costume and dress. (Fig.138,139,140,141,)Most of these designs are just the outline and decoration. Learning how to take such an outline and form a pattern is called flat pattern drafting. Available books can guide you in such a pursuit. Historical dress can also be found in paintings, with accurate portrayal of the colors and fabrics of the fashion season.

It is exciting to make a dress from a very old pattern. It has a flavor of tradition, yet its design is aimed towards modern use. Fabric painting is especially helpful here, as frilly dresses, ruffles, pleats, and intricate and perhaps cumbersome patterning can simply be painted on a dress. Painting can create visual illusion. (Fig.142)

So many sources for design ideas, still there are more! Nature, the fine arts, and the history of textile design are three more areas in

FIG.139: DRAWING OF MEDIEVAL CLOTHING

FIG.140: DRAWING OF RUSSIAN CLOTHING
FROM THE TRIBES OF THE CASPIAN STEPPE.
FROM COSTUME PATTERNS AND DESIGNS-M. TILKE

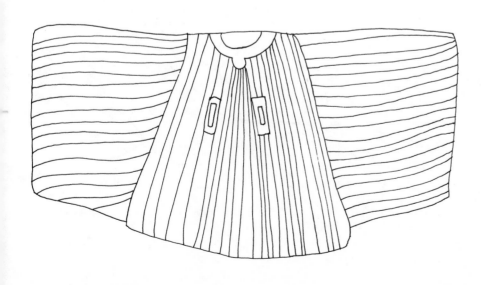

FIG.141: DRAWING OF AFRICAN CLOTHING,
EAST AFRICAN, , WESTERN SUDAN, FROM
COSTUME PATTERNS AND DESIGNS-M. TILKE

FIG.142: DRAWING OF GRECIAN TYPE DRESS.
THE THREE-DIMENSIONAL PLEATING AND FOLDS
ARE DRAWN INTO A TWO-DIMENSIONAL DESIGN.

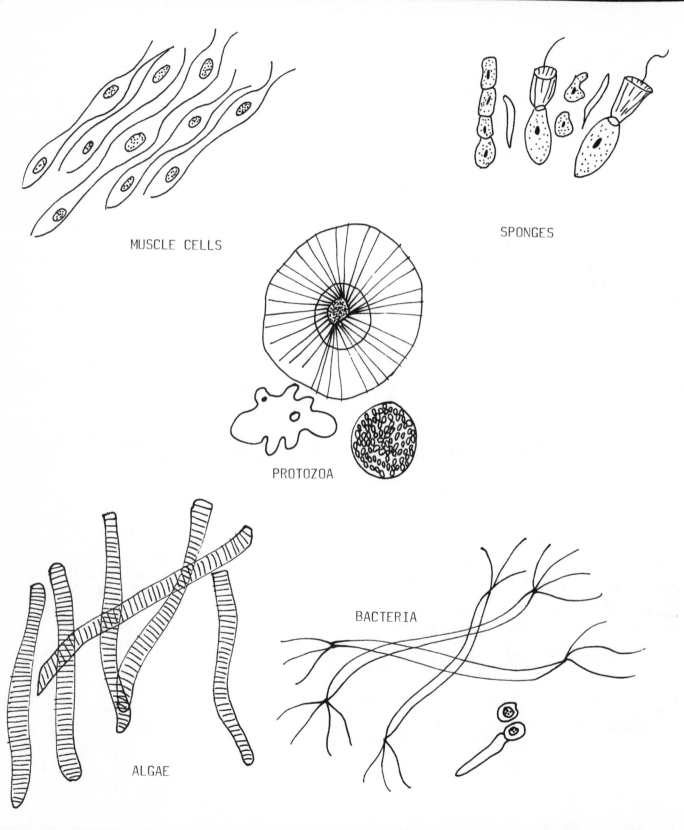

MUSCLE CELLS

SPONGES

PROTOZOA

ALGAE

BACTERIA

FIG. 143: DESIGNS FROM SCIENCE. THESE PROTOZOA, MUSCLE CELLS, SPONGES, ALGAE, AND BAC-
TERIA CAN ALL BE LOOKED AT IN TERMS OF FORM AND TEXTURE RATHER THAN WHAT THEY REPRESENT.

which to look for design ideas.
Design ideas evolving from the
physical and natural sciences
include material from biology,
botany, zoology, human physio-
logy, chemistry, geology, and
astronomy. Such material might
include skeletal structures of
animals, different kinds of wood,
bark, leaves, plants, and flowers,different parts and organs
of animals, drawings from microscope samples of various parts
of plants and animals(Fig.143),
drawings of the arrangements of
atoms, photographs of chemicals,
fossils, minerals, rocks, clay
and earth, and the stars, planets,
and galaxies. This material can
be abstracted, analyzed, or altered to fit specific design needs.

DESIGN IDEAS FROM NATURE

Nature is familiar to us in everyday forms. Art transforms in order
for us to see again, in new but some-
how familiar ways. The eye sees that
which is close and that which is far,
but it cannot see closely enough to
see atoms, nor far enough away to
see the shape of stars. Microscope
eyes and telescope eyes show us other
ways that nature is:the pen and brush
record it and show it to our eyes.
(Fig.146)

Design in nature is abundant.Grass-
es and twigs suggest line. Something
as small as bark, as well as a large
overview of rolling hills interspersed with streams and twigs, suggests texture. Rocks and leaves provide one with simple shapes and forms.

FIG.144: "PERSIAN PONIES I"-BY MAGGIE KENDIS. DIRECT DYE APPLICATION
WITH WAX RESIST. COTTON POPLIN WITH PROCION DYE. 36'X52"

FIG.145: YOUNG BUCK IN THE BIRCHES"-BY MAGGIE KENDIS.PAINTERLY
BATIK DONE WITH DIRECT APPLICATION OF PROCION DYE ON COTTON POPLIN.
22" X 28"

Many different species of flora and fauna can be drawn, both realistically and in an abstract way. (Figs.144,145)As well as rocks, minerals are very good as inspiration. They are crystalline, and offer a variety of composition with their many planes. Some look like paintings themselves, with deep blues and golds and with marbled greens and blacks. Stibnite,microline, and azurite are particularly colorful.

Not only can designs be drawn from nature, as in the previous examples, they can be used directly on the fabric. (This is discussed in detail in Chapter IV, pp.84-85) Bark, pieces of wood,twigs, leaves, seeds and pods can be coated with polymer gel and then glued onto the fabric. Natural or commercial clays can be shaped and fired, and either glazed with a ceramic glaze or painted with acrylic as a sealer. Beads are especially nice when made from clay and then pasted or even strung and sewn down on the fabric, creating a type of organic clothing.

Materials in nature can also be used as stamps and the image can be imprinted onto the fabric. Twigs, grasses, and delicate dried weeds are particularly good, for it is difficult to duplicate their intricacies by brush. The paint is brushed onto the object and then it is pressed onto the fabric. Leaves also produce an interesting though sometimes imperfect replica.

It can be seen,therefore,that there are many design ideas to be found through study of both the natural and physical sciences. Nature is always looked to as a design form, but I feel that the category of nature should be expanded to include other sciences,as mentioned above-sciences which are not so commonly thought of in terms of design or form. Other large categories to explore for design ideas come through an examination of art history and through modern textile

FIG.146: "THETA ORIONIS"-BY FERNE SIROIS. AN EXCELLENT DEPICTION OF THE MULTIPLE STAR IN THE ORION NEBULA. ACRYLIC STAINING ON HEAVY CANVAS.

design.

Although the history of painting and the works of various painters are good as a source of inspiration, not everything is possible on fabric that is possible on canvas or paper. All through the ages, the concept of "design" has been relegated to cloth, while canvas and paper have expanded many painting techniques. Cloth is as equally creative.

However, there are differences in the two materials. Cloth tends to be more textured, and therefore puts up more resistance to paint,especially when doing subtle and delicate techniques of shading, or small lines. You cannot slide paint onto fabric like you can with oils on canvas. Certain types of paint will simply soak into the fabric, while others will stiffen the surface of the fabric. When looking to art history for design ideas for fabric painting, the technical differences between fabric painting and canvas painting should be kept in mind, but you can also keep an open mind to the possibilities of any art form for fabric painting.

DESIGNS FROM THE FINE ARTS

Within art history, there is drawing,painting, sculpture, printmaking, and architecture. The differences and similarities between drawing and painting have been discussed on p 129 . Very simply, drawing is the first part of painting, but it also stands on its own as an art form. Drawing can be simple or complex. You can simply draw lines, one after another on a piece of fabric.Doodle drawings and cartoons are another category. The most popular category of drawing may be figure drawing, and the graceful drawings of Renaissance artists are particularly effective when drawn on long,flowing robes. When a human figure is drawn on cloth, it usually expresses the body in some form of motion-standing,sitting, resting,or moving. It is best that the style of the garment harmonize with the type of movement expressed in the drawing. For example, Degas' full-skirted ballerinas would be consistent when drawn on a loose flowing garment; they would be inconsistent if drawn on a tailored suit, with its emphasis on constraining movement and maximized efficiency. The category of figure-drawing has within it a great many ideas which can be used in fabric painting. One last interesting thought is that drawing figures on clothing is an overlay, for the figures are on clothing which contain within them figures; and if the painted or drawn figures wear clothing, there are four different realities:painted clothing on a painted figure on clothing which is painted, being worn by a real person!

When considering painting, one can look at various artists and historical time periods, or one can look at categories such as still-life, landscape painting, portraiture, religious painting, or abstract. However, since most of the latter categories are emphasized during one or another time period, I will place stress on the historical progression of painting which evolved out of the Western world.

Prehistoric and early historic art was mainly covered earlier in Chapter V, under prehistoric art and cultural motifs(see pp.129, 136-140) Look under Egyptian, Mesopotamian, Sumerian, Babylonian,Persian, Cretan, Mycenaean, Greek,Etruscan, and Roman art for other design ideas and inspiration. In Greek art, for example, vase painting limited itself to a few motifs which were perfected, and painted either as black or red figures. Many different garments could be created from this basic theme from Greek art.

The next large period of art was greatly influenced by the Church, as the various small geographic regions mentioned in the last paragraph were united and ruled by the Church. Early Christain, Byzantine, Early Medieval, and Romanesque art history includes mural paintings, tapestries, and beautiful illuminated books,(see Figs.147-149)

FIG.147: DRAWING BY PHYLLIS THOMPSON AFTER BYZANTINE GOSPEL COVER, MID 900'S. SILVER GILT WITH ENAMEL.AFTER THE ART OF THE BYZANTINE EMPIRE- A. GRAVAR

154

FIG.148: "VENUS"-BY JUDY FELGAR. EXAMPLE OF RELIGIOUSLY ORIENTED FABRIC PAINTING. DOUBLE-WEAVE PICK-UP: WOOL. TEXTILE PAINT.

FIG.149: "NINE" -BY JUDY FELGAR. DOUBLE-WEAVE PICK-UP: WOOL WITH ATLANTIC TEXTILE PAINT

Many of the works done in this time were done by individual artists, but their individuality remained anonymous. Gothic art was also influenced by religion, but less so by the church. Much of Gothic art was expressed through architecture, with the tall spires of the cathedrals pointing to God. Stained glass and painted manuscripts were also popular during these times, and could be easily translated into designs for fabric painting.

From 1400-1600, the influence of Renaissance art was felt, with its emphasis upon the rebirth of the art of classical antiquity.The Italian Renaissance was the beginning of the expression of individualism in art. At this time, names became important:the Van Eyck brothers, who began to use oil paint with good effects, Leonardo Da Vinci, Michelangelo, Raphael, and Titian. Women artists of the time include Elisabetta Sirani, Lavinia Fontana, Barbara Longhi, and Sofonisba Anguissola, among others.Religious art was still important, but there was a variety in art, with expansion into humanism, individuality, and aestheticism.

The last artistic period before Modern art was the age of the Baroque and the Rococo. These periods, which extended from 1600-1800, aimed for dramatic effects and the portrayal of emotional intensity. Paintings stressed space and dissolved form in color and light, unlike the preceding Renaissance, which emphasized form. Some people felt that the Baroque and the Rococo were too theatrical; yet they were created out of a time when science and mathematics reflected an ever expanding universe, and the art of the time rejoiced in this knowledge, with decorative swirls and sweeping golden atmospheres. Some of the artists during this period were Rubens, Vermeer, Rembrant, Velasquez, Caravaggio, Van Dyck, Magasco, Hals, Hogarth, Blake, Reynolds, Gainsborough, Poussin, Lorrain, Watteau, Boucher, and Chardin. Women artists of the time include Artemesia Gentileschi, Judith Leyster, Maria van Oosterwyck, Rachel Ruysch,and Lucrina Fetti.The light touch, light but sensuous, exhibited in the works of these painters, are effective for fabric painting, as fabric painted clothing should suggest a certain effect or emotion rather than be permeated and weighted down by it.

Look to Watteau, Boucher, and Poussin for figures with rich lustrous clothes set in atmospheric landscapes of spacious light. Chardin, Rembrant, and Vermeer portrayed still life, while robust and country life was portrayed by Rubens and Hals. Reynolds and Velasquez painted portraits, Gainsborough and Lorrain concentrated on the countryside, a countryside full of light, space, water and air. Caravaggio and Turner are well remembered for their paintings of light; Caravaggio leaving everything in shadow and dark except for one area of the painting, Turner filling all spaces of the canvas with flooding light. The Baroque and Rococo period is full of interesting ideas for the fabric painter.

Modern art began around 1800 and continues into the present day. The French Revolution and the Industrial Revolution gradually changed art, allowing the artist more individuality. Rather than having many artists following the dominant school of the time, there were several styles in each period. After Napoleon's rise to power, Neo-Classicism was the dominant style, with David, Ingres, and Angelica Kauffmann as the prominant painters of the time. As in Renaissance days, the classical style from the Greeks held the greatest influence. Idealized themes, based on drawings, with an intellectual basis, stressed the traditional values in painting. Lines were singular, color flat, and composition static. This was quite a contrast to the flamboyance of the Rococo. The aim of

the Neo-Classicists was to bridge their present with a selected past. Another Neo-Classicist of popularity today was Maxfield Parrish.

Following Neo-Classicism came the Romantic movement, which rebelled against the restraints of the Neo-Classicists. There was a lyrical manner in the Romantic treatment of color and form. Romantic painting inquired into the actions of humans and nature, depicted contemporary dress(in contrast to Grecian robes of the Neo-Classicists) in exotic and conventional locales. Corot,Millet, Gericault, Delacroix, Caspar David Freidrich, Albert Ryder, Daumier, Inness, and Rousseau were Romantic painters. Women painters of the time include Rosalba Carriera, Francois Duparc, Elisabeth Vignee-Lebrun, and Adelaide Labille-Guiard. Emotions and colors were emphasized; the fantastic, the pathetic, the morbid were acceptable subjects as they were glamourized and made heroic by the Romantic vision.

Romanticism gave way to Realism and Naturalism, midway through the 19th century, and the tragedies portrayed in earlier works changed to an impersonal recording of events. The artist, rather than presenting her own thought or feeling, was merely a neutral recorder of the objects observed. This was most true of Naturalism, which tried to reach the perfectionism of photography. Realism, however, allowed for some distortion for emotional emphasis, a kind of poetic license. What was seen with the eye was fused with the essence into unified imagery. Daumier, Millet, Goya, Courbet, Rossetti, and early Degas and early Renoir were included in this period. Women artists include Rosa Bonheur, Lilly Martin Spencer, Elizabeth Eleanor Siddal, Jane Stuart and Sarah Miriam Peale.

In the late 19th century, a small group of artists in France became intrigued with the effects of sunlight on various objects, particularly outdoors. Monet, Manet, Pissarro, Renoir, Degas, and Sisley watched water, haystacks, and cathedrals at various times of the day, painting "impressions". They sought only momentary occurences; yet the spots of paint fused into a shimmering color field, the effect of which was far from momentary. Impressionism has been an important development in the history of painting.

Berthe Morisot and Mary Cassatt are two important women Impressionist painters. Morisot emphasized painting directly from nature in low-keyed color harmonies. She caught the evanescent effects of light in shimmering color just as her male colleagues did in their paintings. Cassatt's goal was to paint the concerns of "the feminine"- motherhood, the charm of womanhood, in a strong manner. Her success is evident in her now famous pastels and oils.

Seurat took the technique of the spots of paint one step further in Neo-Impressionism. It was a short lived experiment based on the science of optics, and dealt with certain complementary colors being placed next to each other in small dots. The colors would fuse on the retina at a certain distance,creating greater luminosity. This idea would appear in the next century, in Op art.

Among others, Paul Cezanne, Van Gogh, Gaugin, and Suzanne Valadon comprise what is today called Post-Impressionism. Cezanne began a new trend which aimed at form, which evolved into the artist being personally inventive in handling <u>both</u> color and form. Cezanne stressed a solid yet sensitive composition, and the basis of his painting can be found to continue further into modern painting. With their bright colors, textured brushstrokes, and lyrical subject matter, the styles of the Impressionists and Post-Impressionists are particularly adaptable to fabric painting.

Cezanne, Van Gogh, Gaugin, and Valadon planted the seeds of abstract art:Cezanne,with his emphasis on form, Van Gogh, Valadon, and Gaugin with their bright colors and emotional style leading to Expressionism. Abstract art concentrated on a conscious elimination of natural forms, or an abstraction from objects in the environment.

Picasso, Mondrian, and Miro were the beginners of abstract art. Cubism evolved from abstract art,with the emphasis on pure form, with a ressemblance to objects coming second. Cubism was rational, formal, and very intellectual, with classical roots. It destroyed the ordinary forms of things, recreating them into colorful and highly textured decorative compositions. Picasso and Braque were the founders of Cubism, which gained strength in the years before World War I. Gris, Leger, and Alexandra Exter were other followers of Cubism.

There are a number of famous women artists of the Avant-Garde of this time.They include Romaine Brooks, Gwen John, Seraphine de Senlis, (Dora) Carrington, Vanessa Bell, Marie Laurencin, Gabriele Munter, Marianne Werefkin, Paula Modersohn-Becker, and Sonia Delaunay.

Abstract art became the dominant style of modern art. In the 1920's, Cubism was followed by Futurism, Nonobjective art, Expressionism, Fauvism, and Surrealism. Futurism came out of Italy in the early 1900's, with an emphasis on the machine age. Artists painted speed, excitement, movement. Giacomo Balla, Carlo Carra, Russolo, and Marcel Duchamp and Ruzhena Zatkova were artists during this period. Paint was swirled on the canvas, and the form of the object was not seen, only the object in motion. Non-objective art, very similar to abstract art, can be seen in the works of the Russian artist, Kandinsky. By the 1930's, artists were completely free to devise and improvise from their imagination rather than using man or nature as a frame of reference. Kandinsky formed a group called "The Blue Horsemen", which included Paul Klee and Franz Marc. The space relationships in their paintings seem, to the onlooker, to be very free, yet they are formed from calculated relationships. The paintings of these three men have associative properties, but they are not connected to any outer reality. The paintings move us to recognize our inner reality.

Expressionism and Fauvism, the next two art movements, provide the fabric painter with, I feel, a great number of ideas and inspiration. Expressionism, which began in Germany in the late 1800's, emphasized the emotional experiences of the artist; their inner feelings. The colors in Expressionism were bold, vivid, executed with rapid brushstrokes, often symbolic. Van Gogh, Gaugin, Valadon, Matisse,Picasso, Roualt, Kirchner, Nolde, Vlaminck, Munch, Kokoschka, Kollwitz, Dufy, Munter, S. Delaunay, and Kandinsky can all be described as Expressionists, although some of them are included in other groups.Fauvism grew out of Expressionism, with Henri Matisse as the leader. Fauvism emphasized color, swirling bright thick color, unrestrained combinations of color. Faces might be blue or pink, bridges red, rivers yellow. Realism was not a concern of the Fauves; expression was.

The flight from reality continued. Midway through World War I, perhaps expressing the senselessness they saw around them, some artists began rebelling against all existing canons of beauty or logic. The Dadaists, as they were called, felt that the intellectual mind could only produce sterile ideas, when it concerned art.They deliberately pursued chaos. Arp, Breton, and Earnst were Dadaists. Close to Dadaism was Surrealism, which was closely connected to Freud's studies of the unconscious mind. Pursuing a psychological point of view, Surrealism depicted the visual symbols of the unconscious. Space was often seen as endless, with moody dreamlike landscapes and strange figures frozen in space. The Surrealists were very intent upon communicating this new "language" of the unconscious to the general public, so they used traditional painting techniques in order to present their imagery in as clarified a manner as possible. Leonor Fini, Joyce Mansour, Remedios Varo, Leonora Carrington, and Frieda Kahlo are all exciting women Surrealists.

Americans were watching and following from overseas these various forms of abstract art flourishing in Europe. They broke with the European tradition in 1910 and created what is called American Modernist painting. A number of painting groups and techniques abounded. The Ashcan School in New York was unique in that this group of painters focused on painting the city. Edward Hopper depicted the city as a lonely place, while George Bellows' landscapes were peopled with forceful, energetic types.

Regionalism and Social Realism were the two major art movements of the 1920's. Regionalism was a reaction of Americans from foreign influence. People wanted to shut their eyes from the imminence of another world war, so they pretended to isolate themselves. Artists reflected this need by painting romanticized landscapes of the Mid-West, the farms, the people, the simple everyday lifestyles. Grant Wood, Thomas Hart Benton, and John Curry were foremost Regionalists. (Look to their work for good examples for landscape fabric painting.)When isolationism failed, and World War II became a reality, the ensuing emotions in art dealt with death, lonliness, and morbidity. One group, the Bay Area Figurative Movement showed figures in profile, never touching or relating, only anonymous and lonely.

Contrasting with this was Social Realism, which focused on the pain and suffering caused by the economic Depression. Minorities, such as Blacks and Jews, as well as Socialists, figured prominantly in this group. Ben Shahn and Jacob Lawrence are well-known artists of this period. Other schools or groups of painters from 1920-1935 include the Stieglitz group (John Marin, Bluemner, Hartley, O'-Keefe); the Arensberg Circle(Joseph Stella, Katherine Dreier, Charles

Demuth, the Color Painters or Syn-
chromists(who followed the influence of Macdonald-Wright and Mor-
gan Russell in the U. S. and Sonia
Delaunay and Robert Delaunay in
Europe), and the Cubist Realists
(Charles Sheeler, Joseph Stella,
Louis Lozowick, and Georgia O'-
Keefe).As can be seen, some of
these artists overlap various
movements, and their work would
foreshadow approaches and techniques appearing again in the
great movement of the 1940's-
Abstract Expressionism.

Abstract Expressionism began
in New York in the 1940's. Abstract Expressionism, or Action
Painting, as it is sometimes called, is an intuitive activity de-
manding automatic, and nonplanned
responses. The painter empties
herself of conscious direction,
then allows for intuitive direct-
ion.One application of paint demands further applications, the
placement of which depends upon
what happened initially. In a sense,
the painter is building upon im-
pulse,not preplanned thought.The
Abstract Expressionists were not
looking for conventional visions
or traditional techniques when
they painted, and so the paintings
cannot be judged or perceived from
that perspective. The paintings
exist as ends in themselves. Jackson Pollack is well known for his
spatter, or drip, paintings. Hans
Hofmann, a German Modernist who
resided in the U. S. was also instrumental in the beginnings of
Action painting. Other famous members of this group were Mark Roth-
ko, William de Kooning, Adolf Gottlieb, Robert Motherwell, Mark To-
bey, Grace Hartigan, Franz Kline,
Joan Mitchell, Lee Krasner, Arshile
Gorky, James Brooks, Sam Francis,
William Baziotes, Clyfford Still,
and Helen Frankenthaler.

Abstract Expressionism is an
exciting inspiration for the fabric
painter due to its bright colors,
its abstract shapes, and its emphasis on color being the expressive
force in the painting. Modular unit

painting and repeat motifs would
work well with these techniques.
Not limited by form or specific
subject matter, this allows the
painter the free flowing of color
onto the fabric.

Several painters have emphasized painting, or staining, on
raw canvas. In 1953, Morris Louis
began staining his canvases with
acrylics, inspired by the staining of Helen Frankenthaler,who used
acrylic or polymer resins on canvas. By the 60's, this form of
art was being labeled color-field
painting, or Abstract Imagery,and
was a reaction to Abstract Expressionism. Other painters of this
time doing this type of work were
Jules Olitski,spraying colors on
canvas, Sam Francis, and Sam Gil-
lian, who stained and then draped
his canvases so they look similar
to painted fabric. These artists
are, I believe, especially exciting inspirations for fabric painting.

Artists branched out from Abstract Expressionism into a variety of techniques and movements.
Post-Painterly Abstractionists
brought form back into their paintings, while still using the techniques of the Abstract Expression-
ists.John Walker and Richard Die-
benkorn are two such painters.
Hard-edge painting was one form
of this movement. Hardedge painting
is related to the language and
structure of form. It is intellectual painting, with flat color application and abstract subject matter detached from the direct problems of life. The soft-edge form
of this movement was similar, except
that their paintings were soft-
edged!

Pop art bloomed in the early 60's
as a reaction to the intuitive processes of the Abstract Expressionists.
It relied upon mass-media images
such as were used in advertising.Pop
made a mockery of the banalities of
life, and parodied the vulgar culture of the times. Andy Warhol, Roy
Lichtenstein, Jaspar Johns, Robert
Rauschenberg, Wayne Thiebaud,are

some famous names in Pop art. Op art was also popular in the mid-60's. It sought expression thru a sharp stimulus of the retina. It's based on scientific calculations of the theories of vision. There is a kinetic quality to most Op art; the lines seem to "swim" or vibrate before our eyes. Bridget Riley, Goodyear, Hewitt, and Tadasky are some Op artists.

Two more art movements became wellknown in the mid-to late sixties. They are Photo Realism, and Minimalism. Photo Realism was cool and noncommital, like Pop. The artist would often project a photograph onto canvas, then paint it so it looked just like a photograph. Common themes were suburban neighborhoods, cars, city buildings. Richard Estes, Ralph Goings, Idelle Weber, and Robert Bechtle are PhotoRealists. Minimalism emphasized clarity and understatement, and was a reaction against what the Minimalists saw as the excesses of Abstract Expressionism.

Other art movements continuing into the 1970's include Constructivism (an interest in geometric shapes), Conceptualism (focus on the process rather than making an art object), new image painting, and pattern and decoration. Joyce Kosloff's work in pattern and decoration is an excellent source for using peasant design, embroidery motifs, and decoration in painting. Other important painting history to look to for inspiration includes Modern Native American Painting, Black Art, American Folk Painting, and Feminist Art, for these various movements just mentioned have primarily been created by and for white males.

With each day, there are more painters, developing ever new ways of seeing, which, over time, develop into major art movements. One of the distinctions of modern art lies in its versatility; scientific and intellectual schools blossom simultaneously with the very intuitive and the emotional. All of these painting schools and movements, focused on the two-dimensional surface of the canvas and the picture hung upon the wall, can be changed into the painting of fabric, and fashioned into clothes of ones creative choice and fantasy in fabric and color.

While not all paintings are suitable in textile design, there is much to be pulled from these paintings and formed into a three-dimensional statement of color, texture, and balance. Whats important is to look at lots of paintings and get ideas for your own. I personally feel that certain painters and times are more of an inspiration for fabric painting than others, but I wanted to walk you through all of art history, so you can make your choices. I feel that the Impressionists, the Expressionists, the Abstract Expressionists, the Color-Field Painters and the Synchromists and the school of pattern and decoration are especially useful. Look at Paul Klee's whimsical paintings, Sonia Delaunay's brightly colored paintings and sketches for fabrics, Hans Hofmann's brightly colored squares, among thousands of other equally important painters.

It is rarely recognized that the world of painting and the world of fashion can be merged. Because of this, we have an untapped wealth of creativity waiting in all those paintings on the wall, waiting for those of use to consider that fabric is yet another canvas.

DESIGN IDEAS FROM SCULPTURE

There are several basic ways to use sculpture in design for fabric painting. The outline of the sculpture can be drawn on the fabric (Fig. 150), as repeats, in groups or in various compositions. The textures from sculptures can be sketched and used in design. Instead of the outside form of the sculpture, perhaps the textures would form in your mind as a design.

Look to geographic works of art, such as African art, or Russian art, to find sculpture typical of the area. As well, books on the history of sculpture trace their various schools, many of which parallel the trends in painting, and well known artists. Henry Moor, Picasso, Brancusi, and Giacometti are some familiar modern sculpturists.

It is also possible to make very small sculptures which can then be glued onto the fabric . For example, primitive figurines, abstract shapes from wood, clay, or acrylic modeling paste can be shaped and then glued with acrylic gel onto the fabric. It is important that these shapes are not a hindrance to the wearing of the garment. They should be placed where they will not be scratched, or broken.

One way of experiencing the sculptural effect with fabric painted clothing is to put the clothing on a dressmaker's bust, (first covering the bust with plastic so the paint will not damage it) and then paint the clothing. This will give the painter a different experience than when painting on a flat surface.

DESIGN IDEAS FROM PRINTMAKING

Printmaking is another catagory of the fine arts which should be considered for design ideas. Included in printmaking is woodblock printing,etching, engraving, intaglio, and drypoint. Books on printmaking yield interesting ideas which can be painted or drawn onto fabric. An especially diverse book is 101 Prints- the History and Techniques of Printmaking-Norman R.E. Eppink.

DESIGN IDEAS FROM ARCHITECTURE

Architecture should also be considered as a source for design ideas for fabric painting. Buildings are beautiful in three dimensions with real stone or wood, but drawings,diagrams, and paintings of buildings are equally interesting, and especially if the drawing is on such a grand scale

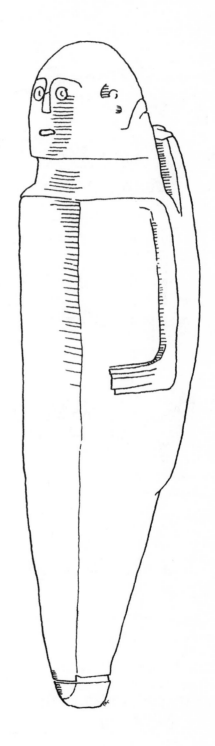

FIG.150: DRAWING BY PHYLLIS THOMPSON AFTER RHODESIAN MALE FIGURE, ZIMBABWE IN AFRICAN STONE SCULPTURE BY PHILIP ALLISON.

161

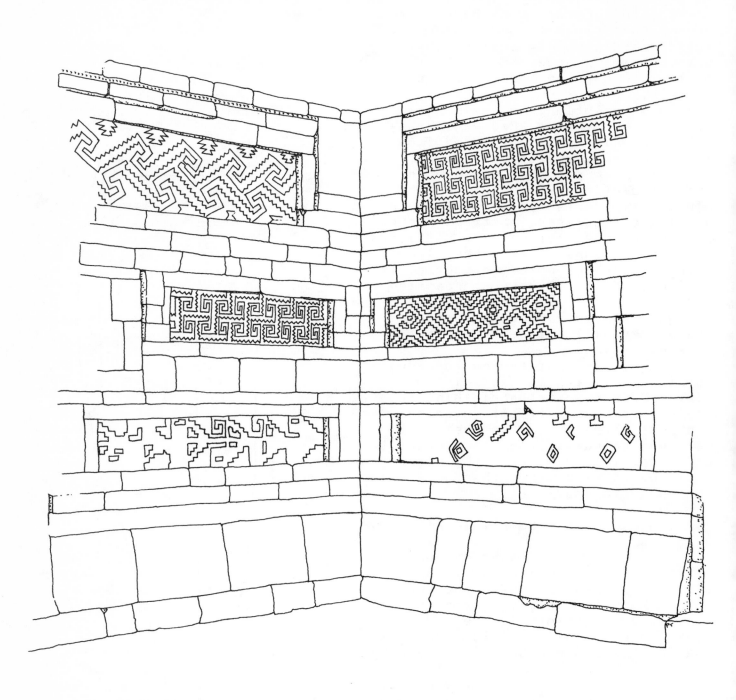

FIG.151 : DRAWING BY PHYLLIS THOMPSON AFTER LATE ZAPOTEC
WALLS, OAXACA, MEXICO, IN _MEXICAN ART_-BY JUSTINO FERNANDEZ

that it would rarely be seen in the
real. Simple tents, yurts, barns,
and huts, (see _Shelter_-Shelter Publications, Random House) or grand-
iose palaces and churches are both
equal as design material. (Fig.151)

DESIGN IDEAS FROM PRINTED TEXTILES

Design ideas from printed textiles is the last catagory that
I will discuss. Printed textiles

should be looked to for design
ideas simply because they are designed for clothing. General
rules for design for clothing
can be followed, but the limitations on design imposed by
technology can be overlooked or
gone beyond with fabric painting.
In some cases, design created by
complex technological processes
cannot be simulated by fabric
painting,and it is best to accept the limitations of fabric
painting,as well. However, fabric
painting can go beyond the repeat
motif, scenes, stripes, and abstract textures of printed textiles to include all of those
effects, if desired, in one length of fabric.

   I find it helpful to analyze
a piece of fabric by verbally describing its components. An overview of several printed textiles
shows: delicate pink flowers with
green leaves in small clusters;
a black background with shapes in
hot pink, turquoise, rose red,
bright orange, and bright purple;

grey, cream and lilac zigzags running parallel; and a geometric
knit with blue,sienna, rust, and
midnight blue. Each of these designs is repeated at some point
in a printed textile. A painted
textile can combine these designs.

163

The magazine, "American Fabrics and Fashions"- Doric Publishing Co.- is an excellent source for modern designs used in textile printing today, as well as clothing designs using these materials. An advertisement for a Color Source book, listed in the above publication, shows the wide range of sources that modern technology uses in designs for printed textiles. The Color Source book lists the following as historic or modern color palettes: Persian miniatures, Egyptian colors, Ancient Peruvian textiles, Japanese woodcut, Illuminated manuscripts, African mask colors, Williamsburg, batik colors, Scottish tartans, Victorian colors, Greek pottery, Indian textiles, Persian carpets, Coptic textiles, Mozarabic colors, American Indian, Gobelin tapestry, Aubusson tapestry, Empire colors, Wedgwood colors, Giotto's Palette, Titian's Venetian Palette, El Greco's palette, Ruben's Baroque Palette, Velasquez Colors, Gaugin colors, Monet's palette, Vermeer's palette, Italian Mannerists, Turner's palette, Delacroix colors, Renoir and Impressionism, Tiffany colors, Fauve colors, Kandinsky colors, Matisse colors, Art Deco colors, the Braque palette, Chagall's colors, Miro's colors, and Pop art colors. It can be seen from the above list that there is much to draw from for inspiration for fabric painting and textile design!

There are many other areas in which one could go to find design ideas for fabric painting. The list is almost overwhelming as it is. I feel it is important to present to the reader an idea of the possibilities of textile design beyond the flowers and nature designs with which we are all quite familiar. It is not to be assumed that every catagory mentioned in Chapter V will provide material for a successful design for fabric painted clothes. I feel it is better to widen the mind a little too much-rather than too little. Areas which I have not mentioned but which may provide interesting material are music history (actual written music, designs of instruments), psychology (mandalas, archetypal drawings,) and geography (maps, diagrams of land usage,etc.) Doubtless there are more.

6 TECHNIQUES AND METHODS

❖❖

Over the centuries, the rules of painting have changed. Painting is not under the strict rules that it was in Leonardo da Vinci's or Michaelangelo's time. Painting is no longer strictly defined. Although many painters do follow the old rules, using oils, doing under and overpainting, and doing many preliminary drawings, many more painters are breaking these rules and following their own. Some of these new found paths are becoming rules, and so there are more techniques from which to choose, more methods of expression. This development in painting goes along with the general increase in technical knowledge in scientific and humanistic fields. As we learn more about the outer world of space and the inner world of the mind, painting expands its boundaries to express in more abstract terms these events.

Techniques of painting which are very basic for beginning fabric painters are discussed in Chapter III(pp.44-46   ). Techniques which are particular to a certain medium are described in Chapter IV(see pp.84-85). In Chapter VI, I will discuss a number of techniques which are used in fabric painting as well as a few other techniques used in surface design.

For our purposes, painting techniques can be divided into three categories: direct, indirect, and spontaneous.(I am indebted to Anthoney Toney for describing these catagories in his book, Creative Painting and Drawing) Direct painting refers to traditional painting,where the paint is put onto the brush and then onto paper or fabric. Direct painting usually involves a general preplanned design, or at least, conscious action and direction. In fabric painting, direct painting occurs when the paint and cloth interact to form a design, usually with a direction and control through a tool, the brush. Indirect painting methods differ from direct painting in that there are stages of preparation needed before the paint contacts the fabric. Often there's a substance needed (besides the traditional brush) to apply paint to fabric. Spontaneous painting refers to painting which allows chance occurences, often concerning nature, to effect the design.

Most of the techniques and methods which have not been described earlier are included in the category of indirect painting, and it is here that we shall begin. Indirect painting includes monopainting, marbling, collographs,stamps and found objects, rubber stamps, airbrush and spray painting,stencils, resist processes including wax resist, cassava paste, flour and starch resist, clay resists, Japanese stencil dyeing with paste resist, and Japanese nori or rice paste resist, rubbings, fold-and-dye methods, bound resists(wrapping,tying, or clamping fabric before painting)and heat transfer painting. As well, a preview to the use of photographic stencils and emulsions is included in indirect painting. Indirect painting is a way of using the advantages of fabric printing and surface design without straying from the idea and techniques of painting. In fabric printmaking, the design is formed on a material other than the finished product and then transferred. The design idea is <u>worked out</u> on other materials. In fabric painting,however, there is a direct relationship between paint, cloth, and brush; the design idea is worked out primarily as an <u>idea</u>, perhaps sketched first, but then put directly onto the fabric.

In the processes of <u>marbling</u> and <u>monopainting</u>, the painted design is formed by the influence of a liquid or a semi-liquid substance, something which forms and shapes the paint differently than would a brush. With <u>collographs</u>, <u>stamps</u> <u>and</u> <u>found</u> <u>objects</u>, <u>rubber</u> <u>stamps</u>, <u>rubbings</u>,<u>and</u> <u>stencils</u>, something solid influences the paint and the design. In <u>spray painting</u> and <u>airbrush</u> <u>painting</u>,the gaseous substance, air, shapes and directs the pattern of paint. <u>Resist processes</u>, and <u>fold-and-dye</u> methods deal more directly with the action of the paint with the cloth. So it can be seen that there are many different "indirect" substances influencing the paint in indirect painting.

The historical sources of indirect painting are drawn from printmaking. Blake, for example, in making a monoprint, would make several prints from one plate. Of course, each print was different,but each has a similar source. This irregular type of printmaking led to a recognition of what is now called indirect painting.

It is important to recognize and accept the differences and limitations in fabric painting when compared with printing methods for fabric. Painting is, in a sense, the primitive or root of printmaking. What ideas can you experiment with, evolve, and extend? Abstract and invent? What ideas are realistically limited to fabric printing as they cannot be repeated by painting without arduous effort?

There are a number of effects which indirect painting create more easily than either direct fabric painting or fabric printing. These advantages include working with intricate designs on certain materials, working with texture, and working with similar forms.Certain effects of texture cannot work on fabrics with a heavy nap(such as cordorory or terry cloth); neither will these fabrics allow for delicate lines with direct painting. By painting the impression or design on a surface <u>other</u> than the fabric, and then transferring it to this type fabric, certain delicate designs are possible in fabric painting on thicker fabric.

Textures are emphasized by many processes of indirect painting. Suppose you want a large painted textured background for a fabric design. Monopainting, marbling, spatter or airbrush painting could be very effective. Designs from monopainting and marbling often ressemble oil on water, frosted windows, or the forms and colors of rocks and minerals embedded in canyon walls. Indirect painting methods differ from direct painting in that something is done to paint, brush, or cloth before the painting is done, in order for a measure of

spontenaity or lack of control in the painting. Because of this spontenaity, the paint is more active in forming the design, and often the mark of the paint is texture.

Another advantage of indirect painting lies in using it for design ideas which are too tedious for direct painting. Suppose you want to use a large number of similar forms in a design. If they were the same shape, size, and color, a block print would work. If they were in a group with a rotation of shape, size, and color, a silkscreen would work. But suppose all you want is a simple repeat pattern of African motifs, say seven or eight, in three different colors. And you want sharp straight edges. And the material you plan on using is thin, with a tendency for capillary action. In this case, a stencil or paste resist would be a better choice of technique. Stamps and found objects are another way of quickly creating a repeat shape. An allover print made with found objects could be an interesting design idea.

Indirect painting, then, can be seen to have many uses different from the painting techniques discussed in previous chapters. Let us now look more closely at the individual techniques.

MONOPAINTING

Monotype, monoprints, and monopainting are terms which all refer to a technique of printing one impression (as opposed to printing duplicate impressions). A discussion of the wide range of interpretations of monotype is found in the book, Printmaking with Monotype-Henry Rasmusen(Watson-Guptill). Monotype is a unique impression produced by painting a design on a surface and then transferring it to another surface.Monopainting was used more extensively than realized throughout the history of art. Blake used the technique for some of his illustrations of "Songs of Innocence and Experience", as well as in other singular works of art. Gaugin was another artist who used monopainting.

When monopainting for fabric,

paint your design on a flat sheet of glass, plastic, or metal. (Use the back of a flat cookie sheet, or the glass from a picture frame,for example).When the design is as you wish it, press the cloth onto the flat surface and pat evenly over the entire surface.Then lift up the fabric. Some paint may still remain on the glass or metal surface,and this serves as the origin for another monopainting. More paint can be added, or another piece of fabric can be pressed upon the remaining paint.

The size of your fabric will be determined by the size of the glass, metal, or plastic surface upon which you use to paint your design. It is possible to use a small surface and a larger piece of fabric, and this will create a type of repeat design. It is not necessary to limit the plain surface to a flat piece of metal, glass, or plastic. With imagination, monopainting with fabric can be extended to painting on large, curved, or cylindrical surfaces,and wrapping or pressing pliable fabric around these surfaces to create unusual designs.

There are other possibilities for monopainting. After mixing your paint material, swirl it on a piece of glass, then press the material into the design. Or put paint onto a piece of glass, then press this with another piece of glass and the paint inside. This will form a design. Or take water or a paint thinner, put this first on the glass or metal surface. The apply the paint onto the surface and press the cloth into it to obtain a delicate

167

running together of color.

MARBLING

Another method of indirect
painting is marbling. It is
sometimes called waterpainting,
as when the paint is dropped
onto the surface of water rather than another type surface.
Marbling is the process of putting paint on a liquid or semi-
liquid surface and letting the
surface tension affect the design of the print. Water, buttermilk, starch paste, and carrogen moss are four such substances used with marbling. The
action of the water or semi-liquid base is similar to the action of wind and water in nature, and many times the designs
created by marbling resemble
the random patterns of oil on water, as well as the mottled vari-
gated look of marble itself.

It's important to find an appropriate container when marbling.
It should be large and flat,ra-
ther than deep, so that you do not
need to use excessive amounts of
starch paste, moss, or buttermilk.
Since only the top layer is used,
one or two inches is deep enough
for the container. Lightweight aluminum baking tins are one good
source, and are easily found. I-
deally, the container for marbling
should be wide enough and long e-
nough to easily place the fabric
flat onto the surface.It is possible to use a large table spread
with plastic wrap for the container,using wooden supports at each
edge. This method will only work
with carrogen moss or starch paste.

Once an appropriate container
is found, the base mixture should
be put into the container. Water
and buttermilk prove no problem;
starch paste can be made by boiling a few tablespoons of cornstarch
with several cups of water,adding
water if the mixture is thicker
than whipped cream. Pour the mixture after it has boiled and thickened into the container.Carrogen
moss is also mixed with water and

(ABOVE AND BELOW: DECORATIVE EXAMPLES OF
MONOPAINTING ON PAPER)

boiled until thick. Instructions
come with the moss.

Paint is then poured onto the
surface. Acrylic, oil, textile,ink,
and dye paint materials have all
been used with success. You can use
nails, a comb, a stick,or other objects to cut across and break the
tension on the surface, thus changing and influencing the design pattern. Also, different types of paints
react differently. Oil on water is
particularly interesting, with the
beads of paint rapidly spreading a-
cross the surface of the water. When
the pattern is as you desire, put the
fabric upon the surface and gently
press it onto the surface. Then carefully lift up the fabric, holding it
by its edge. The pattern of the paint
should have transferred itself onto
the fabric. With a buttermilk surface,
sometimes a layer of buttermilk is also transferred, so not until you wash
it off(after the fabric is entirely
dry) will you see clearly the paint
design. Let the fabric dry and then
fix by pressing or steaming if the
paint material used needs fixing. Be
sure and also rinse off the base mixture for marbling after you've fixed
the paint.

FIG.152: "COLLOGRAPH QUILT"-BY JUDITH STEIN.
DETAIL. OIL-BASE ETCHING INK ON MUSLIN.

COLLOGRAPHS

Collographs are another form
of indirect painting. Although
it is by strict definition a
form of printmaking, I include
it in fabric painting because it
is a unique form of printmaking.
The word collograph explains its
definition. Collo comes from col-
lier(French, to glue or paste),
and graph, meaning to write(from
the Greek, graphein).A collograph
is a process of design where various materials are pasted together on a surface, and paint or
pigment is spread over them, and
then imprinted on paper or fabric.
In many cases, a collograph is a
collection of textures and so it
is well suited for fabric painting.
(Fig.152)

The collograph is fairly recent.
Its roots grew from collage, as
the idea of taking the textures
created by collage and printing
them onto another surface became
apparent. The collograph allows
for a wide range of expression as
much of the design is defined by
the objects used in the collograph.
Since fabric painting can involve
using large amounts of space, the
collograph can expand and use this
space easily. A collograph can be
as large as the artist wishes. The
main creative problem for the artist
is the spacing and choosing of the
objects for the collograph, and
these can be laid out and seen before
they come into contact with the fabric.

To make a collograph, assemble a
number of objects, usually objects
with texture and ones about the same
height, and paste or glue them onto
a sturdy surface,(A piece of plywood,
for example). When they are all as-
sembled, brush the surface with an
acrylic medium, such as acrylic gel.
This will protect the surface of the
materials without obscuring them.
Then brush your paint materials over
the collograph and either press the
print onto the fabric, or press the
fabric over the print. If your col-

lograph is made with objects of different sizes, it might be easier to
press the fabric over and into the
shapes created by the various objects.
Certain types of materials and objects which might be interesting to
try are:crumpled paper, towels,leaves,
string, grasses, metal objects with
textures, fabric, and pins and nails.
The collograph can be painted with one
or more colors at the same time, and
reprints can be made over the same
area of fabric for a different effect.

There are certain other processes
which I include in fabric painting
which are between the printing/paint-
ing process. By using natural materials such as leaves and grasses as
the brush, you can make interesting
textures, and if used in a well-thought
out way, they can be an interesting
composition. For example, rather than
having just a border of leaves,look
at the many variations of patterns of
leaves in a summer tree. Look at the
way nature grows: a field of wheat,
with dense textures, the foliage of
shrubs, the differences of every tree
in winter, a field of flowers with
overlapping shapes and petals on many
linear planes. Using these materials
as brush-prints allows you to focus
on the composition and let the brush
become the drawing.

FOUND OBJECTS

Found objects become a brush-stamp
or brush-print. They are the marks of
our present civilization just as the
American Indian art emphasizes wind
and rain by symbols,showing their in-
volvement with natural forces. Stamps
found in the ancient Pre-Columbian
societies are believed to have been
in the possession of the shamans or
sorcerers, and these were used to
appease the spirit world. Future gen-
erations of scholars may study the
pop top bottle tops imbedded in the
pavement with the same precision that
archaeologists use in their diggings
today. Although we look at the stamp
designs of ancient cultures as something of interest, their perception
of these marks may be as mundane as
our perceptions of Coke bottle tops,

due to the blindness that each gen-
eration has of its own time while
still living in it. Future genera-
tions will notice the marks of these
stamps and found objects as interesting, since they are an important,
if not vital, part of our life today.

Using found objects as art in the
present day is a challenge and most
people have found that by making the
practical use of the object non-appa-
rent, it becomes artistic. Automo-
bile parts, machinery, kitchen utensils, and tools can be used as stamps
without the marks made by them being
identifiable.

STAMPS

Found objects and stamps are objects which can be used to imprint
onto another surface a mark or design. By coating the surface of the
object with paint, and then pressing
it onto paper or cloth, a mark, or
stamp, is made. There are many objects which can be "found" and used
in fabric painting. Pottery shards,
molding scraps, rubber, plastic,
foam, wire, coins, erasers, cork,
broken tiles, old jewelry, kitchen-
ware, nails, pins, bolts, washers,
rocks, shells, twigs, beach glass,
driftwood, pipe cleaners, kneaded
erasers, plasticene, sponges, cor-
rugated cardboard, rubber hoses,
sink stoppers, a rubber plunger,
string, fabric, buttons, lace,
straws, a frosting filler, corn-
cobs, cabbage leaves, potatoes,
cardboard, sandpaper, rubber bands,

leaves, and modeling clay are some of the many objects which can be used for stamps and found objects for fabric painting. For the fabric painter, the found object is a brush, a contact from paint to cloth. And the brush is squeezed, crumpled, broken, and made subservient to the processes and demands of good design.

RUBBER STAMP ART

Stamps and found objects are, in general, an elementary form of fabric painting. However, one type of stamp hit the art world in the late 1970's as a bit of a craze-rubber stamp art-and in the process, elevated and refined the stamping process.

Rubber stamps were being "designer" manufactured at a fast rate for a few years. You can still order a fascinating variety of stamps. Great Atlantic Stampworks(Woodshole, MA), Gumbo Graphics(Ann Arbor, MI),i Stamp(Portland, OR), Good Impressions (Brownsville, OR), Stampworks(Overland Park, KS), Emerald City Stamps (Cincinnati, OH), JGS,Inc.(Reston, VA.), Top Drawer(Hancock, VT), Rubberstampmadness(New Canaan, CT),Donna Childs, (Newburyport, MA), and Bizarro ,Inc. (Providence, RI) have been advertised since 1980(check local phone books to see if they are still in business). Bizarro has a thick catalogue of rubber stamp art including 500 stamps, books on rubber stamp art, inks, marking pens, carving tools, erasers, and even kits to make your own stamps.

Another source for stamps is to salvage them from institutions that use rubber stamps. Three possible sources are grade schools, libraries, and the post office. By the way, don't forget to go scavenging in the toy and school supplies departments of stores. You'll find lots of fun stamps there!

How do you make your own stamps? An excellent book which gives detailed instructions is: <u>Rubber Stamps and How to Make Them</u>-George Thomson. (Pantheon Books, N.Y.1982). General-

ly speaking, handmade stamps are created by carefully transferring a design onto the face of an eraser and then cutting out the design to produce an indentation on the surface. Artgum, Niji soft plastic eraser, Eberhard Faber Rubkleen 6004(a big green eraser), Eberhard Faber Pink Pearl, and Staedtler Mars Grand, are some recommended erasers. Cut foam can also be mounted on wooden blocks for stamps.

Niji wooden carving tools, a stencil knife, a needle, x-acto knives and a small scalpel, are useful tools. Be patient when carving your design, and try to keep the surface edges flat. If nicks or bumps are encountered during the work, you can carefully sand the eraser down to smooth out its surface.

Rubber stamp art is easy! Simply apply your paint material to the stamp and press an impression onto your fabric. You can order an uninked stamp pad from Bizarro, Inc.(Box 126, Annex Station, Providence, RI 02901) or you can make your own using a piece of foam. Carefully brush your paint, dye, or ink onto the uninked pad. Some paint materials which have been used successfully include:Deka textile paints, Deka dyes, Createx pigments, Hot Air Textile pigments, and laundry inks.

Rubber stamp artists go beyond the repeat motif and use their stamps in wild, wonderful ways. Carol Zastoupil makes postcard-shaped canvas pieces with rubber stamped images of travel scenes,while Sam Evans stamps her art on wearables. Cats, dinosaurs, scarry faces, insects, fish, bunnies, stars, stamps and postage markings, hands, alphabets, musical instruments, and cameras are some of the many hundreds of images on pre-manufactured stamps!

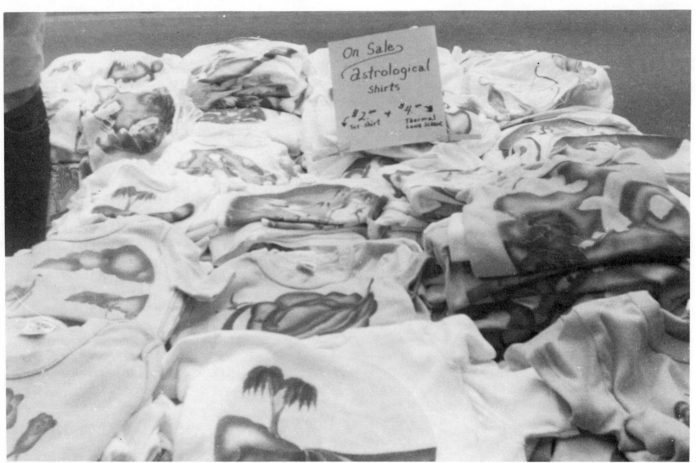

FIG.153:AIRBRUSHED ASTROLOGICAL SHIRTS. PHOTOGRAPHED ON TELEGRAPH AVE. BERKELEY, CA. 1975.

AIRBRUSH AND SPRAY PAINTING

Airbrush and spray painting are another form of indirect painting. Airbrush painting has been fairly popular on clothing since the late 1960's, when the counterculture began decorating their clothes and themselves with buttons, bells, and beads. It has also been used extensively by commercial illustrators for poster art, signs, touch-ups on photographs, as well as for photographic type illustrations for advertising of new products. It is also used for painting toys, ceramics, and automobiles and motorcycles. The airbrush is, indeed, a very versatile tool!

There are two types of airbrushes on the market today:the double action brush and the single action brush. The double action is used for finer work and thinner dyes, and both the flow of the air and the flow of color can be changed simultaneously by depressing two levers with ones' fingers. The single action brush is used with heavier paint materials and the amount of color cannot be adjusted while using the brush. A double-action brush is preferable for most airbrush painting on fabric.

The other important feature in airbrush work is the air supply. You can use a compressed carbonic (CO_2) airtank, an electronic air compressor, or an air compressor with a tank. The first is most common for regular use. A small air-compressed aerosol can is available, but it will not last very long for anything other than small amounts of work.

Although the airbrush is successfully used alone, it is common to use it in conjuction with a variety of masking devices. With these devices, specific effects unique to the airbrush can be produced. Acetate is used as a masking device and can be cut into various shapes for both stencils and templates. Friskets are made from thick paper covered with rubber cement(or can be store-bought) and are used to mask out areas while airbrushing within the masked area. Friskets block the overspray that would occur without them. In the following discussion on "Stencils", more ideas will be given for making stencils which can be applied towards airbrush work.

For fabric painting, it is imperative that you purchase an airbrush with color jars, rather than color cones. The jars screw onto the brush and will hold your paint material. To begin painting, attach the airbrush to the air supply hose. Pour your paint material into the jar, up to 2/3 full.(Thinned acrylic paint, airbrush textile colors, and fiber-reactive dyes have all been used successfully). Regulate your air pressure to 25-30 pounds. Holding the airbrush like a pen, keep it perpendicular to your work. Push down onto the lever to release the air, then pull back to release color. Practice will help you to control your "brush" strokes.

Be sure to clean your airbrush correctly after using it. Improper care with the airbrush is the most common reason for problems. (When you purchase a brush, the accompanying instructions should tell you how best to clean your specific model).

Special effects are possible with an airbrush. These include fine gradations of tone, color overlays(without disturbing the hand of the fabric), and subtle shadings using masking devices. You can draw fine lines, or thick lines, or dots! The following are techniques which are useful in airbrush painting: flat wash, graded wash, spotlighting, and softhandling and hardhandling of common shapes- the cube, spheres, cone, and cylinder. To do a flat wash, go back and forth with the airbrush lightly, from top to bottom. A graded wash is created by working up from bottom to top, left to right, leveling out towards the top. Repeat from the bottom, leveling out sooner as the overspray will build up. For spotlighting, mask the area to be spotlighted and airbrush toward the corners with most of the paint landing on the mask. Start with lighter tones, then add the

FIG.154 : "JAPANESE ACROBATS"-BY FRANCES BUTLER. AIRBRUSHED SILKSCREEN POSITIVE.

FIG.155: "INSECTS DETAIL"–BY FRANCES BUTLER. THE AIRBRUSH IS USED TO CREATE THE DESIGN ON THE SILKSCREEN AS A POSITIVE. YARDAGE IS EASILY MADE THIS WAY.

darker ones. Softhandling of various shapes involves drawing the shape, frisketing around various parts while airbrushing others. The tone gradation with this method is similar to achieving tonal areas portraying volume in oil painting. In hardhandling, each side of the shape has a more similar tonal value than in softhandling, thus having the object appear hard, or solid.

174

Fabric artists use the airbrush in a number of ways. In the 1970's, airbrush painting on T-shirts using stencils of "cosmic" scenes, rainbows, and ecological themes were popular and seen at craft fairs and in boutiques.(Fig.153) This has been expanded to using various stencil methods to create designs for clothing and art pieces. Frances Butler silkscreens yardage using the airbrush to create the silkscreen positive. (Figs.154,155, 156) Cate Fitt handpaints and airbrushes silk wearables using fiber reactive dyes. Melody Weiler makes intricate designs with the airbrush and up to 100 stencils on a shirt. She uses thinned acrylic paint and builds up her image with lighter values, then darker.

FIG.156: " BEACH ROCKS"-BY FRANCES BUTLER. RUNNING YARDAGE. AIRBRUSHED SILKSCREEN POSITIVE.

FIG.157:"PASTORAL BEDSCAPE"-LINDA NELSON BRYAN. PAINTED AND STUFFED RELIEF
(AIRBRUSH AND TRAPUNTO) ON ANTRON NYLON BLEND MATERIAL WITH ACRYLIC PAINT.

Other artists use the airbrush
for surface design, wall hangings,
or art pieces and show the surface
treatment and color effects possible.(Fig.157)

SPRAY PAINTING

Fabric painters also use spray
bottles for another form of airbrush painting. Any bottle with a
spray attachment can be used.
A Pre-Val spray unit, plant sprayers, and old Windex bottles are
good for this type work.

Spray painting is very popular
with fabric painters since it is
quick and easy to use. Diluted
acrylics, textile paints, and dyes
work well with spray painting.
Stencils and templates can be used
just like with airbrush work. Spray-
ed backgrounds for wall hangings
and spray-dyed garments are popular.
(Fig.158)

STENCILING

Stencils have been mentioned
from time to time throughout this
book. Stencils are a very old and
common way of creating a design,
both on fabric and on paper. A
stencil is a stiff piece of paper
or cardboard, or it could be a thin
sheet of metal, acetate, or plastic
upon which a design is drawn and
then cut out. Then the stencil is
placed upon the material upon which
you wish a design, and paint is
brushed in the open spaces, and a-
round the edges of the stencil. Stenciling produces a clear, sharp, design.

Because stenciling is such a common way of creating a design, it is
easy to overlook the creative use of
stencils. It is too easy to see the
simple shapes of flowers, stars, and
animals that are often made into
stencils and sold along with fabric

FIG.158: "SANCTUARY"-BY MICHAEL FORAN. SPRAY PAINTING,
DIRECT APPLICATION. CANVAS WITH ACRYLICS, CUSHING DYE,
BLEACH, TEXTILE PAINT. 19'X9'.

paint or other art supplies, and think that these simple shapes are the extent of stenciling. They are not! There are many sources of inspiration for creative stencil art. Dover publishers carries a nice selection of stencil designs, including designs from Ancient Egypt, Japan, China, Art Deco, Early American, Pennsylvania Dutch, and Victorian. As well, folk art designs such as Scandanavian rosemaling, Islamic designs, African, and Native American are well-suited for stencil work. The design ideas of stenciled folk art symbols which were so popularly used in houses, on doors and doorways, on wooden objects, and on tinware can easily be transferred for use on fabric and clothing.

An easy way to make a stencil is by using lightweight paper, which is then folded several times and cut similar to when one makes paper snowflakes. Scissors can be used when making this "practice stencil". If you use waxed paper, you won't have to worry about the edges of your stencil getting fuzzy, as they may with regular paper.

Once you have made a practice stencil, it's time to make one out of stencil paper. You can find the materials you need at an art store: waxed stencil paper, stencil board, a stencil knife or an x-acto knife (#11 or #16 blades for the x-acto knife are recommended).

You can use the designs you made with the folded-paper stencil and simply transfer them onto your stencil paper. Just trace the cutout parts with a pencil onto your stencil and then cut them out with a knife. A regular design on tracing paper can be transferred with carbon paper.

A successful stencil design drawn from a line drawing is dependent upon connecting strips which are called "bridges" or "ties". These bridges keep the middle of the stencil connected to the outside, so your

design doesn't fall out completely when you cut it. Bridges strengthen stencils- for example, a long, narrow stencil can buckle and warp-bridges will keep it nice and flat. After you've painted your design, if you wish, you can paint in the areas where the ties were, creating an unbroken line.

You can use more than one color in an individual stencil if the shapes are far enough apart or if you use ties. When working with a design where the colors lay side by side, or are superimposed on each other, you'll need to cut more than one stencil. Cut out the center part of your design, and then lay the cutout stencil over another piece of stencil paper. Trace this center shape onto the paper along with the other parts of the design, so that they can "line up" with each other correctly. Then cut out the remaining parts of the design.

Megan Parry, in her book, Stenciling, has explained these methods and more, in great detail. As well, she has expanded the concept of stenciling to an exciting art form. Hers is an inspiring source for designs and projects!

Acrylics, textile paint, block-print inks, oil paint with turpentine, and thickened dyes have all been used successfully with stencils. When painting a stencil, be sure to move your brush from the stencil down into the empty area rather than the opposite way. If you work from the center outwards, the edges of your design will not be sharp and crisp, and paint may seep beyond the area delineated for the design.

Stencils can be used for many types of designs. Many stencils are quite small, from two to four inches. The imposed design is then repeated over and over on fabric or paper. Remember, however, that it is possible to make a very large design, twelve inches square, twenty-four inches, etc. Border repeats with folk art motifs can fit in very nicely on the hems of clothing- they could either be petite and delicate or very wide designs.

Another type of stencil device is <u>masking tape</u>. It can be used where a long straight line is needed. Tape can be used as a design tool by simply putting tape wherever you do not wish paint. Another popular masking device is <u>contact paper</u>. It can also be cut into shapes and used like a stencil. Both of these materials block out areas, just as stencils do. The resist process, which is our next technique, also is a blocking process.

RESIST PROCESSES

There are a number of processes which come under the catagory of resist processes. These include using wax, commonly known as batik, using flour and starch, rice, and clay pastes, as well as more exotic substances such as cassava paste, which is used in Africa

FIG.159: "PERSONAL SPACE"-BY EVE ZWEBEN-CHUNG. PROCION DYE PAINTED ON COTTON WITH INKODYE RESIST, CRAYOLA FABRIC CRAYONS, AND VERSATEX PAINT.

FIG.160: "IRISES"-BY CAROL RACKLIN. WAX LINE RESIST.
COMMERCIAL BATIKDYE APPLIED DIRECTLY WITH BRUSH.

as a resist. As well, many companies now make special resists to be used with fabric design.The resist process allows sections of the fabric to be blocked out while other parts are painted or dyed. Usually the "resisted" design remains white, with other areas of the fabric being colored. Many nice effects can be created in this way.Colored resists are used to add color to areas at the same time that they work as a resist.They are popular with painting on silk.(Fig.159)

Most resists are used in a liquid or semi-liquid state. They can be brushed on, used with a tjanting or cone tips(either the Japanese tsutsu cones or cake decorating tips), or squeeze bottles. After the resist is applied to the fabric, it is left to dry. When dry, textile paint,dye-paste, or cold-water dyes are directly applied to the surrounding areas. The fabric is fixed in a manner appropriate to the paint material used, and then the resist is removed, usually by washing in hot water.

Wax is used as a resist in either hot or cold form. Hot wax as a resist is called batik. Paraffin, beeswax, and sticky wax can be used. Hot wax penetrates both sides of the fabric, and is commonly applied with the tjantung. (Please refer to books on batik for greater details of using hot wax.) I find cold wax resist preferable for fabric painting as it approximates certain features of batik,yet one does not have to deal with the vagaries of hot wax. The cold wax resist is applied to the fabric with various tools and is left to dry. Then the fabric can be squeezed to break and "crackle" the wax. The crackling makes a very nice visual effect.

Color Craft Ltd. carries a cold wax resist solution. It is very pourable and best used with a brush or squeeze bottle. After it dries, color can be applied and set. The cold wax is washed off in hot water and can be used on all types of fabrics. (Figs.160,

FIG.161:"LADY WITH HAT"-BY CAROL RACKLIN. WAX RESIST WITH FIBER-REACTIVE DYES.

161)

Flour and starch paste-resists are easy to mix up and use.Recipes for flour and starch paste-resists don't have to be exact. Basically, if you want a thick paste, use more flour or starch and less water. If you prefer a thinner paste, use more liquid.Here are a few recipes for flour and starch paste-resists.

Take one tablespoon of flour,one tablespoon of rice flour, one-half tablespoon of laundry starch,and one and one half cups of hot water. Boil this for fifteen minutes.Let the mixture cool until it thickens, then brush it,spoon it, or otherwise apply it to the fabric.After it dries, apply your color and fix it, then wash off the paste. Another recipe calls for three tablespoons of flour, one cup of water. Let this boil briefly,then apply it, while hot, to the fabric. This technique allows for interesting yet nebulous shapes, and a somewhat primitive effect.

Very nice effects can be created by using various kinds of flour,cornstarch, and laundry starch. A simple idea for yardage would be to brush on your resist showing evenly spaced brushmarks, then with a wider brush, apply lines of dye-paste going in the opposite direction. Flour and starch paste-resist is an excellent beginning material for the resist process.

Rice flour has been used by Japanese textile artists to create a special resist technique called norizome, or nori.(Japanese paste-resist). This process is derivative of an ancient Chinese recipe for an insoluble resist made from ground soybeans and slaked lime. When the Japanese used sweet rice as a resist material, they found that it was extremely glutinous and had strong adhesive properties. It then became the most desired type of resist process.

The rice flour is mixed with rice bran, water, salt, and slaked lime to create the paste.In the technique of tsutsugaki, the paste is squeezed through cones made from mulberry paper with brass tips, much like a cake decorating tube. Japanese nori paste is also used for katazome, the art of stencil dyeing with paste resist. This technique will be discussed later in this section.

Nori paste-resist is a more complex resist method than the previously mentioned flour and starch resists. General instructions will be given here, but I would like to recommend that you read Japanese Stencil Dyeing:Paste-Resist Techniques-by Eisha Nakano and Barbara Stephan(Weatherhill Publications)for a thorough explanation of norizome and katazome.

Take 1/4 cup sweet rice flour,and 3/8 cup rice bran. Mix these together,then add approximately 1/6 cup of water. Mix this well to make a batter and knead it,just like you would bread dough.Then shape your batter into a few donuts. Wrap these donuts with a damp piece of cotton fabric.

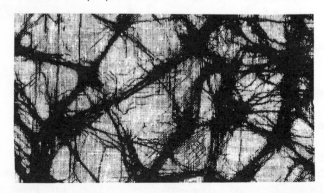

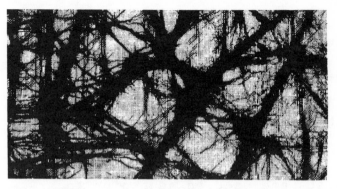

Put them in a steamer(just like a vegetable steamer) and steam them for 45-50 minutes. Remove them and mash them with a pestle or potatoe masher.Gradually add 1 to 1½ tablespoons of uniodized salt,dissolved in 1/8 cup of water. If the weather is humid,you'll need less salt,if it's dry, more. Mix together 1/8 cup of water and ½ tablespoon slaked lime(also called calcium hydroxide). Let it settle for a few minutes and then pour off the top liquid into the paste mixture. Continue beating the paste. Its color will change from light brown to light yellow. Continue adding warm water until you can stir the paste easily. It is then ready to use.

If you are using the Japanese tsutsu cones, first soak them in water to make them more flexible. Attach the metal tips securely and fill the cone half-way with nori paste. If using cake-decorating tubes, attach the proper tips and again half-fill the tube. Squeeze with an even pressure to draw lines and other designs. Let your paste dry(this will probably take at least overnight,)then apply dyepastes or textile paints. Fix your paint material before washing out the paste.

Japanese nori paste is extremely tenacious. For this reason, it is not the easiest method to use successfully for the beginner. Be sure your paste is think enough to flow through the tube-otherwise little globs will come out of the tube and you will have no control over your design.Once you've made up a few recipes and learned how to do it properly, it is a wonderful resist technique!

Sweet rice flour can be purchased at an Oriental food store. Rice bran is available at health food stores. Uniodized salt is available at a regular grocery store. Slaked lime can be ordered through Cerulean Blue,Ltd. P.O. Box 21168,Seattle, WA. 98111, or perhaps found locally.

Clay resists have primitive origins. In Africa, mud and clay were smeared onto cloth,and the metallic salts in the mud sometimes themselves would color the fabric; other times it was necessary to pour a hot dye onto the fabric. To use clay today as a resist, take a small amount of potters clay and put it in a container,a small dish,for example. Add water to soften the clay,then use it as a resist in a manner similar to the flour or starch paste resists.Sometimes the clay will react to the paint material,leaving a nice blending of colors.Clay is an easy resist to try.

Cassava paste-resist also originates from Africa. The cassava root was pounded down and ground into a paste and used much like the starch-resist pastes mentioned earlier. Screen Process Supplies in Oakland,CA. carries an Inkodye Resist which is much like cassava paste. It can be applied with a brush, squeeze bottle,stamps,or through a stencil. After drying,it can be cracked just like wax to produce the batik-like"crackle"effect.It's washed off with hot water.

There are other companies producing ready-made resists today.A line resist is produced by Color Craft, Ltd., called Createx Line Resist. It is a medium-weight water based resist,and is best used with a brush or squeeze bottle.It has to be washed out with Createx detergent and tri-sodium phosphate, both available from the company. IVY Crafts Imports distributes a silkscreen thickener to be used with the French Sennelier Colors for silk and wool. This thickener comes in a powdered form, and can also be used as a resist. It is also of medium weight,and works well with squeeze bottles.

Specific resists are made for painting on silk. Gutta serti is one of the most familiar silk resists. It is a liquid rubber resist,and can be used straight from the can,or or it can be thinned with a gutta solvent.75% gutta to 25% solvent is the standard ratio. Fine lines can be made with gutta with a squeeze bottle or a cone similar to a tsutsu cone. It gently dissolves in water,and will definitely be removed by dry-cleaning. Gutta serti is the resist used for the famous French serti technique of silk painting.

Seidicolor makes a nice water soluble resist called Seidicolor resist. It makes very nice sharp lines and comes in a plastic applicator bottle with a convenient cone-shaped top.It is used primarily for silk painting, but it can also be used on other natural fibers,such as cotton, linen, and wool. It can be thinned with water if necessary. Be sure when applying it that it soaks through both sides of the fabric,otherwise your dye will seep through.

Another nice silk resist is called Rezist Bien. It can be used with squeeze bottles and brushes. It needs several hours to dry. It works best on silks,and washes out with cold water.

Silk painters will find another product advertised along with the regular silk resists. These are the colored resists. IVY Crafts Imports carries gutta and color that you can add. You can also add a dab of oil paint to the plain gutta. Dharma Trading Company carries a fancy line of metallic gold and silver colored gutta. The Seidicolor resist comes in ten colors,and it is unique in that it won't wash or dry-clean out(most gutta resists will come out if dry-cleaned,and this includes the colored ones!) Createx line resist can also be made into a colored resist by adding liquid fiber-reactive dye. After adding the dye, add 2/3 teaspoon of sodium bicarbonate and 2 tablespoons of urea(for every four ounces of resist.

A colored resist using paraffin wax and regular color crayons is described in Batik and Tie-Dye-by Dona Meilach. A particular color of crayon is melted with some paraffin and then applied to the fabric with a brush, squeeze bottle, or tjanting.After other paint materials are applied and fixed, the wax is removed by a hot iron,and the colors from the crayons will remain intact.

As can be seen, the resist process is quite varied and extensive. Its roots are in ancient cultures; resist processes have been found throughout most of the worlds' cultures for many centuries. (The Dyer's Art:Ikat, Batik, Plangi-by Jack Lenor Larsen is an excellent sourcebook which tells of this fascinating history.) Resist processes contain an element of surprise,as they do not adher to hard and fast rules. Part of their appeal comes from the difficulty in pinning their effect down through certain procedures or an exact recipe. As they are part of the process of something handmade,they also have the variety and sometimes the irregularity which is part of the appeal of the handmade item. Their look is the opposite of the hard-edged look of most stenciling, which is interesting in that they both operate under the same basic principle, that of the block-out technique.

JAPANESE STENCIL DYEING WITH PASTE RESIST

The nori rice paste-resist mentioned earlier is also used in another process: katazome, or Japanese stencil dyeing with paste resist. In this resist process, the nori paste is pushed through a cut-paper stencil with a wooden spatula, called a hera, to produce the design. The paste is left to dry, then a dye paste is painted directly onto the fabric.

The process of katazome has many steps,and again I refer you to Japanese Stencil Dyeing:Paste-Resist Technique-by Eisha Nakano and Barbara Stephan, for a description of the complete process. There are also many different types of Japanese stencil dyeing. For example, komon is a technique where a small repetitious design is cut on the stencil and only one color dye is used for the background. This produces a small overall pattern in monochrome. In chugata, the patterns are medium sized and are perfectly aligned on both sides of the fabric. Bingata is a brightly-colored method which combines cone and stencil dyeing. It is an especially interesting design technique,since the stencil can easily reproduce fine textures while the tsutsu cone drawing produces fine line drawing.

Colored paste, or ironori,is used in katazome in the same manner as the colored resists mentioned previously. Yuzen means fine-lined cone drawing of colored paste with delicate hand-painting inside. Stencil yuzen occurs when the colored paste is stenciled onto the fabric.

The design and cutting of the stencil is an art in itself. The two most common stencil design techniques are colored ground, and white ground. In colored ground,or jizomari, the design remains white while the background is dyed. With jishiro, the design is colored and the background remains white. The cutting of the stencil for jishiro would be completely opposite than for jizomari. Other techniques are senbori, or cut outline, and kukuri, or "string", where extensive use of bridges is needed.

There are various types of cutting styles, as well. Awl cutting and thrust cutting create arabesque and floral shapes. Tool punching uses a dot punch, which punches out the design. Pull cutting is a technique which creates very fine stripes.

In order to do katazome, you'll need some kind of stencil paper, a stencil knife or x-acto knife, silk gauze, a wooden spatula or hera, possibly some dot punches, nori paste, soybean liquid for sizing the cloth, and the dye-paste or thickened dyes for coloring the fabric.

In Japan, the type paper used for stenciling is a handmade paper of mulberry bark which is laminated with the sticky tannin-rich juice of persimmons. This paper is very strong and resilant, and much of the success of katazome is due to this paper. This stencil paper, called shibugami, can be ordered through Cerulean Blue in Seattle, WA. Other alternatives for this paper are the regular stencil paper sold in art stores, contact paper or vinyl sheeting(sold to cover kitchen shelves), or firm paper which has been brushed with wax and then ironed between sheets of waxed paper.

To start your design, you can use white tissue paper or special Japanese tracing paper (minogami) over a design and then transfer the tracing paper to the stencil paper with a spray adhesive. Then you're ready to cut your design. This is really the most important part of the process, since the stencils can be used repeated numbers of times. It pays to try and do a careful job of both planning and cutting your stencil. After you've cut your stencil, you can make it solid and secure by attaching a piece of silk mesh, called sha, over the stencil. (I've found that this step is not always necessary). If your stencil design does not have enough connecting bridges or ties(refer to the section on stenciling for more detail on this), you will need to laquer the sha to your stencil.

The next step is to brush your fabric with a sizing of soybean liquid. Secure your fabric and put the stencil on top of the fabric. Then lay the nori paste down onto the stencil, putting the paste in the middle and spreading it outward to the edges. I find a kitchen spatula is sufficient if you do not have the wooden hera. If your paste is of the right consistency, without lumps, this part of the procedure will be very easy. I found that using a blender to mix the nori paste makes it smooth and manageable. Smooth the paste with a firm stroke, so that you will force the paste through the stencil. After laying several layers of paste, carefully lift up your stencil off of the fabric.

The stencil can be washed off and reused many times, if carefully handled. Let your paste dry, then brush the thickened dye over the fabric. Fix the paint material after it has dried, and wash off the nori paste with warm water. You may need to soak the paste before it comes off.

Over the centuries, the Japanese have refined katazome to a fine art. These instructions are but the rudiments of the art of stencil dyeing with paste-resist.

RUBBINGS

The next type of indirect painting is very different from either stenciling or resist processes. Rubbings have recently been noticed as an art form. A rubbing is an impression taken by rubbing a crayon over a piece of paper which is put upon a certain textured surface, which is the desired impression. Subject matter for rubbings include gravestones, stamps and seals on buildings telling of the date of their erection, grates and markers in streets, and other large markers to be found around cities. In order for a successful rubbing to be taken, the object used must be thick enough to create a raised surface in contrast with the paper, but

it must not be so thick or bumpy
that the paper cannot be laid
fairly flat upon its surface. For
example, a large sculpture in a
graveyard or museum which has
great contrasts in its surface,
with some parts out quite far and
other parts barely raised at all,
would not be suitable for taking
a rubbing. A more even texture is
helpful.(Fig.162)

Taking rubbings with cloth varies a little from using paper.
One advantage is that cloth is more
flexible and can be wrapped on a
more uneven surface,like that described above. However, it is still
necessary to move your crayon evenly across the surface of the fabric,
in order to pick up the impression
rather than eradicating it into a
crayon scrawl! A square-shaped crayon,such as a pastel,works more
easily than a round crayon,and the
bigger the crayon,the better. When
first taking rubbings, hold the crayon and move it <u>lightly</u> across the
surface of the fabric with smooth
even strokes. Move the crayon in
<u>one</u> direction rather than in short
back and forth strokes.If you have
never taken a rubbing before, it
might be better to first try it on
paper in order to learn how to use
the crayon correctly.

Some most interesting rubbings
have been made of the ancient Maya
sculptures. The book, <u>Maya</u> <u>Sculpture</u>
<u>of</u> <u>an</u> <u>Ancient</u> <u>Civilization</u> <u>Rubbings</u>
by Merle Greene(Leder,Street,and
Zeus) is full of beautiful rubbings
which were done on rice paper. These
rubbings were made from the various
stelae,sculptures,and the stucco relief and ornamentation found on the
temples.

Two paint materials are especially
suited for taking rubbings. One is a
soft oil-like pastel called Pentel
pastel dye sticks.The other is oil
paint mixed with turpentine or textine. The oil paint can be used with
a brush,and with a very light touch
one can pick up impressions from various textured objects-lace, leaves,
in fact, <u>any</u> kind of textured object. Smooth,fairly thin cloth

FIG.162: "ELK"-BY JEANNE HILLIS. RUBBING
DONE ON POLY-COTTON WITH OIL PAINT.

works best, as it allows the impression to be clearly recorded.

FOLD AND DYE

Fold and dye is another technique which can be used in fabric
painting. Fold and dye is simply
folding the cloth in a number of
sections one way, and then folding
it some in the reverse direction,
and then dipping the cloth into dye,
or brushing dye or paint into corners and on edges of the fabric.
This technique was originated for
use with decorative papers, which
are used in connection with book-
binding or card making. Fold and
dye was seen as applicable for surface design as well.

Flat lengths of material can be
folded and dipped, or a whole garment can be used. The garment does
not have to be evenly folded,and
part of the appeal of the method is
the surprise in finding what kind of
design is created from the random
brushmarks or dippings that have been

done. If, on the other hand,you wish a more even design, simply fold the length of cloth more evenly, and dip the fabric in an even manner.

For the actual process, you will need wide shallow cups for the dye, ink, or other paint material. Fold your fabric,and press the folds with an iron. Then moisten your fabric with water,and gently pat it damp. This is an important step so that the dye will be drawn up into the folds. Clothespins are handy to use as a handle and to keep the folds together. Dip your fabric into the various containers. Let the colors blend and spread. Or, if you wish, use a brush to paint on designs. Gently press the fabric together,so that the designs will penetrate to the innermost folds.

Fold and dye looks simple and easy,but it takes practice to achieve predictable results. The most common error is to not get the dye into the innermost folded areas. If you are sure to moisten your fabric enough, and if you don't have too many folds, this problem should recede.

After you have dipped the material, set it on some butcher paper to dry. Try and keep it in the same shape as when it was dipped. When it is partly dry, it can be spread out for further drying. Set your dyes if necessary.

Fold and dye works especially well with cold water fiber-reactive dyes. Most all types of fabrics can be used,and other types of paint materials,such as acrylics, oil paint,and textile paint, can also be used with good results.The key to good results with fold and dye is practice,since its effects happen somewhat by chance.

BOUND RESISTS

Very close to the process of fold and dye is the bound resist technique. With a bound resist,also called plangi, the fabric is rolled into a rope-like shape,firmly bound with various types of cords,rope,or pieces of fabric,and usually immersed in a dye-bath.For the process of fabric painting, this is modified to applying the dye directly with a brush, or dipping the bound fabric in a manner similar to fold and dye.(In both fold and dye and bound resists,the dye is mixed with chemical water and soda and washing soda in order to be effective. Refer to Chapter IV, pp.101 under"Thinned Applications"for instructions)

Only a few tools are needed for bound resists. String,cord, twine,rope, and strips of fabric are used to bind up the fabric. Sometimes artists will wrap round objects in the fabric as a resist. Seeds, pebbles, stones,beads, rubber balls,marbles,and other round objects are used.

To proceed with bound resist, take your fabric and roll it up into a long"rope". It's best to not have your fabric real wide,but you can have it as long as you wish. If you wish to wrap objects in the fabric place them along the length of the fabric and secure them by tieing them with string or thread.Then continue rolling your rope! The fabric is then bound with various ties,ropes,and strings.It is then dipped in various dyes, just like in fold and dye. The ties will act as a resist. Paint can also be directly painted onto certain sections of your fabric "rope".

For a more complex design, let the fabric dry,then unwrap your ties and strings,and retie them in different ways. Repeat the process and dip areas that are undyed. This process can be repeated several times.After the final drying,unfold your fabric, set your dyes and paints,and untie any objects that were tied in.

For beginners, bound resist processes depend largely on chance. However, in Africa and Asia,where these techniques have been used for centuries, they are highly developed. Again, I refer you to The Dyer's Art-Jack Lenor Larsen as a wonderful sourcebook for bound resists.

Fiber-reactive dyes,textile paints,thinned acrylics, and Inkodye all work well with bound resist techniques. Bound resist is really no more than a "wrap and dip" method. There are many possible effects from changes in wrapping and how the paint material is used. One last point, if you fold or roll your fabric lengthwise,you'll get a linear design. If you wish a circular design,pull your fabric up from the center and begin wrapping it like a rope. This will produce a circular design,commonly seen in tie-dyed T-shirts of the 1970's.

HEAT TRANSFER PROCESSES

The heat transfer process is a technique which uses a type of dye(disperse) which is activated by heat and then adhers to synthetic fibers(such as polyester and nylon). This disperse dye is used in three forms for the heat transfer process: in powder form,to be used with a thickening agent,on premanufactured heat transfer paper,and in a solid wax form-fabric crayons. These three forms have different effects,are applied in different ways,yet can be effectively used together in a complementary fashion.

In the heat transfer process, the design is painted or drawn directly onto paper,left to dry, then the paper is placed,face down, on the synthetic fabric.Butcher paper is placed,beneath and on top of the fabric,and the whole area is ironed until color shows through the top paper. The heat "transfers" the dye molecules from the paper to the fabric.

Heat transfer requires few materials. Have a ready supply of butcher paper-you'll need a lot when ironing your fabric and it's also good for painting designs! Other

suitable paper:heat-transfer Thermal Master paper(available from silk-screen supply houses),or any other smooth,non-porous paper. Various types of brushes can be used for the thickened dyes,and scissors will be needed for the transfer paper.Since this technique utilizes textures, you may wish to collect string,lace, or other items which will create textures when pressed with the fabric.

One of the nicest aspects of this process is that you can reuse your patterns.You can recolor them,in which case they will approximate the original,or you can make a second, weaker image from the original.Areas of a painted design can also be cut out in various shapes for use as an independent image.Any technique that you are used to doing on paper can be done and transferred to fabric. You can tear your paper,or cut it in geometric squares like patchwork,or leave it in big open sheets.Watercolor effects, line drawings,collage, all can be done with the heat transfer process!

The powdered disperse dyes are used with a thickener for direct painting. The recommended thickener is monogum thickener,and is available at Cerulean Blue in Seattle, WA. Take one part monogum to 10 parts water,and sprinkle the monogum over the water. Agitate your container so the particles blend into the water-this should happen fairly quickly. Mix about 1/4 teaspoon of dye with a bit of boiling water(approximately 1 2/3 teaspoon). Then mix the thickener with the dye mixture(I find plastic egg cartons convenient to mix up small quantities of a number of different colors of dye)and you are ready to paint!

I've encountered only a few minor problems in using this technique.The drying time for the paints interferes with a continuous production of craft items. You have to be patient! Also, with the transfer process,the colors are only transferred to one side of your fabric. If you want to make a neck scarf,for example, you might want to repeat a weaker image on the wrong side of the fabric. Sometimes,while ironing,the image will "slip" a bit, but a double-image effect can be used to work with the design rather than against it.

Many nice effects are possible with disperse dyes. The colors blend well,with a softness to them. As mentioned before,watercolor techniques are very effective. The already painted paper can be cut up in various shapes for overlays of pattern and color. And the colors themselves are especially bright,particularly on 100% synthetic fabrics.If you don't wish to mix up your own thickened dye,transfer paints are now available from Deka.They are applied just like the thickened dyes,and come in eleven different colors, lemon,orange,pink, light red, crimson, violet,light blue,dark blue,green,brown, and black.

Heat-transfer paper is also used with the heat-transfer process. This paper has been manufactured with the disperse dyes already on it. It's very easy to use and produces a clear, sharp image. The same method is used for transferring the color from paper to fabric. Simply place the paper, cut or torn in various shapes, face down on your fabric. Cover with white paper, and iron with a dry iron for up to one minute. Your colors will be bright,and very smooth. It's easiest if you cut your shapes from the back of the transfer paper,since the image will be reversed onto the fabric.This way,what you are cutting,and what you see on the fabric,will be the same. Heat-transfer paper designs have been sold as transfer prints for T-shirts commercially. Try making your own T-shirts using this paper- it works well!

Fabric crayons are the last catagory of paint material used in the heat transfer process. A similar procedure is followed,with the design being first drawn on the paper.The wax in these crayons has a tendency to "flick" off from the design,causing miniscule smudges,so be especially precise when coloring,and try and blow off any crayon specks before the ironing process. One solution to this problem is to use the crayons in conjunction with the dyes-they compliment each other wonderfully and your smudging problem is solved.

(Refer to Chapter IV under "Crayons and Fabric Markers" for more details about these crayons.)

All forms of the disperse dye reach out and"grab" the synthetic material, so you do have to be careful when transferring these dyes to not have your pattern accidentally brush up on some fabric. These dyes can be used on white or lightly colored fabrics,and the colors will undergo interesting transformations on colored fabric. Any fabric that is at least 50% synthetic can be used successfully with the transfer processes.Acetate, nylon, polyester,poly-cotton,triacetate,and dacron are some good synthetics to try.Be sure and put a pad of newspaper on the ironing board before laying down the butcher paper-this will give you a cushion when you iron.

The most challenging aspect of heat transfer is the reversibility of the image when it is transferred. One solution to this is to plan abstract designs. Another is to sketch your design in pencil,then turn the paper over and go over the design in fabric crayon or thickened dye. This way the desired image will appear "right-side up" on the fabric. Color blending is also different from other dyes.Rather than the red, blue,and yellow primary colors of color pigments, disperse dyes work on the theory of colored light. Yellow, turquoise,and magenta,are therefore the best colors for mixing.

PHOTOGRAPHIC PROCESSES

There are a number of processes which can incorporate photographic visual images onto cloth. They include photosilkscreen,using photographic positives or negatives, cyanotype, photograms, brown-print, blue-print,copy-transfer,Xerography, photo emulsion, and color Xerox.I refer you to photography books and other books on surface design for most of these processes;however, I would like to describe the last two for you.

In photo emulsion, a photographic emulsion is brushed onto the surface of the fabric. It is then put under an enlarger. The film is put into the enlarger and the image centered onto the fabric.The fabric is then printed as you would a picture.The emulsion can be bought or special ordered at photo stores. The fabric must be dry-cleaned,rather than washed. One idea I have had for use with this process is to take a series of pictures of houses,then make a skirt with the pictures of these houses on it,and go walking down the street in the skirt.

Color Xerox is another popular process. In many ways, it is similar to the heat transfer process. A color xerox machine(specifically color xerox 6500) duplicates color illustrations from magazines or books as well as color slides. It prints the image,using diazo colors (similar to disperse dyes)onto paper. The paper is now treated in a manner similar to heat transfer. Iron the print onto synthetic paper, and peel the backing off. In order to solve the reversal problem, you can have the slide reversed in the machine. Color Xerox machines can be rented,or you can have prints done for around $2.00 each. They can only be used once,unlike the heat transfer process.Robin Becker,Beverly Rusoff, Louise Jamet, Virginia Jacobs, Virginia Davis,and Jan Cochran are some of the many fiber artists using color xerox in their work.

SPONTANEOUS PAINTING

Spontaneous painting is the next large catagory of painting techniques. The roots of spontaneous painting are in the Action painters of the 1940's here in America.Instead of planning out a painting,doing preliminary drawings and slowly building up a picture,painters began to throw paint onto canvas,letting it drip,letting it soak in at random, letting it form its shape with little help from the painters' hand.In general, spontaneous painting allows for chance effects due to motion

and the forces of gravity. Jackson Pollack is one of the more better known"spontaneous"art painters.

For fabric painting as well,spontaneous painting means letting natural circumstances affect your painting. A design book called Design by Accident-O'brien(Dover) has many different techniques to achieve spontaneous design. Chance effects due to motion include pouring the paint around onto the fabric and then tilting the fabric in different directions in order to move the paint around onto the fabric.

Another possibility is to hang a large piece of wet fabric on a clothesline,and pour and drip paint onto the fabric. Again, manipulate the fabric in different ways to affect the direction of the paint. You can press different parts of the fabric together, or squeeze it, while it is hanging. Let the fabric dry, and see if you have the desired effect. If not,repeat the process, letting colors run more thickly in areas where the color is washed out or the design undesirable.

Another possibility: hang wet or dry cloth on a clothesline outside on a windy day. Brush and drip paint onto the surface of the fabric. Let the wind affect the design. Other examples of letting nature affect a design include using the sun, shadows, and water. The paint material,Inkodye(see p. 116) changes color and develops with the use of the sun. Paint fabric with Inkodye and then let it sit outside on a sunny day. Use shadows creatively. Sit under a tree and draw the shadows of the leaves from sunlight. Or sit under a tree in winter with a piece of fabric laid flat on a board. Then trace the patterns of the shadows of the winter tree onto the cloth.

Spatter painting is an easy way to do spontaneous painting. Spatter painting is pouring paint onto a flat surface of cloth from various heights, letting it "spatter" into a design upon the cloth. Plastic containers,such as yogurt or cottage cheese, are useful to mix and pour the paint from. There are real dif-

ferences in effects due to the size
of the pouring containers,the angles at which you pour,and the speed
at which you pour. As well, different paint materials react differently with different kinds of cloth.
Working with four or five colors is
a good way to start with spatter
painting,as these colors blend into other colors without getting too
messy. My favorite combination of
colors is maroon,bright orange,yel-
low,olive green,and navy blue. Experiment with different combinations
of colors.

Pouring and crumpling is another
way to paint spontaneously. This entails pouring paint onto the fabric,
much like spatter painting. Rather
than keeping the fabric smooth,how-
ever,crumple it and then pour the
paint into the cracks and ridges of
the fabric. Then carefully spread
the fabric out. Blowing paint is an
interesting way to get a design. Try
using straws for direct blowing;try
a vacumn cleaner hose or a hose from
an electric hair dryer as well. Think
about how to move the color over the
fabric.

Fingerpainting can be used on fa-
bric.Use the motions of twisting,pul-
ling,pressing,spattering,flicking,and
pushing the paint into the fabric
with your fingers. Try rubbing in the
color.(Be sure and use protective
gloves while doing this)All these ways
are spontaneous,and you will not know
the results until you have tried them.
Spontaneous painting should be looked
upon as experimental rather than de-
finitive. It is not restrictive. It
is,however, subject to certain rules,
in the same way that the effects of
wind and water are governed by certain rules,even if they seem intan-
gible.

DIRECT PAINTING

The last type of painting catagory
I will discuss is called direct paint-
ing.Direct painting is what is normal-
ly considered painting,in other words,
painting as has been recorded in art
history and that which is taught in
art schools. Direct painting is dif-

ferentiated from indirect and
spontaneous painting in that the
paint is applied directly onto
the surface with a tool,usually a
brush. As mentioned in Chapter III,
(see pg. 52) fabric painting is
very concerned with the combination of three things:the paint,the
cloth,and the brush,with the paint
being applied directly onto the
cloth via the brush.

Books on surface design and fabric decoration only give slight
mention to direct painting. They
define it as spray painting,canning,
using eye droppers,paint rollers,
and brushes, but either assume
that the fabric painter is already
an accomplished painter, or do not
realize the diversity of techniques
with direct painting. All art techniques will not transfer exactly to
fabric,but a background in art and
painting will definitely help you
as a fabric painter!

Techniques of direct painting derive from oil painting,acrylic
painting,drawing,pastels,and watercolor. One can also derive techniques from studying still life,land-
scape,cityscape,seascape,figure
drawing,painting flowers,and painting trees.

Much fabric painting creates what
I call a "textile style" of paint-
ing:flat areas of color much like
painting on paper with tempera. Oil
painters,however,will probably want
to transfer their skills to painting in an "oil style"-using oils and
textine,turpentine,or a mix of oils,
turpentine,and enamel paints. Water-
colorists might enjoy using acrylic,
blending it into the fabric using a
variety of watercolor techniques,and
experimenting with a variety of
weaves of fabric(cotton,muslin,poly-
cotton,linen,canvas).Artists who draw,
using a variety of materials such as
pencils,pens,charcoal,and pastels,
could use dye pastels,inks,fabric
markers,and embroidery paints on
well-stretched fabrics for similar
effects.

Direct painting is most effective when the techniques of canvas
painting and the function of fa-

bric decoration methods are blended. To do this, one moves beyond painting a repeat motif on yardage. One moves beyond painting a picture squarely on a piece of fabric. What is really happening is that you learn an "art vocabulary" and transfer the principles of perception,perspective,tonal exercises,color exercises,etc. to fabric and cloth. When this vocabulary is learned, you are much more free to express painting that is unique to the fabric surface and the clothing form.

DRAWING

There are many exercises from drawing that are useful to the fabric painter. Drawing is one of the basics to good painting. It's crucially important to learn how to observe correctly.If one can learn how to see objects in terms of their angular relationships, tones,their relationship to other objects,and the detail of texture, sketching or drawing them is fairly basic. One problem is that the brain can distort what the eye sees. Drawing books are full of ideas in 'training the eye to see'.

One good exercise is to practice drawing lines with various paint materials onto various kinds of fabric. Learn to see angles to draw simple rectangular shapes such as a book on a table,a table on a floor,a house with a yard and a fence. The science of perspective must be learned. For example,parallel perspective means that all parallel lines will converge at one vanishing point(on the horizon of your picture). With angular perspective, lines which are at right angles to each other converge at separate points.

Practice drawing rectangular and cylindrical shapes using the rules of perspective. A line drawn down the body of a cylinder will always be at right angles to a line drawn through the center of the ellipse.Then practice drawing objects by using a grid.Place some cardboard drawn through with grid lines behind some objects-a vase of flowers,for example.Then lightly mark grid lines on your fabric,and practice drawing the object properly,using the grid marks as guides.

Another simple exercise is to practice drawing simple,flat shapes and notice the negative space around them.Place some simple objects in front of you,sketch them with a colored pencil,then fill the shapes in with dye pastels. Then fill the areas around the shapes with color.To learn the beginnings of tone,observe the shadows that objects cast. Practice with a simple sketch,lines to suggest shapes,then shading effects.

The crucial aspect of drawing is to be able to move back and forth from larger shapes to small and then back to large. Let me explain. Draw the outlines of flowers in a round vase. Then focus on each separate object,adding more line and tonal qualities. Continue to reduce these large areas of the picture to smaller detail. Check back to the larger area,wherever it is, to see if your shapes are correctly representing what you are drawing. If you are, continue on with the detail of the smaller areas. If not,adjust whatever mistakes may have been made.

TONAL EXERCISES

Tone creates the illusion of depth. A two-dimensional flat fabric can appear three-dimensional. The easiest tonal exercise is done in only one color.Draw a simple scene,and add tonal variations.Remember that depth is created by thick strokes in the foreground and thin ones in the background. Your one color can be darkened for darker hues,and lightened with white for the highlights.

The light source helps you decide which areas of the picture will be in light,and which in shadow. In this way, each area of the fabric is broken down into three tonal values: light,medium,and dark.With more experience,you can refine your highlights and accentuate your shadows. Your nearby objects will be strong in tone,color,and well-defined. Objects far away will be of a lessened tonality, not as colorful, and less well-defined.

Here's another tonal exercise. Lay in washes with acrylic or textile paint. Lightly sketch your objects or design. First put down the lightest wash,then the second lightest. Add details. Then add the darkest tonalities,adding more details and highlighting with white.Also try working with just white,grey,and black,and paint gradations from light to dark in squares. Then try a simple picture that has perspective,say, looking down a road. Paint this in your whites,greys,and blacks in order to create a sense of depth.

COLOR EXERCISES

After learning about tone,it is a lot easier to put in color. You can work from the lightest tones to the darkest-in color. But first, its helpful to learn just how to mix colors. A good exercise is to mix the three primaries-blue,yellow,and red,on a color wheel.This will give you the secondaries-violet,green,and orange,and then further blends. Then try bands of hues, going from the lightest to darkest, then overlay them with other hues to see blending.

Try a color study all in one hue, with its variations in value and chroma. Choose a variety of objects that are naturally in one color range. A pink flower,a red apple, and a rose tablecloth are some examples. Try a color study,painting the same still life three times,using a different range of colors each time.You can also emphasize the differences in warm and cool colors.(Warm colors go towards red,while cool ones go towards blue.)

An organized palette is important. Try warm colors across the top,and cool down the side. It's very important to mix the colors on the palette

rather than on the fabric! Put colors together on the palette in groups, in order to see how they would look for a particular painting.

Check the color balance in your painting. If one color dominates or is isolated in the picture, it may need to be balanced by being repeated in other areas of the picture.An easy way to practice with color is to work from a color photograph.Use felt-tip colored pens to sketch a drawing,and then paint it onto fabric. There are many other ideas for working with color in painting books.

WATERCOLOR

Watercolor provides the fabric painter with many useful techniques. Watercolor uses both drawing and painting techniques,with line pictures and washes. You can lightly sketch in a design with a transfer pencil,or you can use the color itself to describe shape. Dyes,acrylics, and textile paint can all be used with watercolor techniques.

It's best to practice strokes first without trying to form shapes. Allow yourself a lot of space and work big at the beginning,so you can learn to really move your brush in sweeping strokes! Watercolor is well known for using white space in a positive and unique way. Think of white shapes-sailboats,white clouds, fences, etc.and let your white fabric contrast with the blending of colors around these shapes.

Washes are very important to use. With an even wash,starting at the top of your fabric, brush back and forth across the wet fabric, letting the color run down,and overlapping each successive stroke. In a graduated wash,start at the top of the wet fabric with a brushload of pure paint. As you work down,have less paint and more water.Graduated washes can also emphasize the concentration of color in the middle or on each edge of the fabric. A color wash is created by brushing one color onto the wet fabric in even strokes. It will create a background upon which you can then paint or draw.

There are a number of other watercolor techniques besides washes. Splattering, stippling, blowing, dry brush, wet-on-wet, wet-on-dry, and scumbling are also used in watercolor. Splattering is like spatter painting or spraying. With stippling you make tiny dots with a brush for shading. Blowing just means using a straw to blow the paint onto the wet fabric. With dry brush, you pick up fairly liquid paint with your brush and then flick out most of it before painting. The thicker the paint on your brush, the rougher and more ragged the drybrush effect. Drybrush is used to create textured effects, as the fabric will show through where the brush lays down little paint. Wet-on-wet creates an entirely opposite effect. Take wet fabric and run color through it, letting the color spread out. This process works very well with dyes and acrylics on cotton and poly-cotton. Wet-on-dry allows for overlapping transparent shapes due to applying wet paint onto dry. This modulates the tone of the wet paint as it will show some of the paint below. Scumbling has several definitions. In one process, take thick paint with your brush and apply it with a scrubbing motion. The paint will blur, and take on a broken, rough quality. Another way to scumble is to apply lighter paint over darker, so that the underneath layer shows through. In both of these cases, the scumbling allows some paint to be hidden, while other paint is revealed.

I'll mention a few more of the many watercolor technqiues. (Refer to the bibliography for more books on watercolor). Wet-line drawing means drawing lines with a wet brush on damp fabric. You'll get a softened effect with this technique. Drips occur by drawing through areas of wet and dry fabric with a wet brush. The wet areas will drip onto the dry ones, producing interesting effects. Partial wetting of your fabric can be a very creative technique. It will give you contrasts in tone and types of edges.

Depending on which areas you keep dry and which are wet, you can create totally different effects with the same drawing or design.

Try mixing hard-edged and soft-edged (wet-on-wet) techniques in one painting. When doing a painting in watercolor, look at the white or negative space and try drawing around it as the main area of interest. For example, draw a tree, but leave its shape white. Focus on the areas around the tree shape for your color blendings. And remember, when doing tonal values, a light tone in watercolor has a lot of water and not much paint, while a dark tone has a lot of pigment and not much water.

Salt is a popular watercolor technique. While it can be overdone, if used properly its effects are nice. Throw salt onto your wet fabric. Then paint over with your paint material. (I have found that textile paint works the best, but dye and acrylics are also possible). The wetter the paint, the larger the star-shaped spots be that will occur. Likewise, the drier the paint, the smaller the spots.

OIL TECHNIQUES

Traditional oil painting uses either layering or alla prima. Layering, or glazing, occurs by building up tones and colors with glazes, letting each one dry first. This can be done on a minimal scale with fabric painting, as long as not too many layers are attempted. Alla prima, where wet oil is mixed in and onto other wet paint, is a more spontaneous and freeform technique, and can be successfully transferred with various paint materials.

As with other tonal exercises, you can first sketch your drawing onto the fabric with a transfer pencil. Then add an underpainting with oil and turpentine, and then build up your painting with more oil and turpentine mixture. This can also be done with acrylics and textile paint. Just be sure to limit the number of layers, so that your fabric does not become stiff.

Although drawing is emphasized by many people as the foundation for painting, there are a number of oil painters who feel that it is not a crucial skill. They suggest you sketch out ideas, but primarily focus on painting. Think about color, applying colors and shapes to fabrics and see what happens.

One of oil paints best techniques is one the Impressionists used- that of putting little dabs of color next to each other which would slightly blend into each other. Try this with oil paint and turpentine as well as with other paint materials.

ACRYLIC TECHNIQUES

Acrylic techniques do not vary much from what has already been described in the sections on tonal exercises and oil. However, when using wet-on-wet with acrylics, you may wish to use a gel retarder to slow down the drying time of the paint. You can use acrylics with the glazing technique as previously mentioned.

One of the greatest advantages of acrylics is that they will dry quickly and then can be painted over right away. Acrylic Watercolor Painting-by Wendon Blake is full of interesting ideas and techniques that take full advantage of the special properties of acrylic paint.

To make acrylics more transparent, add gel medium. If you desire to stain your fabric, you may want to use a water-tension breaker with the paint. It will slightly dilute your color, but will help speed the flow of the paint onto the fabric.

PASTEL TECHNIQUES

Short, direct strokes are used with pastels to take full advantage of their delicate rendering. Color is not rubbed in, and textural effects are possible by lightly handling the pastel. Dye pastels are more oily, but can be used in a similar manner and can achieve some of the same effects, particu-larly that of texture.

STILL LIFE

There are several ways of approaching still life. For all still life techniques, however, you'll want to set up the subjects of your painting somewhere where they won't be disturbed. Also, it's important that you have a good light source. Don't try and have too complex an arrangement for a still life. Choose a few, interesting subjects and place them in an interesting background.

One technique for painting still life is to paint the background first. Then paint the foreground. Add the main subject, and then fill out with details. Another sequence is to first draw in the horizon line, usually the edge of a table. Then sketch in the outlines of the shapes, noticing the spaces between the shapes as well. Then add washes for tonal areas. Middle-toned washes can be used to give the objects form, while areas of light can be filled in with a lighter-toned wash. Add shadows and areas of shade with darker washes. Then begin adding colors of the main shapes, keeping to the tonal variations. (It might be best to mix these color tonalities on a palette separately) Then add your finishing details, such as textures, highlights, and shadows.

Still life can be painted in a very realistic manner, with tight control and lots of details. At the same time, it can be rendered with emphasis on color areas and free and easy linear gestures. Flower painting is a popular theme in still life. There are many good books that will give you step-by-step instructions for flower painting. There are two ways you can emphasize a flower painting as a still life. One is to use lots of textured brushstrokes to show the complexity of the blossoms, and carefully detail each stem. The other way emphasizes blocks of color to show flower shapes. For fab-

195

bric painting, a light background with just a few blooms could make a simple and eloquent statement.

LANDSCAPE

Landscape is certainly a subject matter overflowing with ideas! One has only to look outside to find something of interest to paint. Landscape painting is not just a matter of recording this or that tree, a hill, etc. but recreating an entire scene with atmosphere and light. Landscape can be abstract or realistic. Regardless of which one you may prefer, be sure to learn the techniques of both; in this way your painting can be strengthened rather than limited. Think of landscape like a patchwork quilt-there are a number of elements which must be successfully put together!

A sketchbook is crucially important for landscape painting, since ideas can be jotted down and then worked up in the studio. Takes notes, also, of colors and tones.

There are many techniques in landscape painting, many ways to approach a work. You can begin by painting in the background or sky, with the light tone at the horizon. Then add the middle tones and the dark at the top. Add ground color, trees, details, etc. It's important to first draw in the horizon line. Work in masses of tone and color at first rather than shapes, so that you can get your thoughts down. Then work out the lines of trees, fields, etc. Mix your colors on your palette(rather than on the fabric)and think out your color scheme. If you like, put out colors for the trees, sky, hills, etc. on your palette in order to co-ordinate your colors.

Scale and perspective are very important, especially when working with a distant view. It's best to start with a view that is not overwhelmingly panoramic. That can come later! Try painting the same scene over and over again, from different angles. For example, stand at the top of a small hill, sketch the view below. Then walk down the hill halfway, then to the ground level. Remember that, as the forms in your painting recede toward the vanishing point, they diminish in size.

Choose an interesting eye level position. If it is high, the view looks panoramic. If it is low(from a sitting position) you can build a dramatic scene. In the middle of your canvas or fabric, the eye level will create an ordinary looking scene. Choose the one that best suits your purpose.

It can be helpful to divide your "canvas" into foreground, middleground, and background. Make a tonal chart for these three areas, before you start painting. Another helpful technique is to divide the fabric into halves or quarters before sketching in a scene. A grid, with even smaller squares, can help with perspective.

As mentioned before, landscape painting can be realistic or abstract. Abstract painting is especially suited for fabric painting. Landscape color field painting is another possibility, for colors are placed one against the other. A popular technique puts in a background of one overall color, then one particular area is highlighted in a contrasting color. With either color field or abstract painting, don't get involved in details at all. Just focus on masses of color and shape!

Landscape is successful with different mediums. Wet-in-wet watercolor is especially effective, since the blending allows for overall tonal effects of sky, fields, etc. Details can then be filled in with a pen. Washes of receding color can form interesting landscapes. Simply add a few narrow brushstrokes on the horizon for details of trees and sky. Drybrush can give very opposite effects, with rough textures representing tree bark or clods of earth in an unplowed field. Be sure to remember that when beginning a landscape in watercolor, you will start with the lighter tones and move to the foreground with darker tones. However, when working with oil, you start with the darker tones, and work from the foreground to the background with the lighter colors on top.

Fields, skies, clouds, hills, trees; all are important aspects of landscape painting. Painting trees is especially important. Study the shapes of trees, especially in winter, when you can see the branches clearly. Study the silhouette of the tree, and how it enters the ground. See how the main branches split off from the trunk. When the branches divide farther up, notice whether or not one branch is larger than its corresponding mate. (It often is) Notice how the leaves group themselves. Paint trees on the horizon, middle ground, and in the foreground of your painting. Paint them as trunks and branches; also paint them as blobs of color. And most of all, study trees. Sketch them! It's better to really learn a few tree species well than to attempt a partial success with many.

To sum up landscape, have a center of interest in your picture, create a rhythm by leading the eye on a "path" from one area of the picture to another. Contrast this with areas of calm. Make studies and sketches of all the interesting subject matter in the natural landscape.

CITYSCAPE

Cityscape is, indeed, part of our modern landscape. Towns, cities, villages, buildings are all a part of cityscape. They provide an ample opportunity to study shapes and surfaces, especially rectangles and geometric shapes. Telephone poles, bridges, chimneys, brickwork, grates, doors, windows, curtains, shutters, fences, park benches, monuments, roofs, and gaslights are just some of the features that can be used in cityscapes. They can be portrayed either realistically or abstractly, and done in all mediums.

Again, doing sketches is very important, as you will have to set up work in a studio rather than on a city street. Sketches can give you quick impressions that can be worked into future compositions. Perspective and scale are important in cityscapes, so that your buildings are in correct relation to each other. Use a grid if necessary to help you attain proper scale.

To begin a cityscape, indicate the horizon. Divide your surface into background and foreground. Note the changes in scale with a foreground building versus a background one. Use a greater amount of detail in the foreground. Sketch in the main shapes and lay washes for the sky and walls, if using watercolor.

One problem in a cityscape for a painter is the overwhelming amount of detail available. Does one try and draw every brick, every fencepost? The solution is to emphasize certain details, and leave the rest in color masses. Choose what you want to emphasize, with some reasoning; otherwise, your picture will look imbalanced, with certain areas in great detail, and others looking bare.

Figures can be a part of cityscapes. Parks and ornamental gardens can, as well, be a nice place to work and have the city as a backdrop to your picture. The subject of cityscape is a challenge to the dress designer, but with the rectangular shapes, it can be a successful painted clothing design.

WATERSCAPE (SEASCAPE)

Waterscape and seascape are two other interesting subjects for painting. The subject matter is vast: skies, seas, boats, ships, clouds, fishing, shoreline, rocks, sand, pebbles, tides, tidepools, jetties, cliffs, headlands, beaches, sea shells, waterfalls, ponds, rivers, lakes, canoes, and sailboats can all be included in the theme of waterscape. Perspective and scale are very important with waterscape, as water is so fluid and invisible, as well as so mobile. A stable structural background is important.

Waterscape is not the easiest subject to portray. Water can vary from being a perfectly quiet reflecting surface through restless water that mirrors broken images,to the frothy "white" water of ocean waves and wild rivers. As well, when you add the effects of the sun on the water, with the changing light, color,and reflected light that ensues,painting water can become a formidable challenge!

One way of minimizing these problems is to do a seascape in watercolor. First,draw a horizon line.Be sure that it is exactly horizontal, or else your ocean will appear to tilt.Fill in the sky with washes.Then add the foreground. Use the drybrush technique to put the misty spray onto the ocean waves.

Water moves and also reflects a moving sky. Water can ripple and reflect the moving trees overhead. Study the shorelines of water-they provide interesting subject matter. Painting water is also painting what is around the water, and how water reacts with these other elements.

FIGURE DRAWING

Figure drawing doesn't have to be as complicated as it looks. First, look at the figure as triangles,cylinders,and rectangles.Sketch the torso as a triangle(inverted) with a rectangle for the pelvis,and put the cylinders on as arms and legs.

Sketching is crucially important for figure drawing. Sketch people when you are on the bus,walking in town, sketch your friends and family. You can even learn from sketching T.V. figures! It helps to learn simplified basic anatomy,but don't worry about learning the name of each muscle.

A wooden mannikin can be helpful to learn how the various parts of the body work in motion.They are available at art stores.Stick figures are very good to learn about the figure in motion. Practice with stick figures and don't worry about details of modelling. After you feel comfortable with the figure in motion, add tonal areas of light and shadow. Then model the features of the face.

Make studies of hands,feet,and heads. Don't try for too much detail in one drawing.Draw someone doing something. It will be easier for them,as a model,and a repetitious activity,(like sewing, ironing,or even drawing) will help you study the figure in motion.

CONCLUSIONS

Direct painting is indeed an exciting technique. Even with all the specific techniques, each painter will have her own particular style. You will be learning an artistic"vocabulary" which will have your own particular stamp.As well, each painter will pick out of a scene,or a subject, particular details that have meaning to them.Beginners tend to want to paint everything in one particular painting, but as you practice and grow,you will begin to naturally choose certain colors,details,elements that you want to express in a particular work. By isolating a certain element,it can be developed and explored.

Interiors is another subject matter that was not explored in this chapter. Also,practice painting by looking from the inside out. A window facing a garden is a particular favorite.

The shape of your canvas or fabric can be an effective compositional tool. A long narrow piece of fabric,with a vertical emphasis,is different from a skinny horizontal piece. Landscapes,with 2/3 sky, and 1/3 close-up, can utilize this latter form. With long verticals,paint in an oblique direction to maximize the canvas shape.

The point of emphasis is another useful concept. Draw two crossing diagonals on a square,and you will have divided the fabric into four areas. Depending on which quadrant is emphasized, there is a different "point of emphasis".

I hope that these techniques, be they indirect, spontaneous, or direct, will keep you busy creating new and beautiful fabric paintings!

7 *COMPOSITION AND CONSTRUCTION*

Some of the most beautiful clothing I have ever seen has been fabric painted. I have also seen fabric painted clothing that just doesn't "work". Since both possibilities occur with the same process, how can these pitfalls be avoided? The basic solution is to learn to create a design which is harmonious with the clothing.

There are a number of concepts which can be learned which will help the fabric painter to create beautiful handpainted clothing. All these concepts taken together will create holistic design. We can learn about clothing composition, types of basic clothing construction, modern clothing design, differences in ready-to-wear and handsewn clothing, and the elements of color, texture, and form in painted clothing.

CLOTHING COMPOSITION

What clothing means, how it is used, its appropriateness; all these concepts deal with clothing composition. Composition deals with combining the parts of a work of art to become a harmonious whole. Painted clothing <u>is</u> a work of art, and its various parts must be combined appropriately.

Clothing is expression on a grand scale, the expression of culture, of time and place and the attitude about the times. In order to feel comfortable wearing a certain type of clothing, a person must be familiar with the cultural dictates of what is proper to wear in a certain place at a certain time. Then they can decide whether or not to conform to these dictates.

In an abstract sense, clothing is texture, color, form through movement. Clothing is ornamental art. Like all art forms, it is an artificially arranged whole. It has an instrumental value when it is "used for" or "leads to" something else. Many people carefully study how to arrange their clothing to emphasize their best features and minimize their worst. For some people, wearing clothing is a form of art.

It's important, therefore, to develop a sense of appropriateness on where to wear painted clothes, as well as knowing what kinds of painted designs look good with a certain style of clothing. The suitability of the subject matter to the clothing must be considered as well as the suitability of the clothing to the environment.

Regarding painted clothing, it's good to ask the question:what subject matter is <u>unsuitable</u> for clothing? Is that which is appropriate on the museum wall also appropriate on the street and on the body? Is that which is written on the pages of books also suitable as decoration on cloth? Wars are written about and depicted in paintings; why is it that there are so many clothes with flowers on them? It is important to ask these questions as they are themselves frameworks of perception. Each person can decide what their feelings are,and act accordingly.

Clothing interacts with variable environments. How much can it be used as a way of advertisement?Clothing is public,while pictures hanging on a wall are private or at least selective in their audience. Fabric painting opens up <u>any</u> subject matter that can be drawn by the artists hand. Is clothing also an educational tool?(A spelling dress? A French dress?)Is it sacrilegious to have a picture of Christ on a T-shirt? What does it mean to have a picture of Reagan or Nixon on the seat of someones pants?

Painted clothing is mobile and travels with its wearer in many environments,and,as such, makes a statement in those environments.In this way, painted clothing is not merely a decoration, to amuse and divert. I like to think of painting on clothing as an expressive statement of how one feels or what one thinks, and how one wishes to communicate with others.

BASIC CLOTHING CONSTRUCTION

Clothing varies in its form. Clothing ranges from being simply wrapped or draped on the body to very intricately cut and fitted patterns.Very light material can be draped and wrapped around the body,therefore it can be painted and then used for clothing. A simple square can be a skirt,a dress, a shawl, or a scarf. The painting will appear in different ways due to the

wrapping of the cloth. Painted yardage is fairly easy to design.(See Chapter III,p.66   for ideas for making fabric yardage.)What is most important is that you have a recognizable motif which identifies a length of fabric.Other than that,fabric yardage is a gold mine for exploring creativity,as the fabric can go on and on, as long as you wish.

Wrapped clothing evolved into simple shapes still based on the square or rectangle. What we today call folk or ethnic designs <u>are</u> those basic clothing shapes.Though they are what we call the top,dress,skirt,pants, and coat,they also have other names: tunic,smock,huiptl,caftan,jerkin,poncho,and cape.Basic clothing shapes are also fairly easy to paint,for the clothing design does not really detract from the painted design.Some of these square shapes are like a waiting,empty, canvas.(Figs.163,164)

FIG.163 : CAFTAN BY GLORIA RIGLING.CHIFFON WITH DIRECT APPLICATION,THEN TIED,DISCHARGED, AND REDYED.

FIG.164 : TOP BY PHYLLIS MUFSON. CHINA SILK
WITH DIRECTION APPLICATION OF DYE.

MODERN CLOTHING DESIGN

These five basic shapes, based
on the square or rectangle, can
be amplified and extended to create more complex clothing forms.
These include modern-day, historical, and costume. Modern-day clothing forms are simply the styles
of clothing which are in fashion
and go beyond standard attire
which does not change from year
to year. Small details are changed on clothing to make it go in
and out of fashion. These details,
such as wide, baggy pants, or full
gathered tiered skirts, may change
in a few years to a wide cuff on
slim pants and straight skirts
with front slits. Historical clothing forms are specifically
drawn from history. Some examples
are: a Spanish paneled drawstring
skirt, a Tibetan waistcoat, a robe

from the time of Henry the First,
braies and an overtunic from 1066
English wear, or a Byzantine robe.
(Fig.165)

Clothing which is worn for special occasions rather than regular
wear is called costume. It can be
worn on or off the stage. It's very
important for painted clothing not
to look "costumey" unless you wish it
to be. Costume functions to set the
wearer apart from others, to show
off the clothing and the person. In
the right setting, this can be very
appropriate.

Examples of modern clothing forms
are everywhere. Look at Vogue magazine, McCall's and Simplicity pattern books, and American Fabrics and
Fashions, to see good examples of
modern fashions. Advertising for department stores carry the latest in
this seasons fashions.

FIG.165 :(ABOVE AND BELOW) DRAWINGS OF HIS-
TORICAL DRESS FROM 17TH CENTURY FRANCE

READY-TO-WEAR AND HANDSEWN CLOTHING

Fabric painters have available to them two different types of clothing. One is factory-made clothing or ready-to-wear;the other is hand-sewn clothing. There are desirable aspects to using both types.

Ready-to-wear clothing is very desirable to anyone who doesn't know how to sew.It's easily available.If it's new,it's very important that all sizing is washed out of the garment. Permanent press finishes or other finishes will impair the effectiveness of both dyes and paints.Sometimes it is hard to tell whether or not there is a finish that will not come out. Another problem with new clothing is the fiber content may be unknown.If there is a label,be sure and check the suitability of the fabric with the desired paint material.

One drawback to painting on new clothing is that,if you make a mistake,there is little you can do to change it. You might wish to sketch out your design on paper,or make a sample design on similar fabric before painting on the clothing.Another suggestion is to paint on old clothing. For one thing, you have less to lose. Old clothing is good for the beginning painter to practice on,and by painting on a variety of types of clothes(T-shirts,regular shirt,pants, skirt, dress, etc),different design ideas can be tried out and perfected for use with new clothing.Other advantages of using old clothing are that the sizing will be long ago washed out of them,and you may find fabrics that are no longer available to use.

There are several ways to paint handsewn clothing. One is to make fabric yardage,and then cut out and sew the clothing.Another is to paint the design on the already-cut pattern pieces and then sew. Patterns such as simple gathered skirts are simply large squares which can be painted and then gathered. You have more choices when you are painting on hand-sewn clothing,as you are creating both the clothing form and the painted design.(A forthcoming book devoted solely to clothing design will explore the history,use,and design of clothing,including painted clothing design.)

HOLISTIC DESIGN

It is an exciting challenge to choose a clothing style that will be heightened in its composition by being fabric painted.To learn how to do this requires more of a "sense" of knowing how the various elements harmonize themselves than any specific technique.

One easy way to learn this "sense" of holistic design is to observe the way you dress-what kinds of colors you put together, and what types of fabrics you use. Clothes which look good together have a balance of line,weight,and color. If you put,for example,a lot of bold prints together in separate garments(skirt,top,vest),you have an overbalanced pattern and not enough space(created through solid colors).If you draw a very intricate design with lots of slashing lines,and then sew it into a pleated skirt, a shirt with a V collar, and a vest, you probably will once again be overbalancing the element of line.

If you are not so sure as to your own taste in dress, observe others around you and look at pictures of people-people engaged in any number of things as well as people modeling fashion outfits. Costume and clothing history books can be particularly valuable- for you can see how colors and line and other factors in clothing design were used.(Check books on Erte and Poiret for some unusual designs.)

What,exactly, is holistic design? The word holistic describes the wholeness of a thing. All of the component parts of something are put together in such a manner that they form a whole. In terms of fabric painted clothing,the whole is the painted clothing and the parts are the garment form,its type and use;the design idea or the painted design, its type and construction;the paint materials used; the type fabric used in connection with the type of paint;these two factors in connection with the type of design;and the clothing design in relation to its environment.A "sense" of holistic design is also important;in other words, it is something you can intuit. So a simple definition of holistic design is a sense of design which combines various parts into wholeness.

You can ask these questions as a guide for holistic design. First, describe the type of clothing you've chosen. Is it formal or informal?Simple or fussy? Feminine(yin) or masculine(yang)? Is it casual,flowing, box-like,faddish, or sophisticated? Then describe your design idea. Is it bright,colorful? Are the lines slashing?Curved? Or is it delicate, almost weak? See whether you can integrate the concepts of these two items. Next, examine your painting technique. Is the type of paint material that you are using with your fabric the best one for your design idea? (For example, oil paint with turpentine is a good paint material for Impressionistic-type painting techniques).If you verbally describe what it is you are trying to create, and then describe each component,it will be easier to see where you are going with your design!

The painted design should express approximately the same thing as the clothing. If a piece of clothings' statement is 'sophisticated, clear lines, but with a dashing flair', then the painted design should be complementary. In order to be effective, painted clothing must fit into its environment, and not seem out of place or improper. Develop this sensibility. Note the reactions of people when you wear painted clothing. When you become sensitive to this aspect of fabric painting then you will be able to design clothing that harmonizes with its environment and is appropriate to each situation.(Figs. 166,167   )

FIG.166 : SUSAN SPRINGER MODELS A QUIANA BLOUSE SHE PAINTED WITH DISPERSE DYES. PHOTO BY PERRY SMALL.

FIG.167 : LISA HENSLEY MODELLING SILK DRESS PAINTED WITH FLORAL DESIGN.

ELEMENTS OF DESIGN

There are a number of design elements which can be used to analyze painted clothing design. They include color, texture, balance, silhouette, line proportion, rhythm, emphasis, and pattern. Of these, I wish to discuss color in detail. I refer you again to my forthcoming book on creative clothing for an in-depth discussion of the other elements.

Color is a very important element in clothing design. The focusing power of color is strong, so be sure to place your painted design where it can emphasize the person's best bodily features, as well as harmonizing with the dominant theme of the garment.

Color has psychological associations which are reliable and fairly standard. Pink and rose are fragile; red and orange aggressive, lively, and sexual; yellow is luminous and relates to the intellect, the mind, and mental instability. Green is fertile, stable, and cool; blue oceanic and introspective. Purple is associated with royalty, vanity, genius, and creativity. Brown is practical, earthy, durable.

Other properties of color: warm colors, the reds, oranges, and yellows, are advancing colors, while cool colors recede. In terms of design, this means that a painted design with warm colors appears larger than one with cool. The only stipulation to this is that strong intense colors with high value or chroma are also going to look larger than a warm insipid color, such as light pink.

Hue, value, and chroma are important aspects in understanding color. Hue refers to the name of the color: red, yellow, green, blue, purple, yellow-red, blue-green, etc. Value refers to the darkness or lightness of a color. Red is differentiated by value into light red (pink), or dark red (maroon). Chroma, the third aspect, refers to the strength or weakness of a color, in other words, how much saturation of color there is as opposed to neutral gray.

Colors also have apparent warmth and coolness. Warm colors relate to the sun-reds, oranges, yellows. Cool colors relate to the color of shadows on ice or snow-the blues and purples. Green, the color of natural growing things, is inbetween cool and warm. These are apparent values. However, at the red end of the spectrum, it has been proven that the colored light actually is warmer.

You can use a variety of color schemes in planning your painted design. Choose a predominant hue as the thematic color and blend other colors around that basic hue. If you choose to be monochromatic, all the colors will be variations in value or intensity of the same hue. Analogous hues have a color in common; red, red-orange, and magenta all share the red hue. With complementary colors, colors opposite to each other on the color wheel are used together.

Regardless of the type color scheme you may choose, there are certain guidelines in the use of color. Extremes in value do not look well together without medium toned value as well. The extreme, for example. of a dark value with a light tint is uneven. The lack of value contrast, as well, leads to monotony. Too many intense hues is overpowering; while an intense highly saturated color combined with weak tonal values makes the bright colors look garish. All these examples show that extremes do not work.

There are many combinations that do work. Blending of monochromatic and analogous colors are successful and soothing to the eye. Small areas of saturated color can be combined with larger areas of low intensity color with good effect. Bright spots of highly saturated color have a youthful look, with vitality. Often they look good on a white background for fabric painted clothing, such as a skirt with bright spots of red, yellow, bright green, and bright blue. The white background contrasts with the density of the high saturation. A different look can be created with tones of low saturation, such as lilac and pale pink, and weak va ue. This will produce an airy, delicate look, also very satisfying for fabric painted clothing.

How do these other design elements work in order to bring harmony between the painted design and the clothing design? There are some general guidelines that you can follow. For example,if the clothing design is simple,the you are safe in making the painted design complex. On the other hand,if the clothing is quite intricate with darts and pleats and frills, it would be safer to make a simple painted design. Echo or reflect the lines in the clothing within the painted design. One way of doing this is to paint borders on the cut-out pattern pieces. Or reflect the horizontal lines of a big,baggy shirt with painted emphasis of the horizontal. Notice which elements in both the clothing and painting design are complementary,and which are not.For example, if the silhouette(or outline)of your clothing is dominated by vertical lines,then that will be your dominant element to consider when designing the painting.A design with many broken curved lines may be too dissimilar.

In general, verticals emphasize height and narrowness. Horizontals broaden and shorten the overall effect of the design. Diagonals accent the direction in which they tilt. Curved lines soften angular parts of the body and harmonize with the curves of the body.Analyze the line movement in the construction of the clothing-is it primarily horizontal, vertical, or diagonal? Are the lines straight,curved, or broken? Rhythm is the control of the line movement so that one form dominates. Rhythm will be lacking in a garment form when the painted design and design elements in the clothing are so varied that no one form clearly predominantes.The principle of emphasis allows some elements to dominate and others to be subordinate.Establish one dominant interest and then have other things,

such as texture or color, emphasize the lines or forms already planned.

You can organize your design around the balance and proportion of linear elements. There are many possible ways to create a balance of line movement within the clothing and painted design. Using the principle of radiation,an A-line dress can have painted lines radiating out from the solar plexus area of the body. You can choose between symmetrical and asymmetrical balance in a garment. A shirt with most of the visual interest on the right shoulder via pleats or a design in paint will be an asymmetrical balance.This is also an example of focus of interest.

What is it that"catches your eye" when you look at a painting on a wall or a piece of clothing? Whatever,and wherever that is,is the focus of interest. Design your painted clothing so that some of the visual design is placed in an area of the body which is a natural point of interest. You might find a sundress with back interest, another dress or skirt with interest at the hem,the waistline,or along the side seams. Neck interest occurs with blouses,and can be accentuated by painting in the neck area.

Texture is another design element which affects the total look of the garment. A basic rule is,if your fabric is smooth and even textured, the painted design can be varied,with a lot of detail and textural effects.On the other hand,with textured fabric, such as a coarse or hand woven piece, keep your painting minimal. Staining could be a good technique.

TYPES OF PAINTED CLOTHING

There is one last consideration in our discussion of holistic design. Although each of these "parts of the whole" can be individually approached by each artist,I have found through looking at a lot of clothes that there are several types of holistic design which stand out. These types range in a spectrum from the clothing form being dominant and the design idea playing a submissive role, all the way through to the opposite,where the clothing form is very simple and the painting quite complex. In the middle of the spectrum the clothing and the painting design are of fairly equal strength.

The first type of painted clothing is sometimes seen in needlework magazines or fashion magazines.The clothing is complex in pattern and design;the painting,simple-sometimes no more than a few delicate flowers. The opposite type,simply formed clothing with intricate designs,occurs particularly on the basic,folk, and ethnic style of clothing(based on the square or rectangle.)Paintings can range from brightly colored abstract shapes to intricate drawings all over the clothing.

Other types of clothing have more of an equal balance of ground and design. T-shirts with simple center designs are one type.(Figs.168, 170) A very well designed clothing form with a well-designed and integrated painting design is another type. And a very showy costumy clothing form may have equally showy bright designs on it. In

all these cases, it is always the aim to bring into a pleasing harmony the clothing design and the painted design.(Fig.169)

DESIGN NOTEBOOK

As you begin to learn holistic design for fabric painting, you may find yourself jotting down notes and getting ideas from many sources. A sketchbook or design

FIG. 169: ARDEN DALE MODELING WATERCOLOR STRIPE PAINTED GATHERED SKIRT. THE SIMPLE DESIGN COMPLIMENTS THE SKIRT DESIGN.

FIG.168 : DOUGLAS HENSLEY MODELS PAINTED T-SHIRT. ACRYLIC PAINT OVERDYED WITH PROCION.

FIG.170 : BETH BROWN MODELS PAINTED T-SHIRT WITH FRONT DESIGN. ACRYLIC PAINT
OVERDYED WITH PROCION DYE. DESIGN IDEA INSPIRED BY KANDINSKY PAINTINGS.

notebook is helpful for keeping your ideas in order. As well, you may be writing down ideas that may not be used until future ideas develop. These sketches,which may only be vague design ideas in the present, can be reference points for future ideas. You may find yourself repeating basic ideas with variations in techniques and materials. Keeping a written record of these variations is a good way to see your evolution as a designer.

Museums, craft shows, and art libraries are full of designs and good compositions which can be transformed into use for fabric painting. Make simple sketches of things that you really like. Sometimes choose a small design or pattern within a much larger composition. When you look at various things for design ideas, ask yourself: what are your sources of design? What are your favorite parts? Why?

Below, I am listing some jottings from my own design notebooks. I share these ideas with you in case you would like some ideas to start making fabric painted items.There are a number of catagories here from which to choose-both clothing and non-clothing items.

Tops: T-shirts with French words and flowers painted on them. Poems with marking pens look easy. I don't like the stiff center of most manufactured T-shirts. Try large abstract center designs. Be careful of placement on front of women's T-shirts. Some manufactured designs are carefully erotic;others, ludicrous.

Long top,square and loose,out of cotton. Painted Jacobean embroidery. In the center, around edges or sleeves, bottom,and side hems. Leaves flowers, circles. Going towards the center, larger motifs. Interspersed with real embroidery if desired. Round collar.

Women's T-shirt with front cutout and inserts of lacey crochet.V-shaped insert in lower center front with floral and spiral embroidery,

painted. Delicate colors.

Squarish top with dolman sleeves and slight A-line tapering towards the waist.Boat neck. Painted design circling the neck to resemble jewelry. Near bottom, a painted girdle which clasps in front. Painted stones center front.

Man's shirt with names and headlines inspired by newspaper headlines. In foreign languages and English.

Dresses: A long muslin dress, with inset long sleeves. Big flowers on front and back bodice.Pleated skirt,with painted vertical lines. Wide flowers in some of the partitions. Smaller flowers in others. White segments in others.

Crazy-quilt patchwork dress with V-neck and sleeves to elbow. Wide border on hem. Painted sections to resemble patchwork with subdued colors.

Wide,loose dress,made of silk. Dyed with cold-water dyes,thickened, in watercolor overlays. Knee-length.

Simple A-line dress with Impressionistic-type brushstrokes using oil paint with textine. Varying areas of color spread out over dress.

Straight dress in heavy cotton. Painted Chinese trees in black.

Skirts:striped panels painted on a skirt. Bright colors; also bright colors alternating with white .Color range,for example, various shades of blue. Geometrics, hard-edged designs, watercolor stripes. Stripes alternating with motifs; Pennsylvania Dutch, Chinese folk designs, Arabic lattice work,etc.

Reversible skirt. Cut in a circle or as an A-line and lined. Paintings on both sides can relate or be very different. The A-line skirt should be fairly wide at the bottom if the design is to be continuous,so that it is easy to see part of the wrong side.

Hand-painted, hand-woven skirt. Skirt is painted in sections,some being warp-painted and then woven, others being woven and then painted. Weaving done on small table loom.

Procion dyes used, some natural dyes used.

Pants: Drawstring pants, slightly below the knee, with large bright polka dots on a cotton blend.

White duck pants with colorful squares painted up and down the side seam on the outside of the legs.

Drawstring pants,full-length, with spatter painting in pastels on a grey or tan background.

Wrap pants with horizontal stripes across the band of the leg,and vertical stripes 6" or so from each leg edge. Use an analogous color scheme.

ACCESSORIES:

Purses:quilted and painted on lightweight material which is lined. Or,use heavyweight canvas and acrylic paint.

A soft rectangular purse with a long wooden handle. Striped or small painted motifs for the fabric,

A rectangular purse with horizontal strips of:lace knitting,crochet, a strip of heavy fabric, another strip of needlepoint, more painted cloth.

Backpacks: canvas backpacks, painted with stripes, African motifs, and PreColumbian motifs. (Fig.171)

Denim backpack painted with brightly colored motifs.

Painted Hats:Painted hats are fun to make, for each one can express a distinct "hat" feeling. Hats can be made from heavy cottons-such as duck, canvas, or sailcloth. There are some waterproof fabrics which can be used for rainhats. Hats can be completely sewn,or they can be a

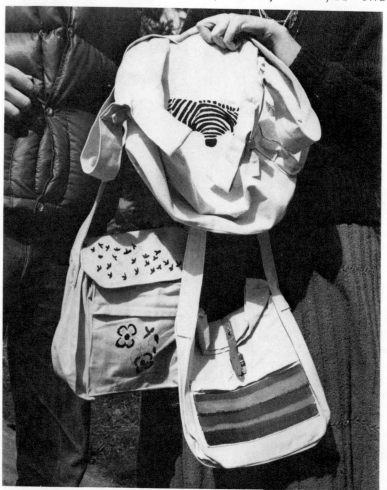

FIG.171: PAINTED BACKPACKS. SEWN BY BETH BROWN. ACRYLIC ON CANVAS.

mixture of sewn material and crochet,for example. They can also be
crocheted out of fabric strips.

Scarves and Shawls: simple square
pieces of cotton painted with dyes,
markers,acrylics, textile paint,etc.
Silk and wool painted scarves
with disperse dyes.
Silk shawl with handpainted flowers.(Fig.172)

Belts and Cummerbunds: soft belts
made from cotton,lightly quilted,and
painted with curving lines.
Woven belt with direct painting,
blending colors.

Socks and Shoes:tennis shoes
painted with acrylics, textile
paints, or acrylics. Cloth shoes
with textile paint. Hand-made moc-
casins painted,dyed,and embroidered.
Painted leggings. Tights painted
with textile paints or dyes. Short
white socks, painted with dyes, a-
crylics,or fabric crayons.

HOME FURNISHINGS

Wall hangings:Try a "natural-
type" wall hanging with trees,grass-
es,and attach small rocks or other
materials on the fabric. Use browns,
natural dyes, acrylics.

Curtains and Drapes:Fiber-reac-
tive dyes are very nice to use with
curtains and drapes,as well as other items through which light shines,
such as lampshades and wall dividers.

Towels:Cotton terry cloth towels
painted in colors to match your bathroom. Dye-painting. Watercolor stripes.
Folk-art motifs. Handtowels in light-
weight cotton with embroidery paint
for cross-stitch or gingham towels,or
flower and fruit borders for kitchens
and bathrooms.

Sheets and Pillowcases:painted
sheets for children with childrens'
stories on them. Use dyes. Illustrations and words. Comic characters.
Delicate floral sheets with flowers on them in pastel colors. Large,

FIG.172: SHAWLS BY SHERRY DE LEON. THE
ONE ON THE RIGHT IS HANDPAINTED SILK.

soft flowers.
Painted double-bed sheets with
tasteful erotic art.
Painted sheets with landscapes.
Mountains,ocean,trees.
Pillowcases with the sun on one
side and the moon on the other."Good
Morning"on one edge,"Good Night" on
the opposite edge.

Lampshades: as already mentioned,
use dyes to emphasize the light
flowing through the material.

Pillows:Pillows come in many
shapes,sizes, and uses. Large bol-
ster pillows for floor or couch use,
down to small head pillows. And all
sizes inbetween!(Fig.173)

OTHER FABRIC ITEMS

Soft books: a soft book made from

210

canvas and painted with acrylic.
   Empty books made from heavy
cloth with watercolor washes,
for poetry or drawings.

CARDS

   Handmade fabric cards using
painted cloth.Cut squares of
painted cloth and glue them to
heavy paper. Add stitchery to
the fabric if desired.
   Playing cards made from
fabric- heavy canvas,painted.
Or a soft tarot deck,made from
muslin and lightly quilted.
Or,with a backing of velvet and
the front painted on silk.Add
embroidery.

SOFT GAMES

   Parcheesi. A soft painted
board with markers made from
modeling paste and then painted. Painted chessboard with
either clay figurines or soft
sculpture.

OTHER

   Painted cloth calendars or
stationary.
   Painted dolls and toys.(Fig.
174) Painted dolls with painted
clothing. Painted cut-out dolls
to be sold and stuffed.
   Painted braid and ribbon.
(Figs.175,176)

FIG.174: PAINTED DOLL BY K.
LEE MANUEL.

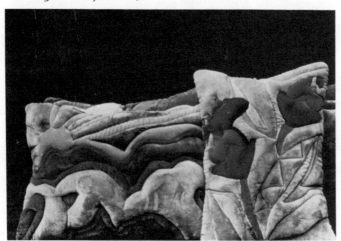

FIG.173 : "TREE FORMS"-LUGENE BRUNO.
WHITE VELVET PILLOWS PAINTED WITH
PROCION DYE.

FIG.175: "PLAITED PIECE"-ANNE MARIE
NICKOLSON. DIRECT DYE APPLICATION,
PLAITING WITH RAYON BRAID.

211

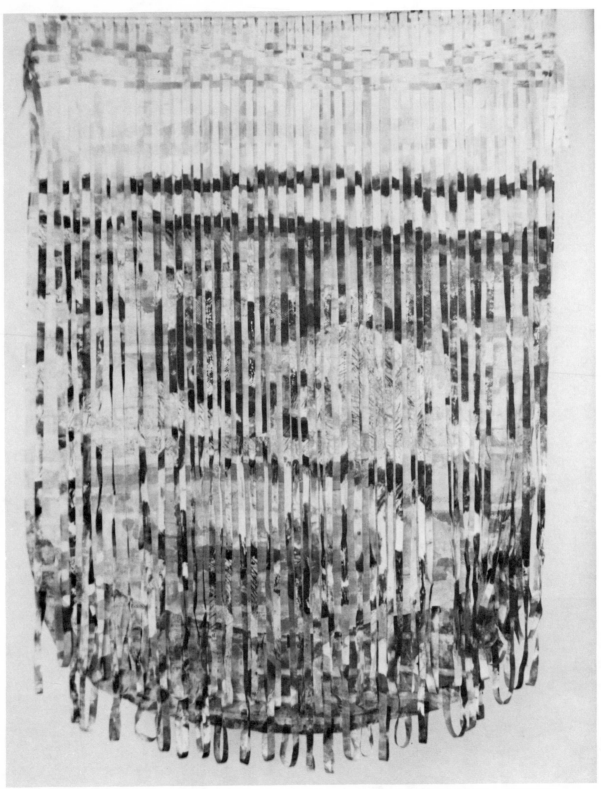

FIG.176 : "SEASONS AT KENTFIELD MARSH"-BY LOUAINE COLLIER ELKE. PAINTED WITH INKODYE,WITH PASTE RESIST. RAYON RIBBON OVER COTTON ORGANDY.

QUICK AND EASY

Rather than continuing with i-
deas and theory,I'm now going to
give you instructions for some of
the most popular fabric painting
projects. This step-by-step method is meant to help give you
practice in fabric painting with
pleasing results! The projects
are divided into those for adults
and those for kids.

General instructions for all pro-
jects:wash sizing out of fabric
or clothing. Let it dry,and press
it flat. Using push pins or masking tape, secure the fabric to a
support such as cardboard or a
flat table.Put newspaper beneath
the fabric if painting on a table.
Use newspaper also to protect layers of fabric when painting on
clothing. Working drawings of the
design may be used,or,if you desire, be freeform and paint spontaneously without the aid of a
sketch.

T-shirt with textile painted,
stenciled design
1) Lay your washed and pressed
T-shirt on a flat table,with a
pad of newspaper underneath for
protection.
2) Sketch,in pencil, a simple
flower design on stencil paper
(purchased at an art store)
3) Cut out your design using a
sharp stencil knife.
4) Put some newspaper between
the two layers of the T-shirt.
5) Lay the stencil onto the T-
shirt,choosing a central loca-
tion or in a corner,if desired.
6) Using a stiff brush,either
a round stiff stenciling brush,
or a synthetic brush used for
acrylic painting,dip your brush
into some textile paint(Versatex, Deka, or Eurotex are all
good choices)
7) Moving your brush from the
outside of the stencil to the
inside of the design,paint the
open areas of the stencil.(If
the stencil is apt to move, it

can be taped down with masking
tape.
8) Remove the stencil,and let
the painted areas dry.
9) Remove the newspaper from
the inside of the shirt,and
fix the paint according to
specific instructions(usually
by ironing).

Pillow front using acrylics,
fabric markers, and embroidery
paints.
1) Cut a 12" square of muslin
which has been washed and pressed. Tape it on a flat surface,
with newspaper beneath.
2) Using fabric markers or other
type markers("magic" markers,de-
sign markers),sketch a flower
shape(it can be similar to the
previous stenciled flower shape).
If desired, make several shapes
rather than just one.
3) Thin acrylics with a little
water and paint the flowers in
pinks, reds, and maroon hues.
4) Use the markers and embroidery paints to draw leaf shapes
and make centers in the flowers.
5) Let fabric dry,then press or
set.
6)To make a pillow, sew a 12"
backing to your pillow front,then
add a pillow form inside. Sew op-
en edge closed with a handstitch.

Potholder(using textile paint,
acrylics, markers,thickened dyes)
1) Cut a 7" square piece of muslin which has been washed and
pressed. Lay it on a flat surface
with newspapers underneath.
2) Using a quilt block as a design, sketch a pattern onto the
square using tracing pencils or a
soft colored pencil.
3) Use small stiff acrylic brushes
and a variety of paint materials.
fill in the areas of your design.
4) Let the paint material dry, then
fix or set it.
5) Cut a matching piece of cotton
7" square as a backing for your potholder. Also cut a thick piece of
quilt batting 6½" square. Press under ¼ inch on all sides of your fa-

bric. Pin edges together with the batting enclosed. Machine sew around the edges of the potholder, then machine or hand-baste along the edges of the quilt design, through the middle of the potholder to secure the batting.
6) Attach a ring to the corner of your potholder if you wish, and you will be all ready to cook!

Painted pockets on a pair of pants or jeans, using oil paint with turpentine.
1) Take a pair of pants or jeans, freshly washed and ironed. Lay them on a flat area, with newspaper between the two layers of fabric. Put small squares of newspaper in the pockets to protect them while painting.
2) Squeeze various oil colors on a palette. Add small amounts of turpentine to thin the paints.
3) Sketch a design of tulips on the pockets. Then begin painting with the oils, using small brushstrokes and blending colors.
4) Let the paints dry, then take the newspaper out and press your pants.

Tote bag, using transfer paints
1) Wash a prepurchased tote bag, or make one out of heavy sailcloth or duck, possibly canvas.
2) Using Deka transfer paints, paint a design onto white paper. Use stripes, circles, and other abstract shapes. If you like, stencil your name on the paper.
3) Let the paint dry, then prepare the bag for painting by putting a thick pad of newspaper or butcher paper on the inside of the bag. Lay the transfer paper face down onto the bag. Put another piece of butcher paper on top of the transfer paper, and press slowly with a dry iron until the design can be seen through the top of the butcher paper.
4) Remove all newspaper and set the paint, if necessary.

T-shirt decorated with cold wax resist and thickened dyes

1) First, mix up some fiber reactive dye with thickener. Dylon with Paintex, Fibrec with thickener, or ProChem with thickener are some good choices. Plastic egg cartons can be used for the separate colors.
2) Take your washed and pressed T-shirt, and fix in a manner similar to the first T-shirt project.
3) Put the cold wax resist in a squeeze bottle. Draw lines up and down and across the T-shirt fabric, on both sides. Let dry.
4) Take a soft brush, like a watercolor brush, medium wide, and dip it into the thickened dyes. Then brush stripes vertically and horizontally on the fabric. Use colors that will blend nicely.
5) Let the dye dry, and then set it. Then wash the wax resist out with warm water.

Wall hanging (or curtain) made with thickened dyes or dye pastels.
1) Take 1 to 1 and 1/3 yards of unbleached muslin, washed and pressed. With pushpins, attach it to a large piece of cardboard (like a broken down cardboard box). You can tape down newspaper below the fabric if desired.
2) Using thickened dyes, and a wide housepainting brush, brush stripes of color vertically down the fabric. At the bottom, leave room for a border of large, soft flowers. (Use a more narrow brush for the flowers). Greens, blues, purples, and maroons are good colors to use.
3) Or, use Pentel dye pastels and color stripes and shapes with the crayons. Make big, bold strokes.
4) Let the dye dry, then set it by ironing with a hot iron. Rinse out the fabric by running it under hot water. This will wash off the "fugitive" dye particles. Set the pastels by ironing.
5) Hem under the raw edges of the fabric for a wall hanging or curtain.

Wrap skirt (or drawstring pants) with acrylic paints

1) Take a cotton wrap skirt or a pair of drawstring pants.They can be handmade or purchased. Wash and press them,lay them flat with newspaper beneath,and, in the case of the pants,fold newspaper inside of the legs and between the fabric at the top of the pants.
2) Gather together your acrylic paints and a palette. Muffin pans are good to mix up a variety of colors.
3)For the skirt, use PreColumbian folk motifs as a design. There are many nice bird designs which can serve as a motif. Using a stiff small brush, paint the outlines of the designs,then go over them with thicker lines to approximate the designs as pictured. Rainbow colors of red,orange,yellow,green, blue and purple can be used successfully. Another idea is to use raw umber,burnt umber, raw sienna, and yellow ochre for an earth-tone palette.
4) For the pants, paint rainbow colored stripes along the bottom hem of the pants and along the border of the pockets. The waistline can also have a painted border of rainbow stripes.
5) Let the paint dry;remove the newspaper(before it sticks to the pants)and press with a hot iron to smooth the paint into the fibers of the muslin.

Silk neck scarf painted in silk dyes or paints
1) Take a piece of China silk 5" wide and approximately 46" long.Wash it out in warm water.
2) After the fabric is dry, press it with an iron set on delicate. Lay it on a flat surface with butcher paper beneath.
3) Use a silk dye or paint that does not need to be steamed.Seidicolor silk paint or Tinsilk are good choices.
4) If desired, use a silk resist (Seidicolor is a good choice)and draw lines vertically all across the fabric.

5) Taking several shades of paint, brush with a soft brush down the fabric.Use black,various shades of green,blue,purple,maroon, and dark shades of pink.
6)If you are using Tinsilk, let it dry for 48 hours,and it will be set. For Seidicolor,after the paint has dried, brush on the silk fixer,and let dry. Then wash off the fixative.
7) Turning under a narrow hem, hem both long edges of the silk. If desired, leave the narrow end fringed.

ESPECIALLY FOR KIDS

T-shirt with Inkodye
1) Prepare T-shirt as in previous T-shirt projects.
2) Take several jars of Inkodye and, with a soft brush,paint a design on your T-shirt.
3) Take the shirt(with the newspaper still in it) outside into the sun and let it soak up the sun's rays.In not too long a time,you will see the colors appear.This heat process will fix the dyes.
4) Wash your T-shirt in warm,soapy water to remove residual dye.

Pajamas decorated with fabric crayons.
1)Take a pair of light-colored pajamas. Lay them flat on a flat surface,putting newspaper beneath and inside the layers of the fabric.
2)Now take some white paper,and with Crayola Fabric Crayons begin drawing designs on the paper.You can make small motifs or one overall drawing.
3)Place the design,rightside down,onto the right side of the fabric.Make a bed of newspapers beneath the fabric,add some butcher paper on top of the colored design,and iron on a cotton setting.When you can see the design coming through the paper,remove the iron. The paint is then set.
4)Be sure to use a fabric with at least 50% synthetic fiber,such as a polycotton;otherwise,the design will not transfer.

Matching pillow,painted with textile paint and fabric crayons
1) Take an old pillowcase. Lay it on

a flat surface. Put newspaper underneath but not between the layers of fabric.
2) Ask an adult to mix up the dyes for you. Use thickened fiber-reactive dyes for your project.
3) Taking a medium large stiff brush, brush on colors onto the pillowcase,letting the dye soak in on both sides. Use swirling motions with your brush.
4) After one side has dried, turn the pillowcase over and fill out the colors that have soaked through. For this second side, use newspaper inbetween the fabric layers.
5) In the center of your pillowcase, leave a white area for a design with fabric crayons.
6) Color one of your favorite coloring book characters with fabric crayons. (If you don't want the image to come out in reverse,trace the outline on the reverse side,then color.)
7) Using the process explained in the previous project, transfer the image onto the pillowcase.
8) Fix your dyes,if necessary.If you have also used coloring book characters on your pajamas,you will have a "matching bedset"!

Painted doll,using dye pastels and fabric marking pens.
1) Trace a flat doll shape on a piece of muslin. Put it in an embroidery hoop.
2) Using dye pastels,fabric marking pens,and embroidery paints,if desired, color in clothing and features of the dolls' faces.
3)Fix or set any paint materials if necessary.
4) Cut out doll ½" beyond tracing marks.Cut a matching back,from muslin or other fabric.Machine sew with right sides together,right along tracing marks.Leave a small opening for turning. Stuff with batting. Handhem opening.

Fish potholder
1) Cut a 12" fish shape out of heavy cotton fabric. Place this fabric on a flat surface with newspaper underneath.

2) Using textile paint,in blue, paint around the edges of the fish shape. Then add an eye,a smiling mouth,and painted on fins,both top and bottom.Paint lines along the tail.
3) Set paint by pressing with a hot iron when dry.
4) Cut out a matching backing and batting for the middle.Follow instructions for earlier potholder to sew potholder together,basting in the middle.
5) Add a ring which has been crocheted over,on the tip of the face to make a nose.

I hope that the theoretical knowledge of holistic design,plus these notebook ideas and projects, will help you towards a greater understanding of the composition and construction of painted clothing.
Good fabric painting takes practice. You are going to have to make mistakes in order to learn these principles.The techniques used in combination with the ideas should provide you with a solid basis of knowledge of good fabric painting.

8   MIXED MEDIA

Materials have different properties. Sometimes you may want to throw every possible material and technique in one garment for its rich interplay. At the same time it is necessary to isolate each materials' characteristics and know what works best in each situation. It makes sense to use a stencil or rubber stamps when doing a series of repeat designs instead of a brush or a pen-<u>if</u> you want them exactly the same. If not, the consideration is whether or not you want to do free-hand painting.

In the preceding chapters, there have been individual descriptions of the paints and their applications. Each material has advantages and disadvantages; each material is limited in its application. Even if you were to use only one kind of paint and made many beautiful things, you would be missing out on the possible effects of other materials. By using materials in combination, it is possible to use the best qualities of each individual material, therefore extending your own growth as a craftsperson.

Fabric painting encompasses such a wide area and large amount of material that I am going to just briefly go over some ideas as to its possible varied application. I am using the term mixed media to describe

three areas: different mediums combined into one whole; fabric painting combined with other fabric techniques, such as needlework, weaving, patchwork, and other types of fabric decoration methods; and the use of different ideas combined into a whole in a painting.

Different mediums combined into one whole simply means that it is possible to use a variety of paint materials, brushes, cloth, and painting techniques in one garment or project. Make sure that the paint material and the type of cloth are compatible; that the various paint materials in an item can undergo the same amount of wear, and that you keep something (a color, form, type of material or painting technique) dominant in the overall design. Try using embroidery paint, textile paint, acrylics, and marking pens on the same cotton skirt. Or, make a skirt with three or four different types of fabric, making sure they hang well together and can be washed together, and paint them with dyes using various size brushes. Just be sure that in your variety there is also sameness.

Fabric painting can also be mixed with other fabric techniques, such as embroidery, stitchery, knitting,crocheting, regular sewing techniques,applique,lace,pleating,quilting,weaving,and patchwork.(Fig.177,178)Painted needlework combines textural interest with variations in color. Embroidery can be both painted and sewn,thus speeding the time it takes to do rows and rows on a skirt. Embroider on woven material,then add painted motifs.

Try making a knitted and crocheted rag rug with strips of dyed and painted cloth. Knit a purse with cotton string,then paint it with thickened dyes. Make a skirt with a crocheted yoke at the top, then add patchwork,painted fabric,and put heavy material at the bottom with thick stitchery. Make a shawl from a heavy soft material, add a crocheted edge,and paint. Make a skirt with applique and painted applique.

PAINTED WEAVING

Weaving lends itself well to painting. A number of fabric artists are weavers who incorporate fabric painting in their work.You can make woven paintings or painted weavings. The warp can be painted(commonly called ikat weaving) before it is put on the loom. As well, the warp threads can be painted after they are on the loom. And the weft can also be painted or dyed.

Ikat is identifiable by the stepped blocks,arrowhead-like patterns, or feathered aspects of the dyed pattern. In native cultures of Africa and the East, the complexity of the patterning of the ikat process has reached a high art form.The warp is bound,like in a bound resist,and then dyed. Dip-dyeing is another possibility in ikat work.

Warp painting creates soft shading throughout,with vertical emphasis. Tapestry weaving works especially well,allowing for a more painterly expression in the weaving. Both textile paint and direct dye application have been

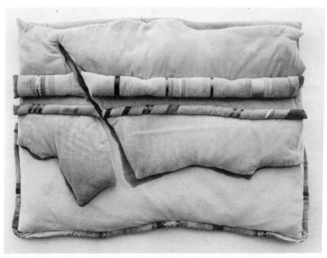

FIG.177 : "UNTITLED-YELLOWS"-VICTORIA RIVERS. PROCION DYE ON VELVETEEN,AIRBRUSH, FLOCKING,APPLIQUE,SCREENED AND HANDPAINTED, QUILTED AND STUFFED. ANOTHER CREATIVE USE OF MIXED MEDIA.

FIG.178 : "RECOLLECTIONS VI"-BY VICTORIA RIVERS. PROCION DYE ON VELVETEEN,SCREENED AND HANDPAINTED,APPLIQUE,QUILTED AND STUFFED. 4X6'. A GOOD EXAMPLE OF MIXED MEDIA.

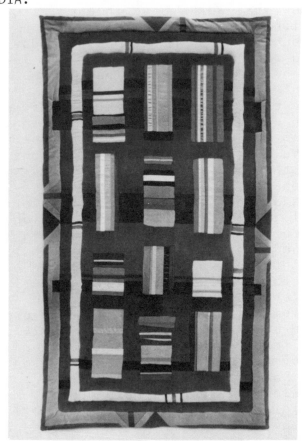

FIG.179 : "JIMMY WHO"-JUDY FELGAR. PAINTED WEAVING, LINEN DOUBLE WEAVE PAINTED WITH VERSATEX AND ATLANTIC TEXTILE PAINT.

used with warp painting.

Woven pieces can also be painted. Dyes, textile paint,and acrylics have all been used with direct painting on weaving. Be sure to plan your design well so as to make no crucial mistakes on your handwoven,time-consuming project! (Fig.179)

PAINTED PATCHWORK

Painted patchwork is a very nice example of mixed media. If you don't like cutting and sewing all those little patchwork pieces into intricate patchwork patterns,yet you like its effect, it is possible to simplify the whole process by drawing and painting them on the fabric.And it is also possible to do the quilting afterwards, so that the sculptural quality is retained. (Fig.178,189)

There are several different approaches to painted patchwork. One method is to paint individual squares in their respective designs;for example,the Log Cabin or the Wedding Ring. The squares are painted in solid colors, either leaving some areas white or filling in all the material with paint. One pattern can be used throughout the work, or a variety of patterns which blend well together are used. (Fig.180)

Another method of work is to paint individual pieces of material with different designs,such as is done when making fabric yardage.Cut this fabric into individual pieces of the quilt pattern, then sew them together. You will then have patchwork fabric with originally painted designs.Another variation is to paint a large piece of cloth with either all solid colors or a mixture of solid areas and patterned areas,all in a patchwork design,of course.

Patchwork is both the small square and the large quilt. There are many ways of combining the individual patterns into large pieces of fabric.Colors and fabric patterns and design patterns must be balanced out in the whole work. When the fabric is to lie flat, as in a quilt or a wall hanging, it is very important that it be well-designed in all areas. However,when the fabric is used in certain garments, especially garments with gathering and pleating, the two-dimensional effect is modified by the body and movement,and becomes a three-dimensional work of art. When this happens, the design must be viewed from a new perspective.(Fig.181)

Machine prints which are often used in patchwork(small prints,calicoes, etc.) are good guides in painting.Materials which are delicately detailed or heavily textured cannot be easily painted; it is easier to use close-weave flat smooth fabric for a patterned painting. Bright,broad splashes of color interspersed with plain colors or white are very effective. Simple rectangular shapes of various colors,sizes,and positions are very pleasing to the eye,easy to paint,as

FIG.180   : DRAWING BY PHYLLIS THOMPSON. AFTER PATTERNS IN THE PERFECT PATCHWORK PRIMER-BETH GUTCHEON.

well as good exercises in working with shades and tones of color.

Another combination of painted patchwork is woven painted patchwork.Any kind of patchwork can be used,but irregular shapes utilize the patchwork process more than squares would, because irregular individual shapes must be

220

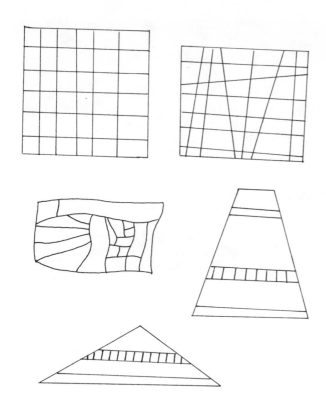

FIG.181 : DRAWINGS OF TYPES OF PAINTED PATCHWORK. FLAT QUILT DESIGNS;SKIRT,AND SCARF.

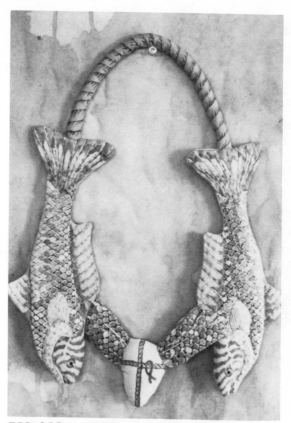

FIG.182 :"FISH TRANSFORMATION" - BY K. LEE MANUEL.

pieced together in order to form a cohesive unit;one large square could be woven rather than small individual pieces.

Woven painted patchwork can be formed by taking various pieces of cardboard and weaving small pieces on them. Then the individual pieces are painted with acrylic washes, textile paints,or fiber-reactive dyes. The pieces are then joined to-gether. A small wall hanging or a sturdy purse are good ideas for this type of work.

SOFT SCULPTURE, DOLLS

Soft sculpture is a favorite technique for use with fabric painting. Many contemporary fa-bric painters use the techniques of soft sculpture to make dolls, containers,toys,soft jewelry, and other soft sculptural items. (Figs.182,183,184,185,186,187.)

FIG.183 : "PAINTED DOLL"-BY K.LEE MANUEL.

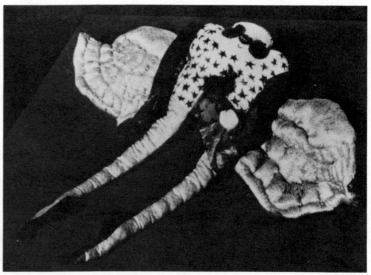

FIG.185 : "MALE DOLL"-BY NORMA ROSEN. COLOR ETCHING ON SATIN. 36" HIGH,54" WING SPAN.

FIG.184 : "FEMALE DOLL"-BY NORMA ROSEN. COLOR ETCHING ON SATIN. 36" HIGH, HIGH,54" WIDE.

FIG.186 :"WINGED BEAST"-BY DOROTHY CALDWELL. COTTON WITH PROCION DYE. THIS TOY HAS A VAR-IETY OF REMOVABLE NOSES,MOUTHS,AND STUFFED ACCESSORIES WHICH CAN BE PUT IN A STOMACH POUCH.

FIG.187 : "LADY DOING HIGH KICK"-LENORE DAVIS.
DYE-PAINTED COTTON VELVETEEN DOLL.

Fabric painting is also used in combination with other fabric decoration methods. Fabric painting can be used in connection with woodblock prints, linoleum block prints, silkscreen,batik,and tie-dye.(Fig. 188).Norma Rosen, a very exciting and talented artist, etches on fabric using zinc plates. Both intaglio and relief methods are used,and she also paints onto the fabric after the initial printing.(Figs.184-185)

COMBINING DIFFERENT IDEAS

Different ideas can be mixed together in a painting. Because fabric painting can use large amounts of space, it is possible to create various moods on different parts of the material.Unlike printed fabric,where the tone and mood pretty much remain the same over the fabric, painted fabric can express a variety of types of ideas. When you paint,open yourself up beyond the safe textile world of flowers and repeat motifs.

I see fabric painting as a bridge between the worlds of art and needlework. In this book, I have gone into detail in the areas of art history, the meaning of clothing,and technical aspects of painting in order to give you the tools to create more expressive,interesting,and varied clothes. Although there are many types of fabrics and designs on fabrics,there are limitations to what machines can do,as machines do not have human minds. The human personality and experience can be expressed through art and design,which then allows fashion design to expand beyond the time limitations of style. Fabric painting,when seen in this way and fully explored,becomes art:transcendent and universal.

THE END

FIG.188 : "LADY IN BLACK"-BY CAROL RACKLIN. BATIK AND
DIRECT APPLICATION OF PROCION DYE ON COTTON.

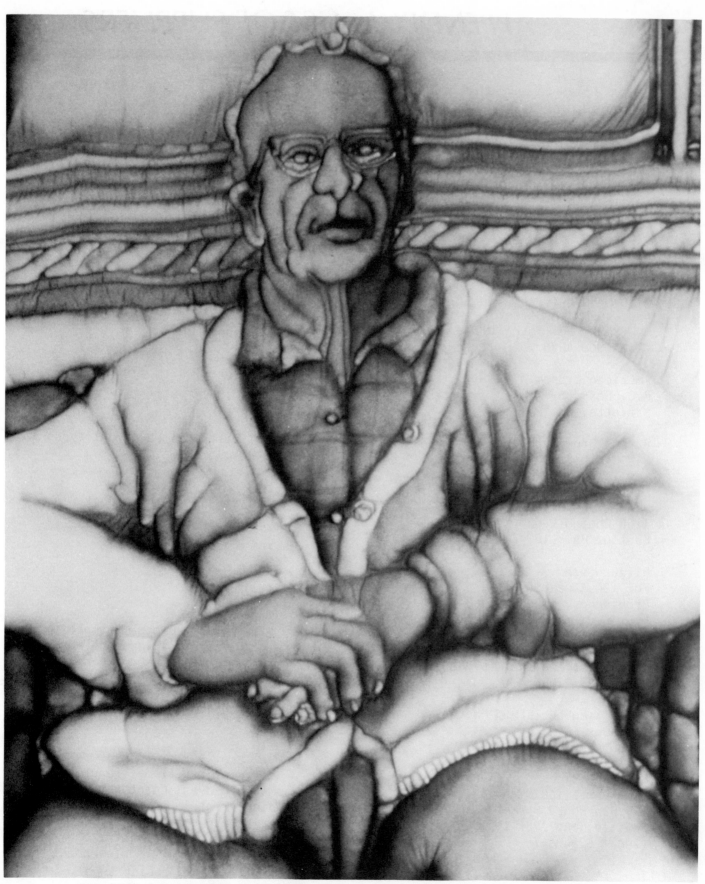

FIG.189 :"MAIN LOBBY #2"-LINDA NELSON BRYAN. PAINTED AND STUFFED RELIEF
(AIRBRUSH AND TRAPUNTO)ON ANTRON NYLON BLEND FABRIC WITH ACRYLIC PAINT.

APPENDIX A: LIST OF SUPPLIERS

I have tried to make this a current list of suppliers. Many suppliers listed in fabric decoration books printed in the last year are already incorrect. These addresses are current as of 1985.

Aiko's Art Materials Import Company
714 N. Wabash Ave.
Chicago, IL. 60611
(312) 943-0745

Miyako dyes, Aritex mineral dyes, Pentel dye pastels, Japanese brushes

Air Waves
555 E. Hudson Street
Columbus, Ohio 43211

Air Waves airbrush fabric paints

Aljo Manufacturing Company
450 Greenwich Street
New York, New York 10013
(212) 966-4046

Acid, basic, direct, and fiber-reactive powdered dyes

American Cyanamid Company
P.O. Box 388
Marietta, OH. 45750

Bulk dyes

Arthur Brown and Bros. Inc.
2 W. 46th Street
New York, New York 10036

Dyes, art supplies of all types

Binney and Smith Artist Materials
1100 Church Lane
Easton, PA. 18042

Liquitex Colors, Permanent Pigments

Bizzaro, Inc.
Box 126 Annex Station
Providence, Rhode Island 02901-0126

Rubber stamps

Bona Venture Supply Company
17, Village Square
St. Louis, Missouri 63042
(314) 895-1008

Prang fabric colors, Versatex textile paints, Flopaque fabric paint, Textile washout pencils

Brand X Rubber Stamp Factory
P.O. Box 6052
Newburyport, MA. 01950

Rubber stamps

Cerulean Blue
P.O. Box 21168
119 Blanchard Street
Seattle, WA. 98111-3168
(206) 625-9647

Acid, disperse, fiber-reactive powdered dyes, Eurotex textile paint, Pentel dye pastels, transfer fabric crayons, Inkodye, books, fabrics, tools, resists, chemicals for thickening, transfer paper, Japanese paste resist supplies

Colonial Printing Ink Co.
180 E. Union Ave.
E. Rutherford, N.J. 07073

Silkscreen inks

Color Craft, Ltd.
P.O. Box 936
Avon, Connecticut 06001
(203) 282-0020
1-800-243-2712

Createx fabric paints, textile colors, metallic colors, and fluorescent colors; Liquid fiber-reactive
dyes, Iridescent fabric paints,chem-
icals for thickening dyes

W. Cushing and Co.
North Street
Kennebunkport, Maine 04046-0351

Cushing 'Perfection' dyes

Decart, Inc.
Lamoille Industrial Park
Box 308
Morrisville, Vermont 05661
(802) 888-4217

Deka fabric paints,transfer paints,
and airbrush paints

Delta Technical Coatings, Inc.
4357 N. Rowland
El Monte, CA. 91731
(818) 579-5420
(213) 686-0678
1-800-423-4135

Delta fabric dye,Delta stencil dye,
'Starlite' fabric dye

Dharma Trading Company
P.O. Box 916
San Rafael, CA. 94915
(415) 456-7657

Versatex textile paint, Deka metallic paint, Sennelier Texticolor
Iridescent textile paint; Tinfix,
Super Tinfix silk dyes; Seidicolor
silk dyes and resists, brushes, gutta, resists, fabrics, Dyehouse fiber reactive dye,disperse dye,steamers

Dick Blick Art Materials
P.O. Box 1267
Galesburg, IL. 61401

Art supplies of all types

Donna Childs
P.O. Box 6052
Newburyport, MA. 01950

Rubber stamps; catalogue-$2.00

D.Y.E. Textile Resources,
see Textile Resources

Earth Guild
One Tingle Ave.
Asheville, N.C. 28801
(704) 255-7818

Deka "L" dye, Deka fabric paints,
Deka transfer paints, Procion MX
dye

Exotic Thai Silks!
see Thai Silks!

Fabdec
3553 Old Post Road
San Angelo, Texas 76904
(915) 944-1031

Procion-M and Procion-H fiber-
reactive dyes

Fibrec, Inc.   Fibrec fiber-reactive dyes
1154 Howard St.
San Francisco, CA. 94103

Floquil-Polly S Color Corporation   Flopaque textile paints
Route 30 North
Amsterdam, NY. 12010

Flynn's Dye and Chemical   Procion-M, Procion-MX, and
Box 11304   Procion-H dyes in powder form
San Francisco, CA. 94101
(415) 621-5968
1-800-824-2168

Guyot, Don   Carroggean moss
Colophon Hand Bookbindery
1902 North 44th Street
Seattle, WA. 98103
(206) 633-1759

Great Atlantic Stampworks   Rubber stamps
P.O. Box 172
Woods Hole, MA. 02543

Gumbo Rubber Stamp Works   Rubber stamps
Box 606
Midland, MI. 48640

IVY Crafts Imports   Tinsilk, Tinfix, and Super Tinfix
5410 Annapolis Rd.   silk dyes; Tincoton, resists, gutta,
Bladensburg, Maryland 20710   disperse dyes, silk and other nat-
(301) 779-7079   ural fabrics, brushes, steamers,
also 6806 Trexler Rd.   frames, pens
Lanham, Maryland 20801

Kasuri Dyeworks   Japanese paste-resist supplies,
P.O. Box 7101   Miyako dyes
Berkeley, CA. 94707
also 1959 Shattuck Ave.
Berkeley, CA. 94704

Mobay Chemical Corp.   Dyestuffs in bulk
Verona Dyestuff Division
P.O. Box 385
Union, N.J. 07083

NIKKO Natural Fabrics Gallery   Suppliers of silk
P.O. Box 71
Kamuela, HA. 96743

Pentel of America   Pentel dye pastels, Pentel
1555 E. Del Amo Blvd.   watercolor dyes
Carson, CA. 90749
(213) 637-0727
or 1100 Arthur Ave.
Elk Grove Village, IL. 60007
(312) 640-7570

or 11 Kulich Rd.
Fairfield, N.J.   07006
(201) 575-7525
or 2715 Columbia St.
Terrance, CA.   90503

ProChemical and Dye Inc.   Procion-M, MX, and H fiber-reactive
P.O. Box 14   dyes;acid dyes, disperse dyes, textile
Somerset, MA.   02726   inks, chemicals for thickeners, Ciba-
(617) 676-3838   cron-F dyes, respirator mask, liquid
                                  fiber-reactive dyes

Rosco-Haussmann   Disperse dyes, Sprila glazing colors,
1135 N. Highland Ave.   fabric colors, textile colors in bulk
Hollywood, CA.   90038
(213) 462-2233
or 36 Bush Ave.
Port Chester, N.Y.   10573

Rupert, Gibbon, and Spider   Deka textile paints
718 College St.
Healdsburg, CA.   95448
(707) 433-9577

Sax's Arts and Crafts   Pentel dye pastels, Pentel watercolor
P.O. Box 2002   dyes; Transfer fabric crayons; acrylic,
Milwaukee, WI.   53201   oil,enamel paint; Colortex textile pig-
or P.O. Box 2511   ments, Prang fabric paint; Dylon Color-
Allentown, PA.   18001   fun fabric paint; Versatex textile paint;
1-800-558-6696   Dylon cold-water dyes, Deka "L" dyes;
                                 Fezandie and Sperrle Professional Batik
                                 dyes; Fibrec dyes; airbrushes; craft
                                 books, china silk, transfer pencils,
                                 Glad Rags markers, other fabric markers
Screen Process Supplies Manufacturing Co. Textile inks, Inkodye, Inko Silk Batik
1199 E. 12th St.   dye
Oakland, CA.   94606
(415) 451-1048

Straw into Gold   SeriTint Liquid dye for silk, Cibacron-
3006 San Pablo Ave.   F Reactive dye, silks and other natural
Berkeley, CA.   94702   fabrics
(415) 548-5247

Sureway Trading Enterprises   Tinsilk, Tinfix, Super Tinfix,Du Pont
826 Pine Ave. Suites 5 and 6   silk dyes; gutta, Pebeo Neotatik, silks
Niagra Falls,NY.   14301   and other fabrics
(416) 596-1887
(416) 596-8899

Textile Resources   Procion-M and H dyes, acid dyes, disperse
P.O. Box 90245   dyes, Setascrib pens, Princefix silk dyes,
Long Beach, CA.   90809   Deco-color pens, Hot Air colors
(213) 431-9611
Thai Silks!   Excellent supplier of silk fabrics
252 State St.
Los Altos,CA.   94022
(415) 948-8611

APPENDIX B: LIST OF TOOLS

There are many tools that are used in connection with fabric painting. The following list may be helpful in planning your work.

AIRBRUSHES: Available in art stores. Can also be ordered from Sax's.

APRON: A plastic apron protects clothes from paint and dye spillage. Order from Cerulean Blue.

BALANCE SCALE: Useful to measure out dyes and chemicals. Order from Cerulean Blue, and ProChemical and Dye Co.

BEAKERS: Plastic beakers are useful to measure out thickened dye-pastes, chemicals, and other liquid solutions. Order from Cerulean Blue,ProChemical and Dye.

COLOR-GRADATION BRUSHES: Used especially in graded washes. Order from Cerulean Blue.

DOT PUNCHES: Used to cut dots or circles in stencils. Order from Cerulean Blue.

DUST MASK: NIOSH-rated dust masks help protect the artist against hazardous dye powders. Order from Dharma, ProChemical and Dye Co., Textile Resources,and Sax's.

EYE DROPPER: Useful for transferring small amounts of dye solution or other liquids. Order from Textile Resources, IVY Crafts Imports.

FAN BLENDER BRUSHES: These are white sable brushes in the shape of a fan. They are good for watercolor techniques. Order from Cerulean Blue.

FLAT BRUSHES: These are from China or Japan. They come in various sizes, up to 2¼" wide. Order from Dharma, Aiko's Art Supplies.

FOAM BRUSHES: Polyurethane foam brushes don't streak. Order from Cerulean Blue,Color Craft , IVY Crafts Imports, Sax's.

FRAMES: Wooden frames are useful for stretching fabric before painting. They are usually adjustable for various widths of fabric. Order from Cerulean Blue, Dharma, and IVY Crafts Imports.

GLOVES: Rubber gloves help protect your skin when working with dyes and chemicals. Order from Cerulean Blue, ProChemical and Dye, Textile Resources, Dharma, Screen Process Supplies.

GOGGLES: Goggles are useful when working extensively with dyes and chemicals. Available from Cerulean Blue.

GUTTA APPLICATORS: A plastic bottle with a very fine applicator tip, to be used with gutta resist. Order from Dharma, Textile Resources, Sureway Trading Enterprises, IVY Crafts Imports.

HAKE WASH BRUSHES: See wash brushes.

HAND CLEANING PASTE: This paste helps wash off any dye residue. Important for health! Order from Cerulean Blue, ProChemical and Dye, Screen Process Supplies.

MEASURING SPOONS: Useful for measuring out powdered dyes. Order from Dharma.

PALETTES: Disposable mixing trays are one type of palette, available from Color Craft. Other types of palettes include plastic trays, disposable containers, and disposable paper palette coated with plastic. From Sax's.

PLASTIC APPLICATORS: Plastic bottles with a fine metal tip, used for resists or thickened dyes. Order from Cerulean Blue, IVY Crafts Imports, or Sax's.

PLASTIC BOTTLES: They are sometimes sold through suppliers for dye storage. Order from Cerulean, IVY Crafts Imports, Dharma, Fabdec, Screen Process Supplies.

RESPIRATOR: Anyone who is working extensively with dyes should consider using a respirator. They are available from Cerulean Blue.

SCRAPER: A wooden scraper can be used in applying resists, especially Japanese paste-resist techniques. Also called a HERA. Order from Cerulean Blue, Aiko's Art Materials.

SPRAYERS: A Pre Val Sprayer is a disposable air brush bottle which is similar to an airbrush, yet much simpler to use. From Color Craft LTD.

SQUEEZE BOTTLES: You can order plastic squeeze bottles with sharp pointed tips to apply thickened dye or resists. Order from Dharma, Cerulean Blue, IVY Crafts Imports, Color Craft, Sax's.

STEAMERS: There are two general types of steamers that can be ordered. One is an ELECTRIC UPRIGHT STEAMER, which either has an electrical unit built into the steamer, or requires a separate heating unit. IVY Crafts Imports and Dharma carry them. The second type is a STOVE TOP STEAMER, which is horizontal and designed to be used over a double burner. Available from Dharma and IVY Crafts Imports.

STENCIL BRUSH: A thick, stout brush used for stenciling. Order from Color Craft.

STENCIL FILM: An adhesive film used for stenciling. Order from Sax's and Color Craft.

STENCIL KNIFE: Used for cutting stencils. Order from Cerulean and Sax's.

STIPPLING BRUSHES: From Japan, used for the stippling technique. Aiko's Art Supplies.

STRETCHERS: Similar to frames, these bamboo stretchers also stretch the fabric for more efficient hand-painting. Order from Cerulean Blue, IVY Crafts Imports, Sax's.

SUMI BRUSHES: Soft round brushes from China or Japan. Order from Dharma, Aiko's Art Supplies, Fabdec, and Sax's.

TRANSFER PIPETTE: Also called PLASTIC EXTRUDER. A transfer pipette is generally used in a lab, but it is useful for measuring small amounts of dye or other solutions. It can also be used to apply very fine lines with thickened dye or resists. Order from Cerulean Blue or Color Craft.

WASH BRUSH: Also called GROUND COLOR BRUSH. From China, a very solid wide brush, up to 5" wide. Useful for watercolor wash techniques over large areas. Order from Cerulean Blue, Dharma, Aiko's Art Supplies, Fabdec, and Sax's.

BIBLIOGRAPHY

You may notice that some titles do not have complete bibliographic information. They may still be available in your library.

FABRIC PAINTING

Bruandet, Pierre. PAINTING ON SILK. NY:Arco Publishing, 1984.

Campana, D.M. TEACHER OF TEXTILE PAINTING. Pampa,Texas: Campana Art.

Dryden, Deborah M. FABRIC PAINTING AND DYEING FOR THE THEATRE. NY: Drama Books, 1981.

Gaines, Patricia. THE FABRIC DECORATION BOOK. NY: William Morrow,1975.

Johnston, Meda Parker,and Kaufman,Glen. DESIGN ON FABRICS. NY: Van Nostrand Reinhold, 1967.

Kafka, Franz. THE HAND DECORATION OF FABRICS. Magnolia, MA: Peter Smith.

Miller, Serene. PAINTING ON FABRIC. Piscataway, N.J.:New Century Publishers,1984.

Proctor, Richard, and Lew, Jennifer F. SURFACE DESIGN FOR FABRIC. Seattle: University of Washington Press, 1984.

Torbet, Laura. HOW TO DO EVERYTHING WITH MARKERS. NY: Ballantine, 1976.

Dember, Sol, and Dember, Steve. COMPLETE AIRBRUSH TECHNIQUES. Indianapolis, IN: Howard W. Sams and Co.,1974.

Miller, Joni and Thompson, Lowry. THE RUBBER STAMP ALBUM. NY: Workman Publishing,1978.

Nakano, Eisha, and Stephen, Barbara. JAPANESE STENCIL DYEING:PASTE-RESIST TECHNIQUES. NY: John Weatherhill,1982.

Parry, Megan. STENCILING. NY: Van Nostrand Reinhold,1977.

Vero, Radu. AIRBRUSH: THE COMPLETE STUDIO HANDBOOK. NY: Watson-Guptill,1983.

OTHER FABRIC DECORATION METHODS

Birrell, Verla. THE TEXTILE ARTS. NY: Schocken, 1973.

Bystrom, Ellen. PRINTING ON FABRICS. NY: Van Nostrand Reinhold, 1967.

Erickson, Janet. BLOCK PRINTING ON TEXTILES. NY: Watson-Guptill,1961.

Gibbs, Joanifer. BATIK UNLIMITED. NY: Watson-Guptill, 1974.

Grey, Robin. ROBIN GREY'S BATIKER'S GUIDE. SF:New Glide Publishers,1976.

Larsen, Jack Lenor. THE DYER'S ART: IKAT, BATIK, PLANGI. NY: Van Nostrand Reinhold, 1976.

Meilach, Dona. CONTEMPORARY BATIK AND TIE-DYE. NY: Crown, 1973.

Nea, Sara. BATIK. NY: Van Nostrand Reinhold.

Proud, Nora. INTRODUCING TEXTILE PRINTING. NY: Watson-Guptill,1968.

_____ TEXTILE PRINTING AND DYEING. NY: Reinhold Pub. Co.,1965.

_____ TEXTILE PRINTING AND DYEING SIMPLIFIED. NY: Arco,1974.

Robinson, Stuart, and Robinson, Patricia. EXPLORING FABRIC PRINTING. Newton Center,MA: Charles T. Branford Co.,1970.

Russ, Stephen. FABRIC PRINTING BY HAND. NY: Watson-Guptill,1965.

Steinmann, Dr. Alfred. BATIK: A SURVEY OF BATIK DESIGN. London: F. Lewis Publishers.

Taylor, W.S. VAN NOSTRAND REINHOLD MANUEL OF TEXTILE PRINTING. NY: Van Nostrand Reinhold, 1974.

Wada, Yoshiko, Rice, Mary Kellogg, and Barton, Jane. SHIBORI: THE INVENTIVE ART OF JAPANESE SHAPED RESIST DYEING. NY: Kodansha International USA,and Harper and Row,1983.

WEARABLE ART

American Craft Council, ART TO WEAR. NY:1983.

Avery, Virginia. QUILTS TO WEAR. NY: Scribner's,1983.

Britton, Kay and Luciano. THE GREAT OVERALL COVERUP. NY: Quick Fox.

Jacopetti, Alexandra. NATIVE FUNK AND FLASH. Oakland, CA.:Scrimshaw Press,1974.

Laury, Jean Ray, and Aiken, Joyce. CREATING BODY COVERINGS. NY: Van Nostrand Reinhold, 1973.

Owens, Richard M. and Lane, Tony. AMERICAN DENIM: A NEW FOLK ART. NY: Warner Books, Abrams, Inc.,1975.

Platt, Charles. T-SHIRTING: A DO-IT-YOURSELF GUIDE TO GETTING IT ON YOUR CHEST.NY: Hawthorn Books, 1975.

Porcella, Yvonne. PIECED CLOTHING. Modesto, CA.:Porcella Studios, 1980.

_____ PIECED CLOTHING:VARIATIONS. Modesto, CA.: Porcella Studios,1981.

Sommer, Elyse, and Sommer, Mike. WEARABLE CRAFTS. NY:Crown Publishers,1976.

Sunset Books. CLOTHING DECORATION:EMBROIDERY,APPLIQUE,DYES AND PAINTS,RECYCLING. Menlo Park, CA.:Lane Publishing Co.,1977.

Torbet, Laura. CLOTHING LIBERATION. NY:

Ballantine Books, 1973.
_____ THE T-SHIRT BOOK. Indianapolis, IN.: Bobbs-Merrill, 1976.

GENERAL TOPICS IN ART

Burke,Edmund. ART AS IMAGE AND IDEA. Englewood Cliffs, N.J.:Prentice-Hall,1967.
Cheney, Sheldon. THE STORY OF MODERN ART. NY: Viking Press, 1958.
Faulkner, Ray,et al. ART TODAY. NY: Holt, Reinhart, and Winston, 1953.
Feldman, Edmund B. VARIETIES OF VISUAL EXPERIENCE: ART AS IMAGE AND IDEA. Englewood Cliffs, NJ:Prentice-Hall, 1972.
Hastie, Reid, and Schmidt, Christian. ENCOUNTER WITH ART. NY: McGraw-Hill, 1969.
Lowry, Bates. THE VISUAL EXPERIENCE: AN INTRODUCTION TO ART. NY: Harry Abrams,1963.
Nordness, Lee. ART:U.S.A. NY: Viking Press, 1963.
Oeri, Georgine. MAN AND HIS IMAGES: A NEW WAY OF SEEING. NY: Viking Press,1968.
Rathbun, Mary Chalmers. LAYMAN'S GUIDE TO MODERN ART: PAINTING FOR A SCIENTIFIC AGE. NY: Oxford University Press, 1949.
Read, Herbert. A CONCISE HISTORY OF MODERN PAINTING. NY: Praeger,1968.
Rosner, Stanley. THE CREATIVE EXPRESSION. Croton-on-Hudson, NY: North River Press, 1976.
Schinneller, James A. ART/SEARCH AND SELF-DISCOVERY. Scranton, PA: International Textbook Corporation, 1968.

ABOUT SCHOOLS OF PAINTING

COLLAGE:Brigadier, Anne. COLLAGE: A COMPLETE GUIDE FOR ARTISTS. NY: Watson-Guptill, 1970.
Lynch, John. HOW TO MAKE COLLAGES. NY:Viking Press.
Wescher, Herta. COLLAGE. NY: Abrams, 1968.
CUBISM: Mocsangi, Paul. KARL KNATHS. Washington, D.C.:Phillips Gallery, 1957.
EXPRESSIONISM: Whitford, Frank. EXPRESSIONISM. NY: Hamlyn, 1970.
FAUVISM: Vogt, Paul. BLUE RIDER. Woodbury, NY: Barron, 1979.
IMPRESSIONISM: Cogniat, Raymond. THE CENTURY OF THE IMPRESSIONISTS. NY: Crown, 1968.
Powell-Jones, Mark. IMPRESSIONISTIC PAINTING. NY: Mayflower books, 1979.
Realities. IMPRESSIONISM. Secaucus, NJ: Chartwell Books, 1973.

Rewald, John. THE HISTORY OF IMPRESSIONISM. NY: Museum of Modern Art, 1961
LANDSCAPE: Clifford, Derek and Timothy. JOHN CROME. Greenwich, CT: New York Graphic Society Limited, 1968.

ABOUT DESIGN

Baranski, Matthew. GRAPHIC DESIGN: A CREATIVE APPROACH. Scranton, PA: International Textbook Corporation, 1960.
Bates, Kenneth F. BASIC DESIGN: PRINCIPLES AND PRACTICE. NY: Funk and Wagnalls, 1975.
Best-Mangard, Adolfo. A METHOD FOR CREATIVE DESIGN. NY: Knopf, 1937.
Bevlin, Marjorie Elliott. DESIGN THROUGH DISCOVERY. NY: Holt, Reinhart, and Winston, 1977.
Bowman, William J. GRAPHIC COMMUNICATION. NY: Wiley, 1968.
Justema, William. PATTERN: A HISTORICAL PANORAMA. Boston: New York Graphic Society, 1976.

_____. THE PLEASURES OF PATTERN. NY: Van Nostrand Reinhold Books, 1968.
Krieger, Lillian Garrett. VISUAL DESIGN: A PROBLEM-SOLVING APPROACH. NY: Van Nostrand Reinhold, 1967.
O'Brien, James F. DESIGN BY ACCIDENT. NY: Dover, 1968.
Proctor, Richard M. PRINCIPLES OF PATTERN. NY: Van Nostrand Reinhold, 1969.
Wedd, J.A.Dunkin. PATTERN AND TEXTURE.
Wilkins, John Gilbert. DESIGN IN NATURE. Chicago, IL: Field Museum of Natural History. School of the Art Institute. 1924-1925.

ABOUT PAINTERS

Breeskin, Adelyn D. THE GRAPHIC ART OF MARY CASSATT. Washington, DC: Museum of Graphic Art and Smithsonian Institution Press, 1967.
Cohen, Arthur A. SONIA DELAUNAY. NY: Abrams, 1975.
Fisher, Robert. KLEE. NY: Tudor Publishing Company, 1967.
Harris, Ann Sutherland and Nochlin, Linda. WOMEN ARTISTS: 1550-1950. NY: Knopf, 1976.
Hunter, Sam. HANS HOFMANN. NY: Harry Abrams, 1964.
Kallir, Otto. GRANDMA MOSES. NY: Abrams,1975.
Loran, Erle. CEZANNE'S COMPOSITION. Berkeley,

CA: University of California Press, 1963.
Moulin, R.J. HENRI MATISSE. NY: McGraw-Hill, 1969.
Petersen,Karen, and Wilson, J.J. WOMEN ARTISTS. NY: Harper Colophon Books, 1976.
Shadbolt, Doris. THE ART OF EMILY CARR. Seattle: University of Washington Press, 1979.
Vriesen, Gustav. ROBERT DELAUNAY: LIGHT AND COLOR. NY: Abrams, 1969.
Warnod, Jeanine. SUZANNE VALADON. NY: Crown, 1981.
Werler, Clemens. JAWLENSKY,HEADS FACES, MEDITATIONS. NY: Praeger, 1971.

ABOUT DRAWING

Jameson, Kenneth. YOU CAN DRAW. NY: Watson-Guptill, 1967.
Rawson, Philip. DRAWING. NY: Oxford University Press, 1969.
Rottger, Ernst, and Klante, Dieter. CREATIVE DRAWING POINT AND LINE. NY: Van Nostrand Reinhold, 1963.
Simmons, Seymour III. DRAWING: THE CREATIVE PROCESS. Englewood Cliffs, NJ: Prentice-Hall, 1977.

ABOUT PAINTING AND TECHNIQUES OF PAINTING

Blake, Wendon. ACRYLIC WATERCOLOR PAINTING. NY: Watson-Guptill, 1970.
_____. ACRYLIC PAINTING BOOK. NY: Watson-Guptill, 1978.
_____. COMPLETE GUIDE TO ACRYLIC PAINTING. Watson-Guptill, 1971.
_____. COLOR IN ACRYLIC. NY: Watson-Guptill, 1982.
Betts, Edward. MASTER CLASS IN WATERCOLOR. NY: Watson-Guptill, 1975.
_____. CREATIVE LANDSCAPE PAINTING. NY: Watson-Guptill, 1978.
Carlson, John F. CARLSON'S GUIDE TO LANDSCAPE PAINTING. NY: Dover, 1958.
Chavatel, George. EXPLORING WITH POLYMER. NY: Reinhold Pub. Corp.,1966.
Chomicky, Yar. WATERCOLOR PAINTING. Englewood Cliffs, NJ: Prentice-Hall, 1968.
Cooke, Hereward Lester. PAINTING TECHNIQUES OF THE MASTERS. NY: Watson-Guptill, 1972.
Derkatsch, Inessa. TRANSPARENT WATERCOLOR: PAINTING METHODS AND MATERIALS. Englewood Cliffs,NJ: Prentice-Hall, 1980.
Dibble, George. WATERCOLOR MATERIALS AND TECHNIQUES. NY: Holt, Reinhart, and Winston, 1966.
Fabi, Ralph. GUIDE TO POLYMER PAINTING.
Friend, David. COMPOSITION: A PAINTER'S GUIDE TO BASIC PROBLEMS AND SOLUTIONS. NY: Watson-Guptill, 1975.
_____. CREATIVE WAY TO PAINT. NY: Watson-Guptill, 1966.
Goldsmith, Lawrence C. WATERCOLOR BOLD AND FREE. NY: Watson-Guptill, 1980.
Herberts, Kurt. COMPLETE BOOK OF ARTIST'S TECHNIQUE. NY: Praeger, 1958.
Jensen, Lawrence N. SYNTHETIC PAINTING MEDIA. Englewood Cliffs,NJ: Prentice-Hall,1964.
Mai-Mai, Sze. THE WAY OF CHINESE PAINTING. NY: Random House, 1959.
Nechis, Barbara. WATERCOLOR: THE CREATIVE EXPERIENCE. Westport, CT: North Light Publishers.,1978.
Owen, Peter. PAINTING. NY: Oxford University Press, 1970.
Richmond, Leonard. FUNDAMENTALS OF OIL PAINTING. NY: Watson-Guptill,1977.
_____. IMAGINATIVE TECHNIQUES IN PAINTING.
_____. LANDSCAPE PAINTING STEP-BY-STEP. NY: Watson-Guptill,1978.
_____, and Littlejohns, J. FUNDAMENTALS OF WATERCOLOR PAINTING. NY: Watson Guptill, 1978.
Simpson, Ian. PAINTER'S PROGRESS: AN ART SCHOOL YEAR IN 12 LESSONS. NY: Van Nostrand Reinhold, 1983.
Szabo, Zoltan. CREATIVE WATERCOLOR TECHNIQUES. NY: Watson-Guptill, 1974.
_____. ZOLTAN SZABO PAINTS LANDSCAPES. NY: Watson-Guptill, 1977.
Tajaylya Productions of Winnipeg. EXPERIMENTING WITH POLYMER PAINT. Manitoba, Canada.
Toney, Anthony. PAINTING AND DRAWING: DISCOVERING YOUR OWN VISUAL LANGUAGE. Englewood Cliffs, NJ: Prentice-Hall, 1978.
Torche, Judith. ACRYLIC AND OTHER WATER-BASE PAINTS FOR THE ARTIST. NY: Sterling Pub.Co., 1967.
Worth, Leslie. WORKING WITH WATERCOLOR. NY: Taplinger, 1980.

ON COLOR

Albers, Joseph. INTERACTION OF COLOR. New Haven, CT: Yale University Press, 1975.
Itten, Johannes. THE ART OF COLOR. NY: Van Nostrand Reinhold, 1961.
Spies, Werner. ALBERS. NY: Abrams, 1970.

ART AND DESIGN SOURCES

PRE-COLUMBIAN: Abbate, Francesco. PRE-COLUMBIAN ART OF NORTH AMERICA AND MEXICO. NY: Octopus Books, 1972.
Bennett, Wendell C. ANCIENT ARTS OF THE ANDES. NY: Museum of Modern Art, 1954.
Bushnell, G.H.S.ANCIENT ARTS OF THE AMERICAS. NY: Praeger, 1965.
D'Harcourt, Raoul. TEXTILES OF ANCIENT PERU AND THEIR TECHNIQUES. Seattle: University of Washington Press, 1974.
Dockstader, Frederick. INDIAN ART IN AMERICA: THE ARTS AND CRAFTS OF THE NORTH AMERICAN INDIAN. Greenwich, CT: NY Graphic Society Pub. Ltd., 1966.
_____. INDIAN ART IN SOUTH AMERICA. Greenwich, CT: NY Graphic Society Pub. Ltd.,1967.
Encisco, Jorge. DESIGN MOTIFS OF ANCIENT MEXICO. NY: Dover, 1953.
Field, Frederick. PRE-HISPANIC MEXICAN STAMP DESIGNS. NY: Dover, 1974.
Greene, Merle. MAYA SCULPTURE OF AN ANCIENT CIVILIZATION: RUBBINGS. Berkeley, CA: Leder, Street, and Zeus,1972.
Innes, Hammond. THE CONQUISTADORS. NY: Knopf, 1969.
Lapiner, Alan. PRECOLUMBIAN ART OF SOUTH AMERICA. NY: Abrams, 1976.
Morley, Sylvanus Griswold. AN INTRODUCTION TO THE STUDY OF THE MAYA HIEROGLYPHS. NY: Dover, 1975.
Nuttall, Zelia. THE CODEX NUTTALL: A PICTURE MANUSCRIPT FROM ANCIENT MEXICO.NY: Dover,1975.
Sawyer, Alan. MASTERCRAFTSMEN OF ANCIENT PERU. NY: Solom R. Guggenheim Foundation, 1968.

AMERICAN INDIANS: Brody, J.J. INDIAN PAINTERS AND WHITE PATRONS. Albuquerque: University of New Mexico Press, 1971.
Canfield, John. PLAINS INDIANS PAINTING. Stanford, CA: Stanford University Press.
Feder, Norman. TWO HUNDRED YEARS OF NORTH AMERICAN INDIAN ART. NY: Praeger Publishers, 1971.
Fewkes, Jesse Walter. DESIGNS ON PREHISTORIC HOPI POTTERY. NY: Dover, 1973.

Mallery, Garrick. PICTURE-WRITING OF THE AMERICAN INDIANS. VOLS.I AND II. NY· Dover, 1972.
Naylor, Maria. AUTHENTIC INDIAN DESIGNS. NY: Dover, 1975.
Sides, Dorothy Smith. DECORATIVE ART OF THE SOUTHWESTERN INDIANS. NY: Dover,1961.
Tanner, Clara L. SOUTHWEST INDIAN PAINTING: A CHANGING ART. Tucson: University of Arizona Press, 1973.

AFRICAN AND OCEANIC: Beier, Ulli. CONTEMPORARY ART IN AFRICA. NY: Praeger, 1968.
Lee, and Woodhouse. ART ON THE ROCKS OF SOUTHERN AFRICA.
Peccinotti and Foreman. LIVING ARTS OF NIGERIA. NY: Macmillan, 1971.
Schmitz, Carl A. OCEANIC ART: MAN, MYTH, AND IMAGE IN THE SOUTH SEAS. NY: Abrams,1971.
Sieber, Roy. AFRICAN TEXTILES AND DECORATIVE ARTS. NY: Museum of Modern Art and the New York Graphic Society, 1973.
Trowell, Margaret. AFRICAN DESIGN. NY: Praeger,1971.
Willett, Frank. AFRICAN ART. NY: Oxford University Press, 1971.
Williams, Geoffrey. AFRICAN DESIGNS FROM TRADITIONAL SOURCES. NY: Dover, 1971.

CHINESE AND JAPANESE:Dye, Daniel Sheets. CHINESE LATTICE DESIGNS. NY: Dover, 1974.
Matsuya Piece-Goods Store. JAPANESE DESIGN MOTIFS. NY: Dover, 1972.
Nakata, Yujiro. THE ART OF JAPANESE CALLIGRAPHY. NY: Weatherhill/Heibonsha, 1973.
Sugimura and Suzuki. LIVING CRAFTS OF OKINAWA. NY: Weatherhill, 1973.
Wieger, Dr. L. CHINESE CHARACTERS: THEIR ORIGIN,ETYMOLOGY, HISTORY, CLASSIFICATION, AND SIGNIFICATION. NY: Dover, 1965.

EASTERN: Erikson, Joan. MATA NI PACHEDI: A BOOK ON THE TEMPLE CLOTH OF THE MOTHER GODDESS. National Institute of Design,1968.
Frankfort, Henri. THE PELICAN HISTORY OF ART: THE ART AND ARCHITECTURE OF THE ANCIENT ORIENT. NY: Penguin Books, 1977.
Gray, Basil. PERSIAN PAINTING. Switzerland: Editions d'Art Albert Skira,1961.
Lloyd, Seton. THE ART OF THE ANCIENT NEAR EAST. NY: Praeger, 1969.

PRIMITIVE AND ANCIENT: Bataille, Georges. LASCAUX, OR THE BIRTH OF ART. Switzerland:

Albert Skira.
Batterberry, Michael, and Ruskin, Ariane.
PRIMITIVE ART. NY: McGraw-Hill,1972.
Boardman, John. GREEK ART. NY: Praeger,1964.
Christie, Archibald H. PATTERN DESIGN.NY:
Dover, 1969.
Koch, Rudolf. THE BOOK OF SIGNS. NY: Dover,
1930.
Petrie, Flinders. DECORATIVE PATTERNS OF THE
ANCIENT WORLD FOR CRAFTSMEN. NY: Dover,1974.
Windels, Fernand. LASCAUX CAVE PAINTINGS.
NY: Viking, 1950.

AMERICAN FOLK:Chapman,Suzanne E. EARLY AMER-
ICAN DESIGN MOTIFS. NY: Dover, 1974.
Lichten, Frances. FOLK ART MOTIFS OF PENN-
SYLVANIA. NY: Dover, 1954.
Mirow, Gregory. A TREASURY OF DESIGN FOR
ARTISTS AND CRAFTSMEN. NY: Dover, 1969.
Sibbett, Ed. PEASANT DESIGNS FOR ARTISTS AND
CRAFTSMEN. NY: Dover, 1977.

OTHER: ATLAS OF ENDGRAIN PHOTOMICROGRAPHS FOR
THE IDENTIFICATION OF HARDWOODS.
Gutkind, E.A.OUR WORLDS FROM THE AIR: AN
INTERNATIONAL STUDY OF MAN AND HIS ENVIRON-
MENT. London: Chatto and Windus, 1952.
Hoffmann, Detlef. THE PLAYING CARD: AN IL-
LUSTRATED HISTORY. Greenwich, CT: NY Graphic
Society, 1972.
Piper, Raymond and Piper, Lila K. COSMIC ART.
NY: Hawthorn Books, 1975.
Pirani, Emma. GOTHIC ILLUMINATED MANUSCRIPTS.
London: Hamlyn Publishing Group Limited,1970.
Purce, Jill. THE MYSTIC SPIRAL: JOURNEY OF
THE SOUL. NY: Avon, 1974.
Ritterbush, Philip C. THE ART OF ORGANIC
FORMS. Washington,D.C.:Smithsonian Insti-
tution Press, 1968.
Waller, Irene. DESIGN SOURCES FOR THE FIBER
ARTIST. Mountain View, CA: World Publishing
Company, 1979.

FROM ALPHABETS: Baker, Arthur. CALLIGRA-
PHIC ALPHABETS. NY: Dover, 1974.
Baker, Arthur. CALLIGRAPHY. NY: Dover,1973.
Douglass, Ralph. CALLIGRAPHIC LETTERING.
NY: Watson-Guptill,1975.
Kepes, Gyorgy. SIGN, IMAGE, SYMBOL. NY: G.
Braziller, 1966.
Lambert, Frederick. LETTER FORMS. Chester
Springs, PA: Dufour, 1968.
Ogg, Oscar. AN ALPHABET SOURCEBOOK. NY:
Dover, 1947.
Rowe, William. EXOTIC ALPHABETS AND ORNA-
MENT. NY: Dover,1974.

FROM PRINTMAKING: Brommer, Gerald. RELIEF
PRINTMAKING. Worchester, MA: Davis Mass.
Daniels, Harvey. PRINTMAKING. NY: Viking
Press, 1972.
Eppink, Norman R. 101 PRINTS: THE HISTORY
AND TECHNIQUES OF PRINTMAKING. Norman, OK:
University of Oklahoma Press, 1971.
Houston, James A. ESKIMO PRINTS. Barre, MA:
Barre Publishing, 1967.
MODERN CHINESE WOODCUTS. Peking: Foreign
Language Press, 1965.
Rasmusen, Henry. PRINTMAKING WITH MONOTYPE.
Philadelphia, PA: Chilton, 1960.
TRADITIONAL JAPANESE WOODBLOCK PRINTS. NY:
Harcourt Brace Jovanovich.
Wenniger, Mary Ann. COLLOGRAPH PRINTMAKING.
NY: Watson-Guptill, 1975.

FROM JEWELRY: Von Neumann, Robert. THE DESIGN
AND CREATION OF JEWELRY. Philadelphia, PA:
Chilton, 1972.
Willcox, Donald. NEW DESIGN IN JEWELRY. NY:
Van Nostrand Reinhold, 1970.

FROM CERAMICS AND SCULPTURE: Barnard, Julian.
VICTORIAN CERAMIC TILES. Studio Vista Pub.,
1972.
Eliscu, Frank. SLATE AND SOFT STONE SCULP-
TURE. Philadelphia, PA: Chilton,1972.
Meilach, Dona Z. CONTEMPORARY ART WITH WOOD.
NY: Crown, 1975.
_____. CONTEMPORARY STONE SCULP-
TURE: AESTHETICS, METHODS, APPRECIATION.NY:
Crown, 1970.

FROM NEEDLEWORK,EMBROIDERY,WEAVING,CROCHET:
Abeles, Kim. CRAFTS, COOKERY, AND COUNTRY
LIVING. NY: Van Nostrand Reinhold, 1976.
Albers, Anni. ON WEAVING. Middletown, CT:
Wesleyan University Press, 1965.
Amsden, Charles Avery.NAVAHO WEAVING: ITS
TECHNIQUE AND ITS HISTORY. Glorieta, NM: Rio
Grande Press.
Birrell, Verla. THE TEXTILE ARTS. NY: Harper
Row, 1959.
Butler, Anne. EMBROIDERY STITCHES: AN ILLUS-
TRATED GUIDE. NY: Praeger, 1968.
Care, Oenone. LINEN CUT-WORK.
Edson, Nicki, and Stimmel, Arlene. CREATIVE
CROCHET. NY: Watson-Guptill, 1973.
Enthoven,Jacqueline. STITCHES OF CREATIVE EM-
BROIDERY. NY: Van Nostrand Reinhold,1964.
Feldman, Del Pitt. CROCHET: DISCOVERY AND DE-

SIGN. NY: Doubleday, 1972.
Gostelow, Mary. THE COMPLETE INTERNATIONAL BOOK OF EMBROIDERY. NY: Simon and Schuster, 1977.
Howard, Constance. INSPIRATION FOR EMBROI-DERY.Watertown,MA: Charles Branford, 1967.
Meilach, Dona Z. and Menagh, Dee. EXOTIC NEEDLEWORK. NY: Crown, 1978.
Rainey, Sarita R. WEAVING WITHOUT A LOOM. Worchester, MA: Davis Mass,1966.
Selenkd, Zuzka. LUDOVE TKANINY ZOKOLIA ZVOLENA(Stenciled and Embroidered Russian/ Hungarian designs).
Wilson, Erica. ERICA WILSON'S EMBROIDERY BOOK. NY: Scribner's,1979.
ANCHOR MANUAL OF NEEDLEWORK. Watertown,MA: Charles Branford, 1975.

FROM QUILTS AND PATCHWORK:Bishop, Robert. NEW DISCOVERIES IN AMERICAN QUILTS. NY: Dutton, 1975.
Dean, Beryl. CREATIVE APPLIQUE.
Gutcheon, Beth. THE PERFECT PATCHWORK PRIM-ER. Baltimore, MD: Penguin Books,1973.
McKim, Ruby. 101 PATCHWORK PATTERNS. NY: Dover, 1962.
Sunset Books. QUILTING AND PATCHWORK.Men-lo Park, CA: Lane Books, 1975.

TEXTILES AND CLOTHING

Albech, Pat. PRINTED TEXTILES. NY: Oxford University Press, 1969.
Arnold, Janet. PATTERNS OF FASHION I(ENGLISH-WOMAN'S DRESSES AND THEIR CONSTRUCTION) 1600-1860. NY: Drama Books, 1977.
Black, J. Anderson, and Garland, Madge. A HISTORY OF FASHION. NY: William Morrow,1975.
Boucher, Francois. TWENTY THOUSAND YEARS OF FASHION. NY: Abrams.
Bolingbroke, Judith M. and the Victoria and Albert Museum. CAROLIAN FABRICS. Plainfield, NJ: Textile Book Service,1969.
Bradley, Duane. DESIGN IT, SEW IT, WEAR IT: HOW TO MAKE YOURSELF A SUPER WARDROBE WITH-OUT COMMERCIAL PATTERNS. NY: Crowell,1979.
Bunt, Cyril G.E. FLORENTINE FABRICS. Plain-field, N.J.: Textile Book Service, 1961.
_____. HISPANO-MORESQUE FABRICS. Plainfield, N.J.:Textile Book Service.
_____. PERSIAN FABRICS. Plain-field, N.J.: Textile Book Service,1963.
_____. SPANISH SILKS. Plainfield, N.J.: Textile Book Service.
Cordry, Donald B. and Cordry, Dorothy M.

MEXICAN-INDIAN COSTUMES. Austin, TX: Uni-versity of Texas Press, 1968.
Davenport, Millia. BOOK OF COSTUME. NY: Crown, 1964.
Dorner, Jane. FASHION: THE CHANGING SHAPE OF FASHION THROUGH THE YEARS. London: Octopus Books, 1974.
Fairservis, Walter A.,Jr. COSTUMES OF THE EAST. Riverside, CT: Chatham Press, Inc.,1971.
Fiberarts Magazine. THE FIBERARTS DESIGN BOOK. Asheville, NC: Fiberarts, 1980.
_____. THE FIBERARTS DESIGN BOOK II. Asheville, NC: Lark Books, 1983.
Gale, Elizabeth. FROM FIBRES TO FABRICS. Plainfield, NJ: Textile Book Service, 1968.
Glazier, Richard. HISTORIC TEXTILE FABRICS. London: T. Batsford, LTD.
Harris, Christie, and Johnston, Moira. FIG-LEAFING THROUGH HISTORY: THE DYNAMICS OF DRESS. NY: Atheneum, 1971.
Hartung, Rolf. MORE CREATIVE TEXTILE DESIGN: COLOR AND TEXTURE. NY: Van Nostrand Reinhold, 1964.
Hawes, Elizabeth. FASHION IS SPINACH. NY: Random House, 1938.
Hillhouse, Marion S. and Mansfield, Evelyn A. DRESS DESIGN: DRAPING AND FLAT PATTERN MAKING. Boston: Houghton Mifflin, 1948.
Hollander, Anne. SEEING THROUGH CLOTHES. NY: Viking Press, 1978.
Hollen, Norma and Saddler, Jane,and Langford, Anna L. TEXTILES. NY: Macmillan, 1979.
Horn, Marilyn. THE SECOND SKIN: AN INTERDIS-CIPLINARY STUDY OF CLOTHING. Boston: Hough-ton Mifflin, 1975.
Kawakatsu, Kenichi. KIMONA: JAPANESE DRESS. Tokyo:Maruzen Co.,1936.
Kleeberg, Irene Cumming. THE BUTTERICK FAB-RIC HANDBOOK. NY: Butterick Pub.,1975.
Langner, Lawrence. THE IMPORTANCE OF WEARING CLOTHES. NY: Hastings House, 1959.
Laver, James. COSTUME THROUGH THE AGES. NY: Simon and Schuster, 1961.
Lewis, Diehl and Loh, May. PATTERNLESS FASH-IONS. Washington,D.C.: Acropolis Books, 1973.
Lurie, Alison. THE LANGUAGE OF CLOTHES. NY: Random House, 1981.
McJimsey, Harriet. ART AND FASHION IN CLOTH-ING SELECTION. Ames, IA: Iowa State Universi-ty Press, 1973.
Mann, Kathleen. PEASANT COSTUME IN EUROPE. London: Adam and Charles Black,Pub.,1950.
Melinkoff, Ellen. WHAT WE WORE: AN OFFBEAT SOCIAL HISTORY OF WOMEN'S CLOTHING:1950-1980. NY:William Morrow.

Metropolitan Museum of Art. PAINTED AND
PRINTED FABRICS: HISTORY OF MANUFACTUR-
ING AT JOUY AND OTHER ATELIERS IN FRANCE,
1760-1815. NY: Henri Clouzot, 1927.
Milinaire, Caterine. CHEAP CHIC. NY: Har-
mony Books, 1975.
Minnich, Helen Benton. JAPANESE COSTUME.
Rutland, VT: Charles Tuttle, 1963.
Minter, Davide C. MODERN HOME CRAFTS.NY:
Johns Hopkins Inc.
Montgomery, Florence. PRINTED TEXTILES:
ENGLISH AND AMERICAN COTTONS AND LINENS:
1700-1850. NY: Viking Press.
Oakes, Alma, and Hill, Margot Hamilton.
RURAL COSTUME. NY: Van Nostrand Reinhold,
1970.
Osumi, Tamezo. PRINTED COTTONS OF ASIA.
Rutland, VT: Charles Tuttle,1962.
Pankowski, Edith, and Pankowski, Dallas.
ART PRINCIPLES IN CLOTHING: A PROGRAMMED
MANUEL. NY: Macmillan, 1972.
Payne, Blanche. HISTORY OF COSTUME. NY:
Harper and Row, 1965.
Pettit, Florence H. AMERICA'S PRINTED AND
PAINTED FABRICS: 1600-1900. NY: Hastings
House, 1970.
Priest, Alan. COSTUMES FROM THE FORBIDDEN
CITY. (CHING DYNASTY ROBES:1644-1661.) NY:
Museum of Modern Art, Arno Press, 1945.
Robinson Stuart. A HISTORY OF DYED TEX-
TILES. Cambridge, MA: MIT Press, 1970.
_____. A HISTORY OF PRINTED
TEXTILES. Cambridge, MA: MIT Press, 1969.
Rosenberg, Sharon, and Bordow, Joan Wie-
ner. THE DENIM BOOK. Englewood Cliffs,NJ:
Prentice-Hall, 1978.
Sloane, E. ILLUSTRATING FASHION. NY: Har-
per and Row,1977.
Strassel, J.L.Co. A COLLECTION OF DISTINC-
TIVE HAND-BLOCK PRINTED LINENS AND CRE-
TONNES. Louisville, KY: Strassel and Co.
Taylor, Lucy. KNOW YOUR FABRICS. NY: John
Wiley and Sons, 1951.
Tilke, Max. COSTUME PATTERNS AND DESIGNS.
NY: Hastings House,1974.
_____. OSTEUROPAISCHE VOLKSTRACHTEN.
Berlin: Wasmuth A-6, 1925.
Ward, Michael.ART AND DESIGN IN TEXTILES.
NY: Van Nostrand Reinhold, 1973.
Wheeler, Monroe. TEXTILES AND ORNAMENTS OF
INDIA. NY: Museum of Modern Art, 1956.
Wiener, Joan, and Rosenberg, Sharon. IL-
LUSTRATED HASSLE-FREE MAKE YOUR OWN CLOTHES
BOOK. SF: Straight Arrow Books, 1971.
_____. SON OF

HASSLE-FREE SEWING. SF: Straight Arrow,
1972.
Wilcox, R. Turner. FOLK AND FESTIVAL COS-
TUME OF THE WORLD. NY: Scribners,1965.
Wilson, Jean with Burhen, Jan. WEAVING
YOU CAN WEAR. NY: Van Nostrand Reinhold,
1973.
Wiseman, Ann Sayre. CUTS OF CLOTH. Bos-
ton: Little, Brown, 1978.

ABOUT DYES AND DYEING

Bolton, Eileen. LICHENS FOR VEGETABLE DYE-
ING. London: Studio Vista Pub.,1960.
Grae, Ida. NATURE'S COLORS: DYES FROM PLANTS.
NY: MacMillan, 1974.
Green, Judy. NATURAL DYES FROM NORTHWEST
PLANTS. McMinneville, RO: Robin and Russ
Handweavers, 1975.
Knutson, Linda. SYNTHETIC DYES FOR NATURAL
FIBERS. Seattle: Madrona Publishers, 1981.
Lesch, Alma. VEGETABLE DYEING. NY: Watson-
Guptill, 1970.
Mustard, Frances E. EASY DYEING. Plainfield,
NY: Textile Book Service, 1976.
Robertson, Seonaid. DYES FROM PLANTS. NY:
Van Nostrand Reinhold, 1973.
Samuel, Cheryl, and Higgins, Carol. GENTLE
DYES. Seattle: Carol Higgins, 1974.
Svinicki, Eunice. SPINNING AND DYEING. NY:
Golden Press,1974.
Thomas, Anne Wall. COLORS FROM THE EARTH.
NY: Van Nostrand Reinhold, 1980.

MAGAZINES, PERIODICALS

American Artist (New York City)
American Craft (New York City)
American Fabrics and Fashions (New York City)
American Home Crafts(Des Moines, IA)
Art News (Farmingdale, NY)
Better Homes and Gardens Needlework and
Craft Ideas(Des Moines, IA)
Crafts Horizons(After 1977 American Craft)
Fiberarts,the Magazine of Textiles (Ashe-
ville, NC)
The Goodfellow Review of Crafts (Berkeley,CA)
Handmade Magazine(Asheville, NC)
Ladies'Home Journal Needle and Craft(New
York City)
McCall's Needlework and Crafts Magazine(New
York City)
Sew News,the Newspaper for People who Sew
(Seattle WA)
Surface Design Journal (Greenville, NC)

GENERAL INDEX

Wool, 49
Words, their meaning, when linked to
    clothing, 134; their size, on
    clothing, 135
Woven painted patchwork, 220-221
Woven paintings, 218-219
Wrap skirt, 214

INDEX OF
PAINT MATERIALS

HOW THIS BOOK CAME TO BE WRITTEN

This book was written over a number of years. It was first conceived in 1974, during the renewed interest in crafts. I noticed that there were no books on fabric painting, although batik and tie-dye were at the height of fashion. I began to paint, learning not through books or teachers so much as by the slow process of experimentation. Each paint material was tested on a number of fabrics; various ideas were tried out on clothing. The research on fabric painting opened the door for me to the whole art world, and I spent much time in art libraries looking at paintings, thinking about what type of paintings would translate into painted cloth.

In 1977, I began the actual writing of the book and completed it 1½ years later. I made the rounds of large publishers and ended up deciding to do the job myself. Then began the learning of self-publishing. I took classes on layout and paste-up and attended workshops on self-publishing. As well, I read as much as possible on these subjects. While supporting myself throughout, I spent evenings hunched over the rented typewriter, typesetting.

There came a year when the book went into storage, along with all my other possessions, while I searched for a job. When I got resettled, out came the partially pasted-up book. I rewrote parts which had become dated, added the many paint materials now available, and finished the book.

This is truely a handmade book, from idea to printed page. I've enjoyed every stage of production and learned many new skills. I hope you also enjoying reading and using this book!

" There is no rest for the messenger
until the message is delivered."

Joseph Conrad

245

ABOUT THE AUTHOR

Linda Kanzinger was born in Louisville, KY. in 1951. She graduated from Waggener High School and the University of Oregon. Her interest in books included being manager of The Book and Tea Shop in Eugene, Oregon. She is presently owner of The Alcott Press. She has been a fabric painter for over 10 years.

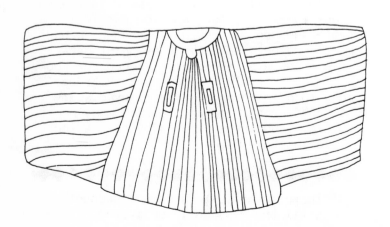

THIS BOOK CAN BE ORDERED DIRECTLY FROM THE PUBLISHER FOR $19.95 POSTPAID.

THE
ALCOTT PRESS
P.O. Box 857
Spokane, WA 99210